TRANSNATIONAL BUSINESS AND CORPORATE CULTURE

PROBLEMS AND OPPORTUNITIES

edited by
STUART BRUCHEY
ALLAN NEVINS PROFESSOR EMERITUS
COLUMBIA UNIVERSITY

A GARLAND SERIES

THE COMMUNITARIAN ORGANIZATION

Preserving Cultural Integrity in the Transnational Economy

JOANN MCDONALD FOSTER

GARLAND PUBLISHING, INC.
A MEMBER OF THE TAYLOR & FRANCIS GROUP
NEW YORK & LONDON / 1998

Copyright © 1998 Joann McDonald Foster
All rights reserved

Library of Congress Cataloging-in-Publication Data

Foster, Joann McDonald, 1941–
   The communitarian organization : preserving cultural integrity in the transnational economy / Joann McDonald Foster.
      p.   cm. — (Transnational business and corporate culture)
   Includes bibliographical references and index.
   ISBN 0-8153-3250-5 (alk. paper)
   1. Corporate culture. 2. Communitarianism. 3. Organization. 4. International business enterprises. 5. Economic history—1900–   I. Title. II. Series.
HD58.7.F67 1998
302.3'5—dc21

98-46217

Printed on acid-free, 250-year-life paper
Manufactured in the United States of America

*In memory of Pearl and Joe McDonald
who were my first community.*

Contents

Preface	ix
Acknowledgments	xi
Introduction	xiii
Chapter I	**3**
DEMOCRATIZATION AND COMPLEX	
INTERDEPENDENCE	3
Liberalization, Democratization, and Transition	3
The New Economic Age	19
Change, Challenge, and Response	23
Chapter II	**29**
CULTURE, ECONOMICS, AND CORPORATE	
BEHAVIOR	29
Culture and Economy	29
Socio-economics and Economic Ethics	32
National Cultures and Corporate Organizations	37
Corporate Culture Sets	44
Global Change and Corporate Culture	51
Chapter III	**61**
THE INDIVIDUALIST MODEL:	
AMERICAN ORGANIZATIONAL CULTURE	61
The Atomized Society	61
American Individualism and Corporate Cultures	71
"Turbocapitalism" or The New Economic Order	84

Chapter IV	95
THE ORGANIC MODEL: THE JAPANESE	
ORGANIZATIONAL PARADIGM	95
Collectivism and The Organic Society	95
Collectivism and Japanese Society	97
The Japanese Organizational Paradigm	107
Challenge to the Japanese Model	123
Chapter V	133
THE COMMUNITARIAN PARADIGM	133
The Communitarian Ethic	134
A Communitarian Epistemology	150
The Communitarian Paradigm for	
Corporate Organizations	156
Business Ethics	166
Human Capitalism: A New Look	177
Internal and External Environments for the	
Communitarian Enterprise	195
Reprise	205
Chapter VI	209
GLOBAL CHANGE, CULTURAL CHALLENGE, AND	209
THE COMMUNITARIAN RESPONSE	
Bibliography	215
Index	227

Preface

Emerging from profound political change in Eastern Europe, Latin America and Africa, and coupled with a proliferation of market economies and technological and commercial interpenetrations of formerly closed societies, the international system has become an interdependent global milieu. New rules of conduct entail enigmatic intricacies and cryptic sensitivities largely superfluous to the experience of past generations of travelers and toilers. Confluence has revealed entirely natural cultural contention among societies who are struggling with the normative implications of economic collaboration and political harmony. Interdependency implies relationships, and the pursuit of entwined cross-cultural relationships carries the social baggage and community traditions of the user and the used, buyer and seller, source and producer, native and alien, haves and have-nots, the We and the Other.

The complexities of these interdependencies have been addressed in disparate theoretical dialogue, but few organization theorists have examined the clear correlation between the present predicament of transnational firms as strangers in an alien land, and the communitarian assumptions regarding individuals in societies. Little attention has been paid to the utility of the communitarian ethic in addressing the cultural conundrums which arise out of the economic and political affinities and antagonism of globalization.

Good theories have sound philosophical moorings; and my research leads me to the conviction that the ideal source for the development of strategies to traverse the dialectic of diversity and unity in the interactions of co-dependent individuals and societies may be as simple as a reconceptualization of the communitarian social ethic, effected through the organizations of civil society, the company of companions, that crucial social link between the individual and her government.

As the communitarian self discovers her membership in society, so solitary sojourners, organizations, and nations have discovered their membership in a global community. The communitarian self is embedded in society, the society in which one finds oneself, which may not be one's native society with its familiar cultural idiosyncrasies and conventions. Organizations, particularly economic ones, are likewise finding themselves implanted in societies with standards of behavior which may not only be unfamiliar, but whose normative principles may be culturally antithetical to both capitalist economics and democratic politics. This imbroglio fuels a demand for new theory which addresses principles of mutual service, reciprocity, responsibility, and communion at the intermediate level of society where individuals join in free association with each other.

The inclusion of a communitarian perspective in organization theory is an appropriate philosophical construct to relieve many of the organic disputations and much of the natural strife of global economic and political interdependencies. Such a theoretical interpretation compels individuals and organizations alike to discover both the constraints and benefits of mutual association and shared purpose. By enhancing the principles of the socially-responsible corporation with the philosophical legitimacy of the communitarian ethic, we can optimize the benefits of cross-cultural enterprise and minimize the social trauma of transformation and penetration.

Acknowledgments

As individuals may not ignore their community, so the single author may not disregard the emotional and intellectual sustenance of her company of companions and collaborators. Although the philosophical journey is singular, there are always those along the way that help you take the next step, or send you reeling backwards in abject frustration. At this point, I thank all of them, because they made me work harder and think more clearly.

But there are those who deserve a special acknowledgment for clearing the intellectual path and pointing me in the right directions. To Cal Clark I am indebted for sharing the journey with me into a theoretical world where no one else wanted to go. Bob Bernstein was the soul of patience, who seemed to understand the intellectual and emotional traumas of the pursuit of perfection which have oftentimes driven me to unreasonable and garrulous ends. Bob Montjoy encouraged me to trust my judgment, and Tom Vocino liked my pretty words. Tom Dickson and Bill Kelly always seemed to find the time to listen and to inspire.

There is another type of appreciation, however, that I must reserve for my family. I am not sure they always knew where I was going, and they may not have understood how I was going to get there, but they were always willing to hold my hand.

Introduction

Fundamental changes in the global political economy during the 1980s and 1990s have created an apparition many observers have euphemistically and somewhat wishfully christened the "global village." In the political sphere, the collapse of communism and the broader "third wave of democratization" which encompassed it resulted in a world dominated by capitalist democracies whose polities and economies operate on the basis of liberal individualism. These political changes, furthermore, occurred against the backdrop of a revolution in the international economy, where technological innovations in transportation and communications fueled "globalization" and "complex interdependence."

The economic and political benefits of these transformation are legion. Yet, there is little reason to think that the momentary triumph of democracy as the political system of choice has solved the world's problems or even resulted in peaceful tolerance and coexistence, since the emerging "new world order" seems far from orderly. In particular, the global changes have provoked a resurgence of localistic nationalism, especially in the Third World traditional societies and former communist countries where unifying trends are defied by historic ethnic animosities. Moreover, turbulent change is not just a problem for the periphery of the capitalist world; the massive "restructuring" movement among corporations in the United States and other industrialized countries has exposed the inability of standard organization paradigms to respond to political and economic anomalies and uncertainties.

I argue that the fissiparous tendencies of globalization may be mitigated through a reconsideration of the organic tradition of society.

In particular, my analysis will seek to demonstrate how the communitarian approach to organization theory may serve as an exemplar for resolving the problem areas in the individualist and the organic model of organizations and will, in effect, spill over to dilute the social strife which attends cultural border crossings.

Organization theory is a dynamic, interdisciplinary field of thought which aspires to articulate both descriptive and prescriptive paradigms of and for organizational behavior. Its developmental pattern is generally the same as that followed in the scientific discourse; its impact is equally profound. Drawing from a variety of disciplines to support an argument for the inclusion of the communitarian perspective in American organization theory, my analysis scrutinizes and questions both the cultural backdrop and the ontological assumptions of contemporary political and organization theory, arguing that the implications of economic enterprise can neither be confined within the organization, nor ignored as an agent of change in the larger society.

The nature of the post-1990 global environment has compelled organization theorists to inject notions of cultural values into their studies of a transformed, tightly coupled global network of diverse nation-states and distinct civil societies whose mutual destinies are increasingly entangled politically and economically. When organization theory thus abuts issues of culture, it necessarily entails social theory.

An exploratory search of the literature reveals a theoretical association between the communitarian perspective and a developing body of social and cultural theory, economic theory, philosophy, and organization theory. These conceptual associations will be examined to determine their appropriateness to the formulation of new communitarianist paradigms of organization theory which address the complexities and particularities of interdependent, diverse cultures with both common and contradictory goals and characteristics.

With all due respect to the quixotic sentimentality of the notion of a global village, I believe the world remains very much a crazy quilt of diverse societies whose ancient customs, values and social arrangements endure. The challenge to organizations and individuals who are crossing those cultural borders is to find arrangements which validate rather than void the values, customs, and norms that identify all of us and each of us.

Chapter I discusses fundamental political and economic changes and the negative side effects of interdependency, exploring the passions of nationalism as an expression of inflamed defiance to the threat of cultural homogeneity raised by the perturbations of globalization. Released to express their nationalist fervor, peoples in numbers of newly-democratic states have tended to generate strife within and among themselves, rather than to reap the promise of a democratic peace. A review of the democratization typology of Samuel Huntington, Scott Mainwaring, Bernard Susser, Adam Przeworski, and others, reveals the vagaries and contradictions in analyses of changes in world political patterns, exposing both the improbabilities and possibilities for consolidation of democratic notions of cooperation and interaction in diverse cultures.

Borrowing from Burke, I argue that legitimate rights and political institutions arise organically in the social relationship of human beings, and interference with the political order jeopardizes civil society. Bearing in mind the premise that natural rights do not exist *a priori*, but in society, I argue that neonationalism is a search for meaningful identity, a reaction to the forces of modernity which threaten traditional societies and indigenous cultures in every part of the globe. The capitalist concept of taking for one's self the profit of one's labor and the private property rights which are attendant to Western capitalist democratic systems may generate both internal social afflictions and regional and international squabbles. The have-nots in new democracies may become impatient with a political system that sanctions an economic system that seems to trigger unemployment, staggering rates of inflation, depleted purchasing power and living standards, financial chaos and debt crises, and human suffering. It is difficult to embrace capitalistic democracy if the disadvantages of competition are allowed to prevail.

Although political commonalities may be the enabler, nevertheless, the engines of change are economic; and the coming age is likely to challenge every theory designed to explain economic behavior or provide guidance for nation-states, as well as organizations and institutions, through the political/economic miasma of disparate democratization, passionate nationalism and unbounded capitalism. Confounding political and economic developments diminish the applicability of standard theories: The political nation-state may be divorced from effective economic activity; institutions and organizations will represent both lateral and hierarchical public and private interests; regions may become more influential than nation-states in global decisionmaking; world leadership will gravitate to those with economic, rather than military strength; ideology becomes inconsequential even as matters of integrity, security, and national interest continue to animate new democratic regimes. Economic power may well displace all other forms of power; markets, as well as production, will belong to those who can make a product or perform a service quicker, more efficiently, and with higher quality than their competition.

The paradox of economic interdependency and cultural nationalism threatens transnational harmony. Nationalism defies cultural homogeneity; even though the state may decline in its political influence, its peoples, its nation or member nations, fervently, adamantly refuse to be absorbed into one another. Perhaps it is the spectre of identity lost to a shrinking world that feeds the nationalist fervor. Regardless, it is the cultural baggage of globalization. Everybody wants their piece of the political and economic pie, but they want it for themselves, not the "other."

Chapter II focuses on cultures, examining two types of cultural impacts on business organizations: (1) cross-national differences, and (2) corporate cultures deriving from the business environment and leadership styles, drawing attention to the links between culture, economics, and social values in diverse organizations and societies. The interdependent and aggregative nature of economic activity and the subordination of the political order to the economic function have conspired to create a new global information and communication infrastructure, enmeshed in a net strung together by billions of dollars in international trade and foreign investment, and weighted by social tensions and clashes among cultures whose values are unwittingly brought into question by abutting and interconnected economic and political purposes. Fueled by international trade and investment and enabled by an ever-increasing tide of international movement of capital, multinational corporations have become intertwined in both coherent and inchoate modes with all manner of the world's cultures. Furthermore, there are important cultural differences among corporations from different nations, defining and distinctive differences which serve to both classify and at the same time diminish the cultural influence over organizational style and substance. As did Hofstede in his seminal work in cross-cultural theory, I argue that the culture of origin remains the most important determinant of corporate value systems.

But organizations are not culturally solitary; they are crucial institutions of civil society, built on politically recognized rights of association and property—economic associations which serve the common good of the community in diverse ways. On the one hand, the private business corporation, independent of the state, enjoying transgenerational legal existence, and outlasting its progenitors, exhibits a unique corporate culture that identifies the corporation just as surely as cultural distinctiveness identifies national cultures. Its voluntary members pursue their own affairs, accomplish their own purposes, and in favorable political arrangements, reap their own financial rewards. The private business corporation is a prime model of voluntary association, common motivation, and mutual dedication. The structure of the economic organization, and the manner in which economic goals are interpreted and pursued, becomes a conscious and subconscious framework within which the physical and intellectual energy of human beings is directed toward a common goal. Ideally, this framework is socially and psychologically healthy for its participants, its culture dignifying rather than demeaning, possessing sound ethical effects which overflow into the larger society in a positive, enriching sense.

While the organization presents its own culture, still it may operate in a different culture, obtain support from yet another culture, and be expected to compete in a global culture. These are multiple communities of action, all of which are dynamic, and each of which may contradict the other. Cultures are social organisms; they may be alternately hospitable and haughty, appeasing and antagonizing, affable and aloof; nonetheless, they are the social cement that binds a people together and gives them the strength and the spirit with which they are identified. At the end of the day, the corporate microculture must be of sound enough character to respond with vigor to the demands put upon it and persist in the face of internal and external threats.

Economic interdependence and information technology have allowed, indeed compelled, the interpenetration of cultures. In a headlong rush to participate in newly expanded markets and take advantage of investment opportunities, organizations have spread about the globe, carrying their own sets of values, rites, and rituals into unfamiliar and antithetical cultural environments. These corporate tribes have become the conduit of change for many societies; they represent new ways of doing things, enabling linkages and opportunities obscure to many peoples of the world.

The transformed nature of the twentieth century economy, and the uncertain challenges of the twenty-first, suggest that the defining corporate culture of the Industrial Age must also be altered. Mass production techniques which stress hierarchy, rigidity, division of labor, and mechanization—a process which indisputably created great wealth, a myriad of products, and millions of jobs—may not be the most effective way to do business in a global economy where new actors, incentives and technology are writing new economic rules of behavior. Fordism, specialization, and the assembly line represent the corporate culture of the Industrial Age; indeed, mass production became society, as the "one way" notion of Taylor mirrored the efficiency and replicability needs of the Industrial Age, and society searched for satisfaction in rationality and reason. Current conditions mandate significant organizational change; the rigidity of the mass production paradigm is no longer seemly. Not only is it unsuitable for the quick response and redeployment of resources required by truncated product cycles and fragmented markets, there is a larger incongruity which suggests that the entire panoply of the social nature of the Industrial Age is dissolving in the accelerated motility of the Information Age. If the way we work is both defined by and defines society, the organizations within which we work are indeed powerful agents for social change, an idea which forces us to consider those organizations as more than the machines of commerce and greed, unless we are content with a society whose defining quality is individual self-interest.

Perhaps the Age of Information is the enabler of the natural next level of organizational change. In the new information society, the key resources are defined as information, knowledge, and creativity—and the only place where the corporation can recover these resources is from its employees. If humanity is seized by its organizations, as well as solaced by them, then it well behooves organizations to reconcile their economic and social goals to human goals—these contexts can no longer be estranged.

Culture is the primary social bridge between economics and sociology, but most modern economists do not worry much about culture. When they do, it is often misconceived as nature, or viewed as exogenous or aggregated preferences and tastes, or as historical or organizational notions of limited interest and regulatory function. But cultural and social attitudes cannot be disregarded as potential restraints to altered economic circumstances in both ascending and declining economies. The resolution of the complexities of economic interdependencies and interactions is unfulfilled without consideration of the countless enigma of accidental, unplanned, and unpredictable cultural phenomena. The debate between economists and sociologists over the breach between human values and economic behavior is fatuous: Economic decisionmaking truncated into value-free science may be abstractly absorbing, but it is neither philosophically or socially defensible.

Chapter III examines America's "individualistic" culture and its consequent economic implications of form and substance. This section offers an in-depth examination into the American commitment to the presumption of society as an aggregate of unrelated wants and wills whose nucleus is the single human being. This individualistic conception, with ancient philosophical roots in the Sophist's notion of society and the state as artificial constructs, decrees that human beings are not innately social creatures, and are not naturally concerned with any greater social good; human beings are observed as individual egotists who are originally and ultimately concerned with their own self-interest. Within this set of psychological and social parameters, social reality is nothing more than mind-set and self will, and it defines the social ethic which enabled the acceleration of the energies of acquisition and entrepreneurship and the growth of the American economic model. Indeed, the American culture is celebrated for its self-made and continually self-making quality; individualism is generally considered the core concept of the American expression of classical liberalism.

This chapter considers the philosophical tradition of American-style individualism from its Greek origins through the early Christians and Protestantism as both a political and economic ideological construct which animated Madisonian democracy and became linked with individualistic atomism and the anti-statist defense of market capitalism during the nineteenth century. Following the historical evidence, however, reveals a shift away from the classical Lockean/Smith legacy of economic liberalism and commitment to the concepts of negative freedom and the minimal state to a new reading of the social contract which created the modern welfare state. Turning from economic freedom to social justice, post-New Deal liberalism is identified with the expectation of government intervention to secure general prosperity and social stability by means of welfare provision and the management of the broader economy.

Consequently, with welfare responsibility vested in the state, American corporations were freed to pursue organizational behavior divorced from the interests of their employees; concomitantly, the individual member of an individualistic organization does not view the organization as her source of stability or long-term security. This combination of ideological individualism and detached organizational social responsibility undermines mutuality and diminishes the loyalty, fealty, and dedication which define the organizations of civil society. The cultural and legal relationship between worker and employer in the American individualist organization is antagonistic, a circumstance exacerbated by laws which stipulate minimum wages and union contracts which compel wage rates, and jurisdictional and seniority arrangements that inflate individual rights at the sacrifice of individual responsibilities. The flow of responsibility-merit-reward is interrupted in the individualist model by the force of the individualist ethic and the framework of law and custom which protects it. Thus there is a confounding paradox: Allegiance to philosophical individualism diminishes individualism in the mass production model and the society in which it obtains.

The characteristics of doing business American-style are simply not acceptable in many cultures. Americans are perceived to be unnecessarily frenetic, disrespectful of authority, pragmatic, loquacious, uninhibited, generous but wasteful, loud, rude, boastful, immature, over-confident, hard-working, and both egalitarian and prejudiced: These traits do not necessarily travel well. This chapter points out that the powerful American organizations that excelled at mass marketing and mass manufacture are equally capable of excelling in a new age, but not without metamorphosis. There is a balance to be sought, the achievement of which will likely affirm or deny American political and economic success and leadership. An organization must be equally complex with its environment if it is to prosper; if it does not prosper, neither do its participants. Uniting pride in accomplishment with the ability and willingness to correct its shortcomings may offer the solution for American organizations whose greater purpose can never be fulfilled solely with the accumulation of wealth.

The examination of the atomist/individualist conceptualization of the American organizational paradigm provides one data set; an examination of the collectivist conceptualization in Chapter IV serves as its philosophical polar opposite. Somewhere in between the two lies a workable foundation to ease the natural inequalities of capitalism as well as to provide a positive model for socioeconomic growth and stability in virtual globalization.

Introduction xxi

Chapter IV describes Japan's "organic" culture and its corollary public/private economic fusion. As Chapter IV presents an examination of the American Model and its individualistic social, philosophical, and economic rationale, Chapter V explores the Japanese model as the organic counterpoint. This organic, or collectivist model, is based on the presumption of society as natural to the human condition; as such, it stands as an antithetical ideological construct to the atomist viewpoint of society as artificial and contrived. The Japanese model is chosen because there are few cultures in which there is greater sensitivity to matters of status, gradations of hierarchy, and an abhorrence of individualism. Writ large, however, the individualistic-collectivist duality describes a bifurcation between the majority and minority of the world's peoples.

The Japanese concept of social order animates Japanese organization theory and is associated with a number of typically-Japanese organizational expressions at both the macro and micro-level, such as lifetime employment and the economic groupings (*keiretsu*) and trading companies (*zaibatsu*) which are so important to the reciprocity and in-common ownership which typify the large Japanese corporation.

My analysis reveals the challenges and weaknesses of the Japanese Model—its protectionist tendencies, the havoc wreaked by the "bubble economy" syndrome, and the general, atypical economic slump in the Japanese economy which began in the mid-1990s and continues, leading many experts to revise their previous plaudits of the strength and fundamental strength of the Japanese economy and its government-managed finance and business sectors. The same forces of changing international market competition and technological innovation that have undermined America's mass production model, forcing American corporations to down-size, outsource, and contract out, are exacting a heavy economic toll on the historic phenomenal growth and productivity patterns of Japan's families of organizations. Some of the most cherished traditions of Japanese organizations may become insupportable relics of economic conditions that are forever past, a construct made vulnerable to the dynamics of both changing external challenges and internal credos that are unsustainable in the face of a re-energized global economy. But one must remember that while the government/private Japanese coalition is by nature and practice committed to certain organistic relational particulars, it is also an extremely malleable system, unashamedly willing to adapt to new contextual conditions while retaining a certain purity of mission. The harmony and cooperation, the fealty and deference, the paternalism and mutual dedication that characterize the Japanese corporate organizational style are a part of their national character as well, but they are endowed with *shukanteki*, a subjective point of view with a depth and wholeness which derives from the whole truth. There is a subtle phenomenological nature to the Japanese culture which allows it to redirect its energies periodically while maintaining its core components.

Chapter V explores the communitarian paradigm as theoretical fulcrum between the two previous models. The communitarian ethic represents a conceptual framework which respects both the unity and the diversity in an interdependent world community of unequal parts. The ethic can serve as systematic input into the stream of organizational and institutional value systems to re-cast the fundamental character of the interactive assemblage of individuals, organizations and societies which comprise the emerging transnational world economy. Weakened nation-states with parochial sovereign interest, transnational economic organizations with market interests, international organizations with interwoven interests, and human beings with personal interests are all a part of a gigantic web of relationships that exhibit both commonality and miscellany of pride and purpose. Globalism may prove the alembic which legitimizes the institutionalization of the communitarian ethic. Communitarianist theory may not replace the power structure paradigm which has historically dominated American organization theory, or the cloying collectivism of the Japanese model; however, it reveals possibilities for the consolidation of new theories incorporating the fundamentally humanistic principles advocated by an interdisciplinary field of organization thought. It is presented as a philosophical foundation to bring coherence to the patchwork, piecemeal, hit-and-miss efforts of corporate organizations in which enlightened leaders are seeking a new value system to animate financial and management techniques to respond to new realities.

The characteristics of communitarianism are presented as clearly implicated building blocks for economic organizations: the embedded self; the assumption of responsibilities; the focus on the moral voice of the community in reinforcing social values, civil society, and civic virtue; and the criticality to society of intimate relationships between human beings and their intermediate associations as the buffer between the individual and the state. The presumption of economic organizations as constituted selves in civil society vests them with civil purpose, obligated to sustain subsidiarity and solidarity as economic and social agents. Organization policies devised to recognize the institutional role in civil society and the responsibilities attendant to the rights of enterprise expand the corporate purpose beyond profit. Quite simply, the organization would discover its role in the community, much as the individual discovers her role in the community. As an embedded self, the organization would then act in concert with the community, not contrary to it. Much like a marriage, there is a presumption of purpose in common, pursued in an attitude of give-and-take which seeks to confirm the values of all parties to the union. This approach does not presuppose that the community would remain unchanged by the organization, nor that the organization would remain unchanged by the community. But it does presuppose that it is the community discovered in this union that will remain the repository of values.

There is no Augustinian and Hobbesian solution unitary state to provide the peace necessary for self-interest to flourish in the post-1990 global society. The elite economic institutions who are reaping the profits of a generally politically-compatible international order may also find that they are vested with the duty and responsibility to sustain it. Plato's admonitions are pertinent. At the end of Book 9 of the *Republic*, in dialogue with Glaucon, Plato articulates the view that justice in the *polis* demands that man conquer the inner monsters of his greed. Indeed, the survival of diverse societies is preserved in the sustenance of their distinct historical ties and traditions, loyalties, and cultures. Without a just consideration of the importance of these characteristics of community, avarice as well as neonationalism will rend asunder global security and strip the international order of its opportunity for creating mutual social justice, reciprocal political support, and sustainable economic wealth.

There is somewhat of an analogy between the individualistic fervor which divides one person from another, and the neonationalistic zeal which separates families of society from their neighbors. An assumption of the communitarian ethic relieves both these pernicious predicaments. An infatuation with a misconstrued neonationalist/individualist ethic should not be allowed to subvert the chances for progress and stability inherent in adopting a communitarian ethic within and among the interdependent communities into which the populations of the world have sundered.

A communitarian organization has a vision of a common good and pursuit of shared ends which enhances individual pursuit; it is perfectionist, in that it is value-laden; it is a theoretical companion of the capitalist economic enterprise, not an epistemological enemy. The communitarian ethic for corporate enterprise corresponds to the "stakeholder theory of the firm" as explained by Igor Ansoff in 1965; and it is the moral component of both liberalism and laissez faire economics. Corporate responsibility to its employees, its suppliers, customers, investors and creditors, debtors, government and the public is basically an expression of the obligations arising out of a new body, a discreet, legal member of the larger society. Such corporate responsibility, which I characterize as an expression of the communitarian ethic, is inseparable from the capitalist system, a natural extension of the created body's need to preserve and secure its place and purpose. The examination of the record of many firms who are choosing to exercise what I describe as the communitarian ethic reveals greater profit, not less, accompanied by greater worker satisfaction and increased assumptions of responsibility for one's own welfare.

In conclusion, Chapter VI summarizes the juxtaposition of the American and Japanese models and demonstrates how both of these major organizational models suffer from their own excesses, the consequences of which spill over into the societies they serve. Elite economic institutions are powerful harbingers of social and personal well being; in an interconnected world the dualities of diversity and unity in individualistic and collective societies take on new significance. We are coming to realize our membership in a community beyond our cultural boundaries. The either-or's of individualism and collectivism are displaced and interpenetrated. As we proceed to learn our way around this larger social and economic order in which we have discovered ourselves, the communitarian ethic allows us to look beyond reliance on the unfettered market or the bureaucratic regulatory state for steerage and guidance through global change.

The communitarian ethic is an appropriate theoretical bridge between the corporate organizational styles of the American and Japanese models. Both philosophically sound and morally correct for the individuals, communities, and organizations who constitute the modern global society, the communitarian ethic is both corrective and alimentary. For individuals, the ethic relieves the estrangement and alienation of both faceless and servile labor, leaving a whole human being who is more aware of her self-worth and more emotionally and intellectually equipped to meet her broader responsibilities to herself and to others. For society, the ethic re-unites and uplifts work and civil communities of all cultural preferences, strengthening the democratic process and the intermediate civil institutions of normal life. For organizations, the ethic enables full-fledged partnership with all the stakeholders—the owners, stockholders, managers, workers, and customers—melding the profit motive with moral responsibility.

Great conceptual theories are generally idealistic; I do not contend that such is not the extant case. What I do contend, however, is that the communitarian ethic holds great promise for organizations who more often than not find themselves caught between a presumptive Scylla and Charybdis of high returns on investment and moral rectitude. And to make implementation even more difficult, the incorporation of the communication ethic into organization theory requires an epiphany of sorts—a moment of profound which must then be translated into meaningful action by leaders who recognize the rich and complex blend of economic, social, and political purpose.

A Hungarian minister in site negotiations with American executives for investment in his country stipulated "rebuilding our community" in his vision statement. The same poignant sentiment was discovered among the Lithuanians. (Foster, 1998) These political and economic leaders recognize the symbiosis between work and community as a reflection of the moral content of economic development. I would submit that the communitarian ethic is the natural expression of that moral content.

The Communitarian Organization

CHAPTER I
Democratization and Complex Interdependence

Political transformations in the last three decades have swept authoritarian and totalitarian governments into a new array of emerging democracies unversed in democratic forms and processes. Released to express their nationalist fervor, peoples in these newly-democratic states have tended to generate strife within and among themselves, rather than reap the promise of a democratic peace. Equally profound economic change has tailed political conversion, sharpening and directing the pangs of change of unaccustomed forces of capitalism, exaggerating cultural differences, and creating zig-zag paths to growth and development. Accompanied by increasing technological sophistication swiftly sweeping the world economy from the Industrial Age to the Information Age, dynamic expectations and market demands are washing away the old paradigms of mass production, leaving in their wake new forms of organizations who continue to struggle to keep up with extraordinarily diffuse and vigorous market metamorphoses.

LIBERALIZATION, DEMOCRATIZATION AND TRANSITION

Samuel Huntington describes a "Third Wave" of global regime democratizations between 1974 and 1990, in which as many as thirty-five countries shifted from various forms of authoritarianism to democratic systems. But these democracies are as yet incomplete; while they satisfy the Huntington criterion of elections as the essence of democracy, they remain in varying stages in the democratization sequence. (Huntington, 1991, 5) Huntington argues that given the complex interrelationships of contemporary global society, the implications and associations of democracy are not only the strongest determinants for individual freedom and liberty, they also constitute the greatest hope for global peace and stability. Huntington will also posit, however, first in an article for *Foreign Affairs* in 1993 and continuing in the 1996 publication of *The Clash of Civilizations and the Remaking of World Order*, that however unifying the spirit of democratization, the promise of a world democratic order is subsumed by the divisive forces of culture and cultural identities.

Huntington's democratization process rests on five essential factors of change: (1) declining regime legitimacy and performance dilemmae; (2) global economic development and economic crises; (3) religious changes; (4) changing policies of external actors; and (5) snowballing, or the demonstration effects of other democratizations. But this pentalogical procedure is but a skeleton; the body is the historical experience of those countries he considers as a part of the third wave and how that experience reveals the mosaic of the democratization process. He warns that "In any particular country, democratization was the result of a combination of some general causes plus other factors unique to that country." (Huntington, 107) And the final catalyst for any and all change was political leadership: "In the third wave, the conditions for creating democracy had to exist, but only political leaders willing to take the risk of democracy made it happen." (Huntington, 108)

Huntington's typology is an expression of his perceptions and analyses of societies, their histories, their cultures, their leaders, and their reactions to conditions. His list of factors is rather extensive, and he points out that each country moving toward democratization exhibits different combinations of the factors, omitting some, or proceeding to democracy regardless of the presence or absence of some of those factors.

Not all of Huntington's factors appear to be endorsed by other scholars. Mainwaring points out that, in general, new democracies (of the same period of Huntington's examination) proceed primarily through an expansion of political contestation. Mainwaring begins his analysis of the factors of democratization with the process of liberalization, but he warns that even when liberalization begins as a precursor to democratization, it is sometimes aborted and leads to renewed repression, rather than to democratization. According to Mainwaring, joining Kaufman (1986), O'Donnell and Schmitter

(1986), Chalmers and Robinson (1982), and Przeworski (1986) liberalization begins for a variety of reasons, some of which reflect some commonality with Huntington's factors, and some of which bring new factors into the dialogue. For example, in his works and the works of the referenced authors, liberalization begins with a schism within the authoritarian coalitions, perhaps because of the failures of the regime, but, paradoxically in some cases, because authoritarian elites believe they have little to lose and much legitimacy to gain by leading a liberalization process. And according to Mainwaring, the new democracies in Latin America have generally failed to reflect a democratization process based on popular interests. This is not to say that the masses are not important, Mainwaring continues: "Democratic politics is a system of interactions and accountability between rulers and ruled. One need not romanticize how effective accountability is to perceive that the position of the rulers depends on their ability to appeal to the majority." (Mainwaring, 1992, 304, citing Dahl 1956 and 1961; Sartori, 1987)

Susser argues that genuine democracy involves the presence of a communal ethos, that it is dependent on an "inner psycho-social reality that binds citizens together into a unit." (Susser, 1995, 92) Fowler and Orenstein propose that democratization is a consequence of the creation of a culture that arises out of the free exercise of ideas, coalescing in the belief that citizens have a moral right and collective capacity to pick their rulers. (Fowler and Orenstein, 1993, 162-163) Przeworski juxtaposes two explanations for regime changes to democracy: loss of legitimacy, and conflicts within the ruling bloc which cannot be reconciled and which drives one faction to appeal to outside groups for support, a process he labels "extrication," a condition which is dependent on the development of a civil society. (Przeworski, 1985 and 1986, cited by Mainwaring, 304; Przeworski, 1992, 107-117)

Huntington's argument is anchored on his first general factor of democratic change, the development of what he calls a "world democratic ethos" (Huntington, 47) produced by the Allied victory in World War II, an ethos which by the 1980s appeared the only viable alternative to the inadequacies of authoritarian regimes. Faced with ideological, performance, and procedural dilemmae, absent traditional legitimizations for nondemocratic rule such as religion, divine right, and social deference, and void of a credible enemy to nationalism and ideology, eventually all types of authoritarian regimes succumbed to erosion and/or demise of legitimacy. According to Huntington, the regime transitions of the third wave reveal a trend to democracy as a consequence of an absence of authoritarian mechanisms for self-renewal. (Huntington, 46-58)

With respect to his second factor, Huntington joins Lipset (*Political Man*) and Dahl (*Polyarchy: Participation and Opposition*) among others, to affirm the correlation between wealth and democracy: "Most wealthy countries are democratic and most democratic countries—India is the most dramatic exception—are wealthy." (Huntington, 1991, 60) According to Huntington, the data reflect such a close correlation as to imply at what level of economic development countries may be expected to resort to democratization, based on their per capita GNP. He labels this point the "transition zone," and declares that:

> ... the post-World War II surge of economic growth that lasted until the oil shocks of 1973-74 moved many countries into the transition zone, creating within them the economic conditions favorable to the development of democracy. In considerable measure, the wave of democratizations that began in 1974 was the product of the economic growth of the previous two decades. (Huntington, 61)

The synergist in the economic factor, however, is the rate of economic growth, which "raises expectations, exacerbates inequalities, and creates stresses and strains in the social fabric that stimulate political mobilization and demands for political participation." (Huntington, 69) If economic crisis and/or failure accompanies substantial levels of economic development, as Huntington found in the third wave regimes, conditions become most favorable for a transition from authoritarian to democratic government. (Huntington, 72)

Huntington stands alone in our examination of the liberalization-to-democratization continuum in his proposal that there is a strong correlation between Western Christianity and democracy. His observations are based on his findings that Catholicism and/or Protestantism were the dominant religions in thirty-nine of forty-six democratizing countries. While denying that the correlation proves causation, nevertheless Huntington believes it strong enough to "hypothesize that the expansion of Christianity encourages democratic development." (Huntington, 73)

Democratization and Complex Interdependence 7

Catholicism was second only to economic development as a pervasive force making for democratization in the 1970s and 1980s. The logo of the third wave could well be a crucifix superimposed on a dollar sign. (Huntington, 85)

But since numbers of Huntington's democratizing countries in the third wave are in Latin America, and Catholicism is the traditional religion of the region, there may be some overrepresentation in the data. In addition, the power of Catholic Liberation Theory in Latin American countries may not be discounted in these regime changes. Led by Catholic progressives, the theology of liberation prescribed new political and pastoral practice for the Church and society. Beginning in the 1950's, many priests and nuns who worked with the poor and oppressed across Latin America and the Caribbean began to exercise a new political activism, and sought new, sometimes revolutionary, ways of securing social justice. Liberation theology proposes that the Church should be concerned not just with the needs of humanity, but with political and economic repression as well, with priests directly involved in transforming repressive political regimes. Franciscan priest Leonardo Boff is perhaps the best known theorist of liberation theology. His arguments for the oppressed to organize for immediate reform, and his exhortations to seek a new society characterized by widespread participation cannot be entirely rejected as a force for democratization in Latin America. (Sargent, 1996, 215-221; Baradat, 1994, 266, 285)

Huntington's fourth factor of change addresses the relationship between democratization and the actions of governments and institutions outside that country. He proposes that this factor is associated with economic and social development in that the effects of external influence depend on where in the transition zone it intervenes. At the time of the third wave, the major sources of global power and influence were those of liberalization and democratization. The consolidation of human rights policies as a major issue in international relations brought about by a host of international actors in the 1970s and 1980s "altered the international environment." (Huntington, 94, citing A. Schlesinger) Citing the Helsinki Process of 1975, the American attachment of trade practices to human rights, and a variety of international economic pressures and sanctions, propaganda, diplomatic action, material support, military action, and multilateral pressures designed to promote human rights and democracy abroad, Huntington affirms the positive/negative authority of external power when he surmises that it was the exercise of American power which fueled democratization in Latin America and East Asia, but it was the abdication of Soviet power that effected Eastern European democratization. (Huntington, 100) This somewhat contradictory analysis on the part of Huntington reveals the complex nature of democratization in diverse cultures. Huntington is very resolute in his warning that "The search for a common, universally present independent variable that might play a significant role in explaining political development in . . . different countries is almost certain to be unsuccessful if it is not tautological." (Huntington, 38) Just as in one country one factor may outweigh the others, there may be a complete absence of numbers of factors in other democratization cases. He reminds us that "In politics, almost everything has many causes." (Huntington, 38) The multiplicity of theories and the diversity of experience reveal substantial differences from place-to-place and from time-to-time, with no single factor being both necessary and sufficient for the development of democracy in all countries in general, or in one country in particular. (Huntington, 38)

But Huntington is persuaded that third wave demonstration effects owe their significance to advanced communication and transportation technology which "made it increasingly difficult for authoritarian governments to keep from their elites and even their publics information on the struggles against and the overthrow of authoritarian regimes in other countries." (Huntington, 102) This "snowballing" is a pattern of contagious reactions to the substance, method and consequences of democratization from one society to another, and it is both a factor and product of democratization. While the earliest democratizations of the third wave occurred out of a combination of events as described by the other factors of change, snowballing may have later substituted for those changes, and acted independently when the other factors may not have been present. According to Huntington, issues of proximity and cultural similarity produced a profound tide of snowballing democratization in Eastern Europe: "Everyone knew from their neighbors' experience, that it could be done." (Huntington, 104) This is not to imply, however, that democratization is so alluring as to preclude serious, indeed catastrophic, pitfalls in the path. While the former Yugoslavia might well have been expected to serve as a prime democratic model for Eastern Europe, based on its atypical Soviet history, nevertheless, the political and social anguish of Bosnia, Croatia, and Serbia are a constant reminder that predictions of behavior

Democratization and Complex Interdependence

in times of extreme political change may well be an exercise in futility. Huntington will address this phenomenon in later treatises on what he calls the "clash of civilizations."

Robert Jervis' analysis of changes in patterns of world politics in Eastern Europe after 1990 reiterate Huntington's interdependency assessment. While Jervis believes that the development of democracies in the region does indeed create the possibility of new, broader ties of mutual interest and peaceful coexistence through the persuasion of democratic values and causes, nevertheless, he is unconvinced that Eastern European democracies have grasped the democratic notion of cooperation and interaction necessary to prevent disputation and conflict. (Jervis, 1993, 19-20) Bruce Russett's remarks on a democratic peace are pertinent:

> [D]emocratically organized political systems in general operate under restraints that make them more peaceful in their relations with other democracies . . . the relationship of relative peace among democracies is importantly a result of some features of democracy, rather than being caused exclusively by economic or geopolitical characteristics correlated with democracy. (Russett, 1993, 11)

But Russett proposes that there are serious flaws in the arguments that propose that transnationalism and the creation of alliances explain peace between democratic states, although each of these factors may be related to democratic linkages that help resolve conflicts. Russett believes, as does Jervis, that the most important theoretical explanations for peace between democratic states are situated in the development of democratic norms and cultures which allow for dissent and structural and institutional constraints which serve to reduce the likelihood of violence. (Russett, 24-42) Jervis appears to share this assessment, insisting that the countries of Eastern Europe lack "stable, democratic governments that have learned to cooperate and have developed a stake in each other's well-being." (Jervis, 20)

Crockatt points out that there is a continuing, vigorous debate among practitioners and theorists of political science to explain both the end of the Cold War political system and perspectives on the kinds of structures which might develop in their place. On the one hand, those who considered the period of the Cold War as stable, diminishing its dangers, tend to view the future as dangerously unstructured. On the other hand, however, those who considered the period of the Cold War as an artificial brake on a global tendency toward interdependence and multipolarity are more inclined to consider the end of the Cold War as an opportunity for the establishment of some sort of new world order. While Francis Fukuyama asserted the triumph of liberal democracy in his essay "The End of History?" in 1989, and liberal scholars such as R. O. Keohane credit the role of human-created institutions and the importance of changeable political processes as the instruments of change, nevertheless, Crockatt claims that there is a need for consideration of both the historical and empirical evidence as a means to understand the structure of the Cold War, its demise, and possibilities for the nature of its successor international system. (Crockatt, 1993, 59-64)

Crockatt claims that "The Cold War system has not so much collapsed as been bypassed, and to that extent it is an example of system change without war." (Crockatt, 77) But that is not to imply, according to Crockatt, that human beings are forever released from fundamental ideological conflicts. While the United States could ". . . afford to fight the Cold War with one hand while making money with the other," (Crockatt, 77) the costs of the Cold War were much higher on former Soviet states. Viewed in this light, the political enmities of the Cold War system were in a tangential relationship with the growth of the world capitalist system. According to Crockatt:

> From this perspective it is possible to view the postwar period as one of an interplay between two distinct but intersecting systems, the Cold War system possessing a political and military dynamic of its own, and a globalising capitalist system whose growth progressively undermined the stability of the Cold War system. (Crockatt, 78)

But, warns Crockatt, there is little reason to believe that war and conflict are at an end: "All one can say is that one particular phase of history, characterised by a particular arrangement of the international system, is now over. What its outcome will be is as yet unclear." (Crockatt, 77) The events in Chechnya and Bosnia-Herzegovina illustrate the immense range of variables which must be considered in interpreting tendencies or events which are not only always in motion, but are also only partly known. (Crockatt, 78) While it is true that the Soviet Union disintegrated without war with the West, it has fallen victim to internal strife and warfare so severe as to involve the international community in securing a peaceful resolution of its conflicts, and raising the spectre of future conflicting alliances.

In 1992 Fukuyama expanded his earlier perspective on the legitimacy of liberal democracy, explaining the present process of democratization from an Hegelian point of view. Hegel, and later Marx regarded History as an evolutionary process, flowing inexorably to, for Hegel, the liberal state, and for Marx, a communist society; hence the designation "The End of History." But it is the philosophy at the core of these perspectives that Fukuyama explores; that is, if the present course of democratizations coupled with the almost worldwide acceptance of liberal principles in economics is indeed an Historical destiny. (Fukuyama, 1992, xi-iv)

Mike Bowker focuses on the social, ideological, and economic conditions and changes of the period pre-dating the Reagan and Gorbachev eras to support his premise that internal change brought about at the inter-state level by socio-economic problems in the Soviet Union fueled the demise of Soviet policy and the democratization of Eastern Europe. Not unlike Crockatt, he argues that the Soviet perspective during the Cold war was based on a combination of variables. While he argues, with Kennan and Brzezinski, that the ultimate goal of the Soviet Union was to destroy the international capitalist system, or at the least, to undermine the basic Western interests of free enterprise and free trade, he also joins those scholars who have stressed the totalitarian structures of the Soviet Union and the peculiar Russian political culture as explanations for Soviet behavior. (Bowker, 1993, 82-86)

However, Bowker claims that the choices made by the Soviet leadership which were to eventually culminate in radically new political thinking were only influenced, rather than determined, by external events. Examining the ideology of the totalitarian model and Slavophile and geostrategic perspectives of the Russian culture, Bowker concludes that it is short-sighted to ignore the internal forces for change. He observes that there was little direct pressure on the Kremlin in 1985 to embark on any program of radical reform, and that *perestroika* was a revolution designed from above to benefit the elite and burgeoning professional groups in the Soviet Union. According to Bowker, pressure for change was the culmination of long-standing problems, including economic difficulties and disaffection in Eastern Europe: "As Soviet writers have noted, capitalism has not been successful everywhere, but communism has not been successful anywhere."

(Bowker, 106) Bowker also argues that in effect Gorbachev's abandonment of Eastern Europe, specifically East Germany, in 1989, allowed, even encouraged momentous change:

> ... it was the Presidential spokesman, Gennadi Gerasimov, who publicly fired the starting pistol for radical reform in Eastern Europe. In October 1989, Gerasimov formally declared that the Breshnev (sic) Doctrine was dead, and said it had been replaced by the Sinatra Doctrine. In other words, the people of Eastern Europe were free to leave the Soviet embrace and do things their way. (Bowker, 107)

According to Bowker, it is this release of Eastern Europe from the geostrategic web of the Soviet Union that provides insight into the Gorbachev policy. Gorbachev, already convinced that the East and West were not necessarily in conflict on every issue, and that the "zero-sum concepts of the Cold War were redundant," (Bowker, 89) perceived that the region had lost its former strategic importance. If the West was no longer a threat, and if there would be substantial economic benefits accrued with Soviet withdrawal from Eastern Europe, rationality permitted, in effect mandated, the release of Eastern Europe. (Bowker, 88-110)

But, like Jervis and Crockatt, Bowker recites the warnings of those who fear democracy may still be overthrown, not by communists, but by the nationalist forces which were constricted by the forces of the former Soviet system:

> Economic and ethnic crisis is gathering pace. The new leaders confront enormous difficulties in restoring any kind of stability to the country. In the circumstances, authoritarian measures may be perceived as an increasingly attractive option. Viktor Alksnis . . . prominent member of the conservative group, Soyuz, may be right when he predicted that even the reformers will be compelled to use tanks to quell future food riots . . . . (Bowker, 91)

When the political order is drastically changed, as it has been in numbers of nations around the world in the recent past, the members of those societies flounder for firm footing. A host of newly democratic states exist precariously in an unfamiliar world system, states which may be only minimally democratic, i.e., through the incorporation of the election process, or what Sartori calls "popular power," (Sartori,

1987, 482) but have yet to traverse to a commitment to democratic norms and institutions. "In 1993 Freedom House reports 75 free nations, up from 55 a decade earlier, with only 31 percent of the world's population, and most of that in China, living under repressive regimes, down from 44 percent ten years ago." (Bartley, 1993, 16) Manifested first in southern Europe in Portugal, Greece, and Spain in the early-to-mid 1970's, democratization was effected in Latin America in Ecuador, Peru, Bolivia, Uruguay, and Brazil, among others. These countries would be joined in the 1980's and early 1990's by, for example, Chile, Grenada, Panama, Nicaragua, and Haiti. In Central America Honduras installed a civilian president in January of 1982; in May 1984 Salvadoran voters participated in a hotly contested election for president; Guatemala chose a constituent assembly in 1984 and a civilian president in 1985. In Asia, India returned to democracy in 1977; the Turkish military regime gave way to civilian government in 1983. They were followed by the Philippines in 1986, a civilian presidency in Korea in 1987, significant liberalization in Taiwan in 1987 and 1988, and an end to military rule in Pakistan in 1988. By the end of the decade Hungary, the Baltic republics, and Poland joined the growing list of liberalizing/democratizing states. With the collapse of the communist regimes in East Germany, Czechoslovakia, Romania, Bulgaria, Mongolia, and eventually Russia, Belarus, Ukraine, and a host of former Soviet states, democratization in most cases, and liberalization in others, became a global political norm. (Huntington, 1991, 21-24)

Singer and Wildavsky are convinced that eventually democratic regimes will take root among the majority of the peoples of the world, even in the face of sporadic failures in the search for stable governments. The legitimation of government, the creation of democratic institutions, and the development of a public democratic consciousness are qualitative components of a democratic continuum that reflects power that comes not from force, but from widespread civil debate and negotiation. The position of individual "democracies" on this continuum is necessarily variant; of course, the more inclusive, stable, and representative the government, the higher quality the democracy, and the higher its position on the continuum. (Singer and Wildavsky, 1993, 50-56)

But while world democratization is certainly a welcome political development in the sense of the opportunities it affords for greater attention to issues of human rights, and less coercion through participatory forms of government, democratization is far from a panacea. Indeed, democratization may simply be a momentary palliative, a temporary substitute for regimes which, when the growing and consolidation pains of democracy take hold, will seem favorable in retrospect. It may be an exercise in futility to make firm predictions that the third wave of democratization will indeed be permanent; indeed, that is why Huntington refers to it as a "wave," a process which has happened before, and may be transitory in those nations and cultures unfamiliar with its institutional and economic ramifications.

Neonationalism

The post-1990 global village is an international community of unlike tribes, a tightly coupled global network of diverse nation-states and distinct cultures whose mutual destinies are increasingly entangled politically and economically. Relationships among the new and renewed democracies of Latin America and Africa and the reconstituted and transformed nation-states of the former Soviet Union with the regimes of the Western democracies remain in flux. Although anxious to interact economically with the world, the structures of these societies, liberated from old constraints of ideology and tyranny, remain culture-bound and passionately nationalistic, challenged by the dialectic of becoming modern without becoming Western. (Huntington, 1993)

Huntington is not sanguine about what Fukuyama labels Universal History, or Singer and Wildavsky's view of extensive democratic regimes. Expanding an argument published in an article in *Foreign Affairs* in 1993, Huntington proposes that the world remains a fractious place, with viable peace and the international order threatened by the forces of cultural divisiveness. There is a good deal of scholarly support for Huntington's argument that "In the post-Cold War world, the most important distinctions among peoples are not ideological, political, or economic. They are cultural." (Huntington, 1996, 21)

Zbigniew Brzezinski refers to these societies as the "shipwrecks of communism and . . . the deprived masses of the Third World," (Brzezinski, 1993, 66) who see the West as model, not idol. Whether a consequence or instrumentality of change, rising tides of nationalism have intermixed with the allure of the free market system and the democratic idea to bring about the collapse of communism as both system and ideology. (Brzezinski, 61) However economically ambitious, having shed familiar, coercive patterns of politics, economics, and society, these new democracies are loathe to enter into arrangements that threaten their new sense of national integrity. While worldwide democratization bears some promise of a peaceful future among transformed centers of power, persistent threats of Western domination and cultural friction challenge the new democracies and baffle more established democratic states. Many of the new democracies, struggling to establish unfamiliar systems of internal order, concomitantly discover that there are some elements of democracy and liberalism that encourage nationalistic fervor. The *desencanto* that inevitably follows democratization threatens to rip apart nascent strands of liberty and freedom in societies with few historical democratic precedents and practices. (Mainwairing, et al, 1992, 2) Depersonalization and alienation tend to spring from the confounding political turbulence of nation-states that are first structurally demolished and then reshaped in new and unfamiliar forms. In many cases, such as in Eastern Europe, the collapse of the bonds of totalitarianism and artificial associations have left their societies unprepared socially and politically for the vagaries of self-rule. They have not passed through significant phases of liberalization; while they exhibit some of Huntington's factors for change, the demise of the Soviet Union was so abrupt, so sudden, and so bereft of the citizen/leadership coalition most authors on democratization find necessary, they have been forced to struggle unprepared through regime change, pitifully oblivious to the advantages and consequences of democratization. Long-suffering traditional communities and local cultures, fueled by ethnic anxiety and the impulse to cultural distinctiveness, glorified religious zeal and an apocalyptic quest for martyrdom, challenge a sense of optimism for global serenity.

Some of these new democracies have no generational experience with the prescriptive elements of democracy; they have no passion for liberty in the sense of its loss at some point in the past. Having never experienced democracy, they may be ill-served by an unfamiliar ideology which ennobles self interest at the expense of community traditions and responsibilities. What is the sanctuary when the accustomed virtues, certitudes, and obligations of community are diminished? Does individualism as an *a priori* for democracy ever work in cultures in which the *demos* has hitherto been unable to decide nothing? (Sartori, 482)

We can look at Burke's comments on the French Revolution for clues to some of the unrest and discomfort that find expression in violent nationalist confrontation. According to Burke, legitimate rights and political institutions arise organically in the social relationship of human beings, and interference with the political order jeopardizes civil society. (Brenkert, 1991, 28) Civil society is the natural state of human beings; the society that emerged when men came together as social creatures had almost mystical qualities, which enabled civilization itself. The social nature of man is the source of natural rights: ". . . rights do not exist *a priori* or abstractly, but concretely in society." (Nelson, 1996, 263)

The paradox is inescapable: The same forces that have brought world peace have also begotten local strife. According to Graham Fuller:

> Nationalist feelings and aspirations will acquire a new assertiveness, springing from international relaxation of tensions and rising expectations. Many states of the world had little opportunity in the Cold War period to settle old scores or redraw national boundaries after independence. Their nationalism will no longer be directed against former colonial rulers but against an "unjust international order" of winners and losers. Although the West will still undoubtedly come in for its share of attack, these new nationalist movements will take aim at rival proximate nations, or at other communal groups within the same state boundaries . . . . The more alien the democratic tradition is to the state, the rawer the forms in which neonationalism will express itself." (Fuller, 1991/1992, 15)

Neonationalism represents more than the reaction to political restructuring and newly-acquired freedoms. "Its most characteristic features spring from far deeper roots: the search for meaningful identity in the modern world. Indeed, anomie—alienation and a sense of loss of self-identification—is a problem that affects the entire world, capitalist or socialist, advanced or undeveloped." (Fuller, 16)

Neonationalism is also a reaction to the forces of modernity. Feelings of localism and particularism, cultural pride, and animosity flourish in indigenous cultures and traditional societies in every part of the globe where one group's way of life is threatened either by other more advanced or powerful ethnic and religious elements, or by the powerful, inescapable forces of modernization itself. (Fuller, 15-16)

The new nationalism is an emotional response of a culture to a threat to its integrity. William Pfaff calls it "an expression of the primordial attachments of an individual to a group," (Pfaff, 1993, 196) neither synonymous with nor limited to the nation state, a form of group identity which is inexhaustible, hopeful, frequently irrational, and ferocious when frustrated. (Pfaff, 196-200)

The general problems associated with democratization are exacerbated by its association with capitalism and market economics, a process which exerts a certain double-bind on the system. Liberalism, with its emphasis on private property and political equality, can also lead to greater poverty and social inequality. It comes with no guarantee of a "chicken in every pot." It is a fair system only in the sense of its support of equality of opportunity, not equality of results. Successful democratization in those states experiencing severe initial economic inequities and social trauma is not a foregone conclusion. Reinhold Niebuhr's Myth of Democratic Universality suggests that democracy may not be a universal option for all nations. (D. P. Moynihan, 1993, 168-169)

In order for political arrangements to be sustained, they must maintain legitimacy with the governed. It is therefore incumbent that new forms of political systems must effect a match with the historic values and cultural pillars of their societies. (Weisbord and Janoff, 1995, ix) But since all ideologies condone some inequities and condemn others, in times of systemic change, society may be called upon to simply switch its allegiance from one set of inequitable arrangements to another. This is not a process unique to liberalization or democratization. New Communist regimes, fascist regimes, theocratic regimes, monarchies, or socialist regimes all face this problem when first established. But the capitalist concept of taking for one's self the profit of one's labor and the private property rights which are attendant to Western capitalist democratic systems may generate internal social afflictions and international squabbles. If the allure of personal gain offered by the capitalist system is unrestrained by respect for the certitudes of community values and traditions, economic growth and development may become the antecedent of civil disorder and the harbinger of increased social stratification. The have-nots in new democracies may become impatient with a political system that sanctions an economic system that seems to trigger unemployment, staggering rates of inflation, depleted purchasing power and living standards, financial chaos and debt crises, and human suffering. It is difficult to embrace capitalistic democracy if the disadvantages of competition are allowed to prevail. "Economic adjustment to improve competitiveness in international markets and fiscal and monetary restraint to fight inflation are hardly compatible with the political agenda of democratic consolidation." (Mainwaring, et al, 9)

While democratic aspirations as ideals have traversed international borders, extending the opportunity for representation and the development of political institutions and self-determination and democracy in-country, it is also clear that "the proliferation of transnational activities and decisions reduces the capacity of the citizens of a country to exercise control over matters vitally important to them by means of their national government." (Dahl, 1994, 27)

> The globe may be in the process of shrinking, but in many ways this has served merely to make people in the various parts of the globe more aware of their differences. (Ray, 1979, 361)

Robin Brown suggests that these international and transnational processes may create a dialectical relationship between sovereign states, with which Liu concurs, proposing that new arrangements may lead to conflicts between civilizations seeking to improvise new means of balancing their own peculiar interests in a global struggle. (Bowker and Brown, 1993, 14; Liu, 1993) Denying the Fukuyama's end of history model, Huntington's notion of a world divided by cultural diversity into a "clash of civilizations" is fulfilled by widespread evidence of regional strife in the post-Cold War world. (Huntington, 1996, 31) His vision of a "Velvet Curtain of culture" (Huntington, 1993, 31) which shrouds civilizations and drives societies to resist the allure of Western universalism also impels newly identified groups to deny to the "other" what they seek for themselves. Quoting Michael Dibdin's nationalist demagogue in *Dead Lagoon*: "There can be no true friends without true enemies. Unless we hate what we are not, we cannot love what we are." (Cited in Huntington, 1996, 20)

Huntington claims that civilization identity will become increasingly important in the future; in a reprise of the Western Culture Thesis he asserts that the line which defined the eastern boundary of Western Christianity in 1500 may well be the most significant dividing line in Europe:

[T]he world will be shaped in large measure by the interactions among seven or eight major civilizations. These include Western, Confucian, Japanese, Islamic, Hindu, Slavic-Orthodox, Latin American and possibly African civilization. The most important conflicts of the future will occur along the cultural fault lines separating these civilizations from one another. (Huntington, 1993, 25)

THE NEW ECONOMIC AGE

Global economic changes have produced an international transformation fully as profound as political re-orientation and upheaval. Resting on the foundation of post-World War II investment and economic restoration of Europe and Japan, high levels of economic intercourse have significantly increased the wealth of many nations, while other economies continue to struggle. While the post World War II economic dream was to create countries equally as wealthy as the United States, the success of the GATT-Bretton Woods trading system, the Marshall Plan, and the European Coal and Steel Community is noteworthy. (Drucker, 1989, 22-23) With the tremendous expansion of the world economy, foreign aid, and an open, easily accessed American market, the record for the years 1950 to 1980 reflects a quadrupled world real GNP, from 2 trillion to about 8 trillion in U.S. dollars. (Kennedy, 1993, 48) And it is a world in which no one doubts that trade is necessary for prosperity; while people in one country might blame those in another for unfair economic competition, the belief that one's economic well-being is linked to that of others is a strong impetus for the development of interconnected systems that are mutually beneficial. (Jervis, 13-14)

Economic development, the creation of modern wealth, and increased productivity have established fertile conditions for governmental arrangements that enable individuals to receive most of the benefits of their labor. (Singer and Wildavsky, 44-50; 56) "The combination of instant information, economic interdependence and the appeal of individual freedom is not a force to be taken lightly." (Bartley, 16)

However, the features of transformed global arrangements are neither solely perpetrated nor singularly produced by democratization; increasingly, inter-relatedness exhibits a transnational nature dominated by regional units and transnational economic enterprise. (Drucker, 115-

116) Absent political barriers, democratic commonalities may be the enabler; but the engines of change are economic. But such engines of change are proceeding at different speeds and in diverse directions, creating numbers of states tenaciously pursuing the brass ring of capitalism, regardless of their level of readiness or existence of the infrastructure associated with modern economies. Where investment once followed trade, now trade follows investment. Maximization of market standing has become everything in a transnational world where the components of production can be scattered about the globe, wherever the economics of manufacturing dictate. (Drucker, 120-124)

Democratization has stimulated an opportunistic, transnational economy which exhibits what Luttwak calls "geo-economics," a central arena of world competition characterized by aggressive national technology programs, predatory finance schemes, and ambush-like tariffs and technical standards. Absent military/political threats to world peace, economic priorities emerge and become dominant; under these conditions, the unifying external threat is geo-economic. (Luttwak, 1993, 40) Driven not by a quest for gold, or pure wealth, in geo-economics the ultimate purpose is to maximize high-grade employment in advanced industries and sophisticated services, a game of pursuit played by countries that have ruled out war among them, yet who have yet to determine the extent of participation and the rules of the game for themselves and others. (Luttwak, 41-42)

According to Kennedy, response to global change has been and will continue to be uneven: "While some are in distress, others are booming—but what else ought one to expect when analyzing nations ranging from Singapore to Burkina Faso?" (Kennedy, 218) Change may also be discomfiting to existing habits, ways of life, beliefs, and social prejudices. Any transformation is likely to be perceived as a threat to entrenched cultural norms; but Kennedy posits that "it . . . seems fair to assume that most peoples of the world, *if they so choose*, can respond positively to the challenges of change." (Kennedy, 16)

In addition to differing rates of GDP growth, economic performance may also be characterized by the measure of basic human needs, which defines a country's development only in terms of conditions in which more of its people "are gaining adequate diets, clean water, decent shelter, basic health care and education, and a peaceful means of making their views known to the government." (Bronfenbrenner et al, 1990, 454) Economic development therefore means different things to different people; situations in which "the numbers prosper while the people suffer," (Bronfenbrenner, et al, 454 citing G. Papandreou) may represent growth, but not necessarily development to all societies.

A significant consequence of developmental disparities has been the advent of *dependencia* theories of exploitation which argue that the prosperity of the First World is dependent upon the poverty of the Third World, and the poverty of the Third World dependent upon the prosperity of the First World, a structural position in a hierarchical world division of labor, sustained by inherently exploitative linkages between local elites in penetrated societies and advanced capitalist states. Dependency theorists contend that international capitalists make decisions for the whole world, determining the political and social consequences of those decisions through exploitation and domination. (Bronfenbrenner, et al, 460-461; Kegley and Wittkopf, 1993, 142-144)

But historians such as Walt W. Rostow argue that traditional societies must pass through a series of developmental stages to reach similarity to the high mass consumption societies of the West. Rostow's optimistic five-part institutional stage theory, initiated in traditional society and passing through phases outlined as preconditions for takeoff, takeoff, drive to maturity, and high mass consumption or maturity, describes the attainment of a society characterized by various combinations of the factors of militarism and imperialism, the welfare state, and high mass consumption, and gives little credence to the effect of more developed countries on lesser developed ones. (Bronfenbrenner, et al, 462-463; Kegley and Wittkopf, 142-143) But Rostow's analysis is based on the experience of Western societies; it may not hold for the experience of non-Western countries.

Nevertheless, the trauma and variable rates of development point to growing pressures on the traditional states. For example, while admitting that the attachment of citizens to their nation is a strong, valuable force, Singer and Wildavsky suggest that the developing overall international order may call for the reorganization of governments, in recognition of the convergence of political and economic function in government:

> The idea is for countries to transfer responsibility for the economic part of government from their single national government to multiple regional or provincial governmental units. Since most politics follows the money, this transfer would make the politics of the province at least as important as that of the nation. (Singer and Wildavsky, 123)

Calling their idea one of "competitive subnational governments," Singer and Wildavsky envision a future increasingly linked by a complex web of overlapping local, regional, national, and supranational governmental units each with their respective specialized functions, source of authority, form of politics, powers, and constituency. Subnational units, with authority for business and commerce, exercising their power apart from the national government responsibility for defense and foreign policy, national culture and identity, would enable competition, make for smaller governments, and preserve the democratic vitality, honor and authority of the national government. Believing that dividing up power can make learning to live together easier, Singer and Wildavsky's proposal suggests a rebirth of federalisms as a remedy for bad government, big government, and conflictual nationalism. (Singer and Wildavsky, 122-129)

Peter Drucker argues that theory which assumes that the sovereign state is the sole, or even predominant unit, is already passe. He is convinced that the transnational economy already exhibits four partially dependent, linked, interdependent units: The national state; the region; the world economy of money, credit, and investment; and the transnational organization. (Drucker, 116)

In addition to growing international interdependence, the very nature of economic activity has undergone a fundamental transformation as well. Alvin and Heidi Toffler argue that change and transformation evident in the post-1990 global environment are the consequence of a "Third Wave of Civilization," which brings with it "new family styles, changed ways of working, loving, and living, a new economy, new political conflicts, and beyond all this an altered consciousness as well." (Toffler and Toffler, 1995, 19) Convinced that the agricultural revolution and the industrial civilization are giving way to a third, Information Age, or age of knowledge, the Tofflers describe:

> A new way of life based on diversified, renewable energy sources; on methods of production that make most factory assembly lines obsolete; on new, non-nuclear families; on a novel institution that might be called the "electronic cottage;" and on radically changed schools and corporations of the future. The emergent civilization writes a new code of behavior for us and carries us beyond standardization, synchronization and centralization, beyond the concentration of energy, money and power. (Toffler, 20)

Democratization and Complex Interdependence

Believing that the tide of industrialism peaked in the mid 1950s coincidentally with the introduction of computers, commercial jet travel, and the birth control pill, the Tofflers are convinced that although today's high technology nations are slipping out of the "obsolete, encrusted economies and institutions" of the Industrial Age, (Toffler and Toffler, 23) they have yet to emerge full blown into the Third Wave. The irreconcilable differences between a yet unconsummated Industrial Age and the onset of the age of knowledge creates political and personal incoherence which exhibits in attitudes and behavior, in even the nonindustrial countries of the world, where struggles between feudal interests and industrializing elites are clarified by approaching obsolescence. (Toffler and Toffler, 20-26)

Another reference to the age of which the Tofflers speak is that of the "digital age," in which high-tech companies weave computers, cellular phones, modems and microchips into the workplace. The development of global information technology in recent years has accelerated exponentially, rapidly transforming industrialized societies from service to information economies. (Palvia, Palvia and Zigli, Eds., 1992, 3) In the interdependent global marketplace, information technology is likely to be one of the best sources of competitive advantage.

> Increases in global trade have been followed closely by a rapid growth in services transactions and paralleled by international monetary transactions and foreign direct investment. In this environment of interdependence, the enhanced role of Information Systems (IS) and Information Technology will be a major issue that business executives will face in the future. (Palvia, Palvia, and Zigli, Eds., 215)

CHANGE, CHALLENGE, AND RESPONSE

Many observers are troubled by the implications of economic changes which appear not to bode well for American industry, suggesting that the challenges of a global economy must be accompanied by a fundamental change in thinking, much like the Tofflers' recognition of a new age of knowledge. Convinced that there has been a seismic shift in the way the global economy works, Hedrick Smith argues that the historical characteristics of American industry, such as size and scale, low cost, and bureaucratic, depersonalized organizations are trivial given the circumstances of new economic competition. (Smith, 1995, xx-xxi)

These pressures have resulted in major changes in the ways that leading corporations do business, both in the United States and globally.

Bennett Harrison describes a contemporary global economy composed of networked, large company organizations, boundary-spanning networks of firms operating in different industries, regions, and countries. According to Harrison, these coalitions were created as a deliberate strategy for attaining greater flexibility in the face of the chronic uncertainty and market fragmentation of the new world order. Harrison predicts that these spatially extensive production networks, governed by powerful core firms and their strategic allies, are the economic vanguard of the future. But Harrison argues that in pursuit of downsizing, lean production, outsourcing, and networking these allied, global organizations are causing a negative fallout in the form of polarized wages, labor market dualism, the erosion of employment security, and an extraordinary growth in the numbers of contingent workers whose status is temporary, seasonal, part-time, and unstable. (B. Harrison, 1994)

According to Adrian Wooldridge, multinational firms are actually relics of the Industrial Age, the legacy of Taylorism and the doctrine of economies of scale, more suited to command-and-control management than the contemporary production whirlwind of fickle fashion and quicksilver markets. Wooldridge argues that giant companies with bureaucratic bloat, mammoth factories with alienated shopfloor workers, and massive corporations staffed by unimaginative employees must pursue the course of downsizing and streamlining in order to survive and compete with smaller companies who are, in the Information Age, privy to the sort of information processing and information-dependent innovation that was once a preserve of the giants. (Wooldridge, 1995, 3-5)

Wooldridge claims that globalization has exposed the weaknesses of multinational organizations, that deregulation and lower trade barriers have opened up world markets to smaller competitors, who are forcing the classical multinational to break itself up into constellations of profit centers, shrink its managerial staff, and combine economies of scale in product development with sensitivity to local tastes. Standardized products have fallen victim to fashion-and value-conscious customers who increasingly want goods tailored to their particular needs. Traveling the multidomestic road, many multinationals have discovered it is no longer profitable to set up clones of themselves in all the countries where they operate, complete with head offices, engineering and design facilities, and production plants. Instead, partnering in design, production and marketing appears to be the only sustainable strategy; where vertical integration was once the pride of the multinational, now they are focusing on their core business and contracting out everything else, or breaking themselves up into smaller units and giving those units plenty of freedom to do things their own way. "Even the world's oldest multinational, the Roman Catholic church, has contracted out the management of its worldwide data network to General Electric." (Wooldridge, 5)

Many multinationals, particularly in Europe, have begun to devolve power to regional levels, as well as to create global systems to deal with global customers on a global basis. Numbers of companies have been giving subsidiaries responsibility for global products and functions in order to disperse decision-making throughout the organization and capture local expertise. IBM, AT&T, and Hewlett-Packard, as well as Johnson & Johnson have all moved the worldwide headquarters for some of their products from America to Europe, with Johnson & Johnson giving world-wide responsibility for pharmaceuticals to its Belgium subsidiary. (Wooldridge, 5)

Research by the McKinsey Global Institute concludes that multinational firms contribute directly to higher levels of domestic productivity and transfer knowledge of best practices to other domestic producers. Global corporations, free of national borders and identities, liberated to source and manufacture anywhere, move billions of dollars in capital and goods daily. (Lash, 1996, 3F) Yet, with all these alliances, there is little evidence of any cabal of powerful firms dominating the globe. The United Nations estimates 35,000 multinationals now operate through 170,000 foreign subsidiaries, and according to *The Economist*, in mid-1996 the 100 largest multinationals control about 16 per cent of the world's productive assets, with perhaps the 300 largest firms controlling 25 per cent of these assets. (Lash, 3F)

While the United States, Germany, and Japan remain the world's leading sources of economic dynamism, as they have throughout most of the twentieth century, the general harmony among them and the other developed and developing nations is tested by the interests that flow from their different locations, cultures, and historical experiences.

The gains resulting from open economies around the world are accompanied by the friction between distinctive social policy priorities. Countries differ substantially on the proper role of the state in promoting business; in the importance of protecting individuals and social harmony from the excesses of the market; on macroeconomic policy issues such as whether to focus on consumption or investment; on issues of antitrust; on methods of corporate finance; and on a myriad of social and cultural matters whose domestic social and cultural roots make harmonization excruciatingly difficult. (Tonelson, 1995, 353-357)

The international economy is being shaped by the capital, technology, and management practices that are mobilized by corporations when they move into new markets. Increasingly, those who venture into different regions and countries are discovering that borderless economic mobility has a cultural and social dimension sustained by distinctive local traditions and cultures. "In an increasingly mobile world, they are stubbornly immobile resources." (Wooldridge, 7) Companies must thus become insiders, in full response to the social and cultural norms of numbers of host countries without bastardizing their own corporate mission. The coming age is likely to challenge every theory designed to explain economic behavior or provide guidance for nation-states, as well as organizations and institutions, through the political/economic miasma of disparate democratization, passionate nationalism, and unbounded capitalism. Confounding political and economic developments diminish the applicability of standard theories: The political nation-state may be divorced from effective economic activity; institutions and organizations will represent both lateral and hierarchical public and private interests; regions may become more influential than nation-states in global decisionmaking; world leadership will gravitate to those with economic, rather than military strength; ideology becomes unimportant as the majority of the world's member states pursue some variant of democracy.

The world of the future is likely to be one in which anything can be made anywhere, and with unbounded information technology, what was once remote becomes as near as a computer monitor. Economic power may well displace all other forms of power; markets, as well as production, will belong to those who can make a product or perform a service quicker, more efficiently, and with higher quality than their competition. Vast new markets of once closed societies beckon with a siren call to countries and companies who in recent history could only dream of the opportunities for growth and profit that are ripe for the plucking.

Paradoxically, as the economic world becomes more interdependent, societies seem to be seeking a stronger sense of identification. Nationalism defies cultural homogeneity; even though the state may decline in its political influence, its peoples, its nation or member nations, fervently, adamantly refuse to be absorbed into one another. Perhaps it is the spectre of identity lost to a shrinking world that feeds the nationalist fervor. Regardless, it is a force to be reckoned with, a potential impediment to globalization.

CHAPTER II
Culture, Economics, and Corporate Behavior

Globalization implies convergence and integration, yet it is accompanied by conflict and disintegration. The interdependent and aggregative nature of economic activity and the subordination of the political order to the economic function have conspired to create a new global information and communication infrastructure, enmeshed in a net strung together by billions of dollars in international trade and foreign investment, and weighted by social tensions and clashes among cultures whose values are unwittingly brought into question by abutting and interconnected economic and political purposes. Fueled by international trade and investment and enabled by an ever-increasing tide of international capital, multinational corporations, largely from the United States, Japan, Germany, and Switzerland, (Lodge, 1995, 4-5) have become intertwined in both coherent and inchoate modes with all manner of the world's cultures.

CULTURE AND ECONOMY

Culture is the primary social bridge between economics and sociology. "If by culture we mean shared cognition, values, norms, and expressive symbols, and by economics we refer to scarcity and choice, then our scope is coterminous with the social sciences, for symbols and scarcity are ubiquitous." (DiMaggio, 1994) But culture is taxonomically elusive. It has cognitive, expressive, and valuative aspects; it is the source of goals; it is foundationally related to preferences, attitudes, and opinions; it is both constitutive and regulatory; but laws and principles for its classification are illusory. (DiMaggio, 27)

Most modern economists do not worry much about culture. When they do, it is often misconceived as nature, or viewed as exogenous preferences and tastes, or as historical or organizational notions of limited interest and regulatory function. DiMaggio explains:

> Faced with anomalies in human decision-making, economists prefer cognitive psychology to cultural anthropology; how much easier to incorporate into one's models decision heuristics that are invariant and hardwired than to deal with perturbations caused by culturally varying schemes of perception and value. (DiMaggio, 23)

A determination of the confounding relationship between culture and the economy is fraught with substantive theoretical hazards. In one sense, the relationship is far too broad to be approached in generalities about causal, constitutive, or regulatory effects, demanding particular attention to scope conditions and contexts. Further, cultural effects on economic behavior are profoundly ambiguous, giving rise to obfuscation and confusion in interpretation, even in those cases where it can be determined that cultural factors are significant to matters central to economics. (DiMaggio, 46-47)

Culture is always evolving; while it may exhibit a given pattern, "this pattern is an abstraction imposed on the culture from the outside." (Morgan, 139) Culture is more than the hoopla and ritual that decorate the surface of life; it is the fundamental structure of society which ". . . allows people to see and understand particular events, actions, objects, utterances, or situations in distinctive ways." (Morgan, 128) And culture as symbols, ideals, and views of reality is organizationally and institutionally embedded. (Rueschemeyer, Stephens and Stephens, 1992, 275)

Cultural and social attitudes are also potential obstacles to altered economic circumstances in both ascending and declining economies. Just as surely as economic change threatens traditional societies of developing nations, it also creates uncertainty and anxiety in advanced societies challenged by changing social priorities and new/old notions about the relationship between the individual and society. (Kennedy, 16-17) "The most important influence on a nation's responsiveness to change probably is its social attitudes, religious beliefs, and culture." (Kennedy, 16) Yet the Tofflers argue that the entire structure of society is changing from the state-centered sovereignty of the Industrial Age to an Information Age interdependency which pierces the veil of sovereignty. They speculate that the consequences of the yet-unconsummated Third Wave will invoke profound changes on sovereign states:

> As economies are transformed by the Third Wave, they are compelled to surrender part of their sovereignty and to accept increasing economic and cultural intrusions from one another. Thus, while poets and intellectuals of economically backward regions write national anthems, poets and intellectuals of Third Wave states sing the virtues of a "borderless" world and "planetary consciousness." (Toffler and Toffler, 33)

Huntington argues that the overriding, central aspect of the new phase of global politics is to be found in diverse civilizations that share identifying and distinctive cultural features. He argues that the interdependent world will be shaped by the interactions of major civilizations in part because "the processes of economic modernization and social change throughout the world are separating people from longstanding local identities," driving them to seek a basis for identity and commitment beyond national boundaries. (Huntington, 1993, 26)

George Lodge likens globalization to a child's kaleidoscope, whose patterns give way with every movement of its countless complex parts into new patterns which appear accidental, unplanned, and unpredictable:

> Everything is related to everything else: the flows of trade and investment impacting the differing roles and relationships among government and business, in turn constrained by the necessity of ecological integrity and shaped by different value systems. (Lodge, 28)

Frank Mueller proposes that the behavior of large economic organizations need not be antithetical to indigenous societies; rather, he believes there is a capacity for complementary action in the relationship. But he makes a distinction between cultural and societal effects, and suggests an "institutional specificity of culture," in which only certain sectors of cultural and societal behaviors are transnational. (Mueller, 407-409)

Differences in culture are not always matters of either-or; they may often be simply peculiarities that distinguish one society from another. Cultural stereotypes, while not a guarantee of universal individual behavior, are general rules which suggest particular cultural propensities in societies. Cultural precepts are both explicit and implicit, abstract values which affect how one thinks and behaves, but more importantly, determine the kind of criteria by which one person makes a judgment about another. For the most part, culture is a result of subconscious absorption, but its violation may be perceived to be quite overt and purposeful. (Goman, 89-90) In an interdependent world, because the basic assumptions for doing business in one culture are often not the same as the assumptions and attitudes in another culture, abused cultural sensitivities, whether for cause or out of ignorance, represent cultural imperialism, and seem to introduce all sorts of images of the disappearance of the local or the authentic under a tide of imported culture. (Lealand, 1994, 34)

It is probably useful to take a pragmatic approach to the issue of cross-cultural theory. The flow of culture is an ongoing element in the political, social, and economic life of a society. Culture has a natural resilience which is not to be denied, but this is not to say that the recombinant force of a people's history, customs, and the materials of their everyday life may not be, or have not already been, recontextualized over time as new traditions and customs are created and the practices of everyday life change. (VanMaanen and Laurent, 1993, 307-308)

Clark advises that "Broad cultural patterns shape institutions, but are far from deterministic . . . Various contextual circumstances . . . determine what aspects of a culture become operative in particular historical circumstances." (Clark, 1993, 58 citing Clark, 1989; Lam, 1993; Pye with Pye, 1985; Wong, 1986) Globalism is a contextual circumstance; its effects on and the degree to which it will be affected by the interpenetrations of economic enterprise have yet to be discovered.

SOCIOECONOMICS AND ECONOMIC ETHICS

The forces of democratization, the proliferation of market economies, and dense interactions among an array of culturally diverse and unfamiliar societies expose the socio-economic context of globalism, a frame of reference which explores the social and cultural bias in

Culture, Economics, and Corporate Behavior 33

economic choices and enables a synthesis between the duality of self and community:

> Socio-economics assumes that economics is embedded in society, polity and culture, and is not a self-contained system. It assumes that individual choices are shaped by values, emotions, social bonds, and judgements—rather than by a precise calculation of self-interest. (Morong, 378, citing the Society for the Advancement of Socio-Economics, quoted in Coughlin, 1991b. p.3

As a frame of reference, socio-economics allows us to focus on the role of the community, rather than the individual, in the study of economic behavior. (Morong, 377-378) Indeed, Buscher's theory of economic ethics warns that without the consideration of sociocultural foundations in designing economic policy, economic liberalism as the cohort of political liberalism may become a new form of social coercion. (Buscher, 1993, 320-321)

As articulated by Amitai Etzioni, socio-economics, rooted in Kantian philosophy, humanistic psychology, and sociology, focuses not on rational, individualistic, greedy, economic man as economic decisionmaker, but rather on individuals who make economic decisions within the context of values, beliefs, ideas, and guidelines installed in them by others and reinforced by their social circles. (Etzioni, 1991, 4) Socio-economics is the study of how individuals resolve the conflict between personal self-interest and shared values of one's community. The relief of this conflict is found in the realization of the "web of interlacing *socioeconomic* interdependencies that now infolds the planet." (Morong, 375)

The subjection of economic theory to the rigors of social values is telling, suggestive of a broader orientation which considers not just markets, rationality, and instrumentalities, but also the investigation of the value-relationship of the acting self and his/her community, exhibiting a cultural and social inclusivity which becomes significant in times of dramatic political change and extreme economic transformation. (Etzioni, *Public . . .* , 1993) Socio-economics considers on first principles the social man, loathe to accept the tenets of the liberal tradition which often minimizes the significance of institutions in defense of individuals as free-standing units. Socio-economic theorists regard individuals as members of a variety of social and ethnic groups, classes, and subcultures with a variety of values, beliefs, ideas, and social arrangements, who make economic decisions based on those social identities. (Etzioni, 1991, 3-7)

> Socio-economics was born of a need to understand man and how hard he works, how much he saves, and what he purchases. This new science challenges the basic assumptions at the root of neoclassical economics, including the assumption that people are basically rational beings, interested in maximizing their personal interests, unswayed by friends and outsiders alike. (Etzioni, 1991, 3)

Socio-economics is a conceptual response to the narrow vision of mainstream economics, which remains constrained by utilitarian ethics, maximization, the rationalist-individualistic approach, and the concept of cognitive limitations. Swedberg argues that "The demand for complexity emerges as a major dimension of socio-economics, if we contemplate that one of its major tasks is exactly to synthesize or reunite the social and economic analyses." (Swedberg, 1991, 29) Multidisciplinary, substantive, and value-based, socio-economics represents a paradigm shift away from and beyond that of neoclassical economics. (Swedberg, 13)

The reality surpasses the view of economics as a value-free science: "Economics deals with choices involving the production, distribution, and consumption of scarce resources and in that process it greatly impacts human life." (Wilson, 1991, 233) John Oliver Wilson has developed a theoretical model which integrates human behavior into the essential behavioral characteristics of an economic system. He argues that the debate between economists over the issue of human values and economic behavior is fatuous:

> Philosophers and theologians have never suffered from such ambiguity. Economic arrangements "can be sources of fulfillment, of hope, of community—or of frustration, isolation, and even despair. They teach virtues—or vices—and day by day help mold our characters. They affect the quality of people's lives; at the extreme even determining whether people live or die. Serious economic choices go beyond purely technical issues to fundamental questions of values and human purpose." (Wilson, 233 citing the National Conference of Catholic Bishops 1986)

Similarly Amartya Sen rebukes the narrow connotation of rationality as a basis of analysis of both the economic and sociological context of human behavior. Sen, rather, argues for incorporating both goals and values, and their relationship to each other in society:

> ... there are no internal consistency conditions which can be thought to be invariably appropriate, irrespective of the context. In fact, the internal consistency conditions that we can insist on as part of rationality of behavior are thoroughly dependent on the external context. The idea of endogenous internal consistency is ... bizarre. Each time, there is a particular context to look at and what counts as consistent will depend on it. And quite often that context ... is a *social* context. (Sen, 1990, 262)

Sen believes that the gap between sociological and economic literature is of recent origin, reminding us that both Weber and Emile Durkheim were basically sociological thinkers, Adam Smith was a moral philosopher, and the literature of Bentham, Mill, and Marx "had sociological elements in it as well as what can be seen as narrowly conceived economic elements." (Sen, 253) Sen makes a compelling argument for an understanding of the commonalities of economics and sociology: "One can, in fact, say that ultimately economics and sociology look at different aspects of the same phenomenon, viz, the lives of human beings in society." (Sen, 266)

Daniel Hausman and Michael McPherson claim that economics is linked to both ethics and theories of rationality. They argue that "empirical work often has to take into account moral matters, for ethical commitments are among the causal factors that influence people's economic behavior." (Hausman and McPherson, 1994, 255) While they make no claim that ethics either pervades every area of economics, or that ethical issues should be a major preoccupation of most economists, nevertheless, they conclude that:

> There are, however, important areas of economic research where the ethical dimensions of human behavior and the moral appraisal of actions and institutions quite naturally arise. Acknowledging and working with those aspects of economic problems, where they are relevant, will strengthen both the explanatory power and the practical relevance of economics. (Hausman and McPherson, 272)

Suggesting that ethics and the role of normative influences are particularly important in matters of labor markets and workplace organization, Hausman and McPherson reiterate the connections between moral philosophy and everyday economics: "[T]he relevance of economics to ethics is as evident as the relevance of ethics to economics, and it may be just as important." (Hausman and McPherson, 273; Wilson, 241)

Martin Buscher's argument for economic ethics also challenges the methodological and normative foundations of the analytical school of economics as neglectful of the historical changes in the sociopolitical setting of its doctrine. Buscher declares that contemporary economics remains dominated by the methodology of Carl Menger, producing an unhistoric, individualistic, and universal model which "suggests that there are economic phenomena which are independent from non-economic surrounding factors and support[s] the research about the autonomous relations of prices, interest and exchange rates, and economic growth and development." (Buscher, 313)

Buscher argues that economic theory in a period of international competitiveness and social and political restructuring cannot rely on neoclassic economic liberalism. Warning that "The market can become the new dictatorship," (Buscher, 320) Buscher's theory of integrative economic ethics seeks to interject changes in philosophical, social and political foundations into the overwhelmingly dominating school of analytical economics in an effort to construct economic theory for the 1990s. Although Buscher believes that the notion of the historical, philosophical roots of economic ethics is theoretically enhanced by the concept of the *Soziale Marktwirtschaft*, which integrates life order and economic order, arising out of the work of the German ordoliberals in the postwar period, he does not believe that the systematic and sociotechnical elements of the concept have yet been modernized. According to Buscher, there is a social void in the prevailing classic liberal and ordoliberal interpretation, created when the basic idea of the market is considered without the contextual background that gives it meaning. Economic policy based on international competitiveness is incomplete without the incorporation of the factors of a socially sustainable competitiveness, the intermediary institutions and general cultural infrastructure of the social aggregate. (Buscher, 318-320)

Economic goals, growth, and standards in the Buscher model are a matter of sociopolitical setting and historic, philosophical inquiry: "The old foundations do not exist any more. Conclusions, though, are still drawn as if nothing had changed. What implications are to be taken from this insight?" (Buscher, 312)

NATIONAL CULTURES AND CORPORATE ORGANIZATIONS

Corporations exhibit two types of cultural differences, both of which have been subjected to exhaustive research and analysis. There are strong extant national cultural differences which inhere, but there are also distinct and diverse corporate cultures which exist within the same society. These two concepts of cultural differences may be both complementary and contradictory to one another in that they represent value systems and social and economic baggage that direct corporate behavior.

There is a rich body of literature showing important cultural differences among corporations from different nations, defining and distinctive differences which serve to both classify and disaggregate national cultures as powerful influences over organizational style and substance.

Geert Hofstede's work on cultural differences among nationalities is fundamental to the study of cross-cultural theory in organizations and has served as the analytical basis for volumes of other cross-cultural studies. Since the publication of *Culture's Consequences* in 1980, Hofstede's work has focused on culture around and within organizations. Led into the cultural domain by his own earlier research in the comparative study of values, Hofstede continues to avoid disciplinary boundaries in the behavioral sciences, creating new avenues of investigation in organizational psychology, organizational sociology, and organizational anthropology. Believing the three domains to be inseparable, Hofstede cuts a broad swath through the disciplines to examine the embedded institutional structure and stability of the mental programming of national culture. (Hofstede, 1994) Hofstede's 1980 study arose out of years of research on over 100,000 employees of IBM in over forty different countries. From the analysis of this data he discovered a set of four cultural dimensions which outline how a nation of people view their own reality and their cultural niche and explain the differences that were evident between the widespread offices of what was essentially a very unifying corporate organization. The dimensions that derived from the research were ecological dimensions of collective national cultures, not dimensions of individual personality. (Goodman, 1994, 137; Hoecklin, 1995, 39)

The first of Hofstede's four cultural dimensions, Power Distance, measures the degree to which a society accepts the unequal distribution of power. If the power distance rating was high, power is more centralized and subordinates expect and are expected to be told what to do; superiors are believed to be entitled to privileges, and visible signs of status and the trappings of power; organization pyramids are steep; and managers are seen as both autocratic and paternalistic in their decision-making. (Hofstede, cited in Hoecklin, 30-31) In a low power distance organization, in contrast, organizations tend to be more decentralized, with flatter hierarchies and limited numbers of supervisory personnel; privileges of rank and perqs are essentially undesirable; abuse of power is unacceptable; and there is more interaction between superiors and subordinates, much of it arising out of the management philosophy. (Adler, 1986 cited in Hoecklin, 29-30) Lisa Hoecklin cites a 1991 report in the British newspaper *The Independent* describing the power distance variations involved in an attempt by British Petroleum to mix 40 workers from thirteen different nations in a European finance office:

> Germans felt more comfortable in formal hierarchies, while Dutch members had a relaxed approach to authority. UK, Scandinavian and Dutch managers all expected their decision-making to be challenged, while French managers thought that authority to make decisions came as a right of office. (Hoecklin, 29)

The second dimension, Uncertainty Avoidance, indicates how much control of the future was favored by a culture, or the degree to which a society feels threatened by ambiguous situations and tries to avoid them by providing rules and discouraging deviance. High uncertainty avoidance is associated with dogmatism, authoritarianism, traditionalism and superstition. Low uncertainty avoidance indicates a certain willingness by that society to take each day as it comes, with less emotional resistance to change. From the perspective of organizations and uncertainty avoidance, Hofstede's research suggests that in high uncertainty avoidance cultures there is more loyalty to employers and more long-term employment, more fear of failure, more expectation for managers to be experts, more adherence to organizational rules, less subordinate initiative, and less risk-taking.

Low uncertainty avoidance, however, is associated with greater optimism about the future, the acceptance of conflict within the organization, and more willingness and acceptability of the delegation of power. (Hofstede, cited in Hoecklin, 31-32)

The third rating, Individualism-Collectivism, is said to reflect which cultures are the most, or least, collective in their behavior, or the amount of independent thought and action which is acceptable in that society. When individualism is rated at low levels, people expect more help from family, friends, and organizations, in exchange for more commitment on their part. But in that minority of world societies where individual interests prevail over group interest, people tend to classify themselves, and each other, by individual characteristics, independent of others, and able to stand on their own two feet. (Hoecklin, 35)

The individualist-collectivist dimension in organizations contains a moral element, in that in low individualism cultures employees expect organizations to look after them much as a family, and can become very alienated if the organization is not satisfactorily meeting that need. In high individualism cultures, however, the relationship between the individual and her organization is seen to be primarily calculative; there is certainly no pretense of cradle-to-grave alliance. While organizations are assumed to have a moderate influence on their members well-being, employees are expected to defend their own interests, using their own initiative, and retaining a private life and opinion disassociated from that of the group. (Hofstede, in Hoecklin, 36)

The fourth dimension differentiates between gendered roles in societies. In his research, masculinity was associated with ambition, assertiveness and the desire for achievement, while its opposite, femininity, was concerned with inter-personal relationships, the environment, and a sense of service. (Hofstede, in Goodman, 137; in Hoecklin, 37) In low masculinity cultures, there is less gendered occupational segregation. High masculinity cultures exhibited higher levels of job stress and more industrial conflict than the low masculinity cultures; in addition, in high masculinity cultures there was a recognition of the legitimacy of the interference of organizational interests in one's private life, while low masculinity cultures tended to reflect a belief that organizations should not interfere with people's private lives. (Hofstede, in Hoecklin, 37-39)

Hofstede's research prompted Mant to chart certain industrialized countries according to these same four dimensions in a 1983 publication, *Leaders We Deserve*. In general, his work plotted an

Anglo-Saxon bloc of countries (the United States, the United Kingdom, and Australia) as much more individualistic and masculine, and less characterized by higher levels of power distance and uncertainty avoidance than, particularly, Japan, which appeared to be not only far more collective, but also much more cautious, authoritarian and materialistic than both the Anglo-Saxons and the Scandinavian bloc of Sweden, Denmark, Norway. (Mant, 1983, cited in Handy, 1993, 7)

A fifth dimension called "Confucian Dynamism" was later developed by Hofstede and others (Hofstede, 1991; Hofstede & Bond, 1988) in an effort to explain the sudden economic growth in Japan, South Korea, Taiwan, Hong Kong, and Singapore, "The Five Dragons." Research conducted in twenty-two countries revealed that rapid economic growth was found in societies that valued and practiced certain specific Confucian values, while de-emphasizing other Confucian values. These studies revealed that "culture in the form of certain dominant values was ... necessary for economic growth." (Hoecklin, 75) In the societies that experienced robust economic growth, the Confucian values of persistence and perseverance, adherence to status relationships, thrift, and a sense of shame were emphasized. The de-emphasized values—personal stability, protecting face, adherence to tradition, and the reciprocal giving of favors and gifts—were seen as factors that could retard growth if practiced too rigidly, by subverting the need for change or reducing the likelihood of risk-taking. (Goodman, 140)

Hofstede's analysis of cross-national differences in corporate organizations has been replicated by many other scholars as well. Charles Hampden-Turner and Alfons Trompenaars based their 1993 research on 15,000 managers from around the world who had taken part in seminars conducted by the Center for International Business Studies in Amstelveen, The Netherlands. They assert that there are seven specific, distinct cultures of capitalism which represent unique habits and traditions of economic practice. Each of these cultures is represented by a capitalist, free enterprise nation—the United States, Britain, France, Germany, Japan, Sweden, and the Netherlands—but according to Trompenaars and Hampden-Turner, the similarities between their economic cultures are few and their differences are legion. (Hampden-Turner and Trompenaars, 1993, 1-2)

These researchers claim that the culture of origin is the most important determinant of corporate value:

Culture, Economics, and Corporate Behavior 41

Cultures that work upon products originate within nations, within sects or groups therein, and increasingly within organizations deliberately incorporated by industry. The qualities of work performed by these corporations depend as much on the durable values of their work cultures as they once depended on the values of their founders. (Hampden-Turner and Trompenaars, 4)

According to their analysis, there are seven sets of both complementary and conflictual value systems specific to the economic process, a typology along the lines of Parson's Pattern Variables and David Reisman's categorizations in *The Lonely Crowd*. They argue that the degree of economic success of each of the considered countries will depend on that culture's ability to balance the scale between the tensions inherent in these valuing processes. Their seven sets of values are: (1) Universalism vs. Particularism, or how exceptions to the rule are resolved; (2) Analyzing vs. Integrating, or whether phenomena are analyzed as parts or in the wider context; (3) Individualism vs. Communitarianism, whether attention should be paid to the enhancement of each individual or to the corporation as a community; (4) Inner-directed vs. Outer-directed Orientation, whether decisions are guided by internal commitments or external trends and demands; (5) Time as Sequence vs. Time as Synchronization, which is concerned with systemic sequencing; (6) Achieved Status vs. Ascribed Status, which speaks to issues of merit and performance; and (7) Equality vs. Hierarchy, which addresses matters of treatment of employees and authority systems. (Hampden-Turner and Trompenaars, 10-11)

Hampden-Turner and Trompenaars argue that these issues are passionately ideological; each of the seven nations considered has a unique perspective of these values, which the authors refer to as an "economic fingerprint," which correlates with economic achievement and failure. Their study points out the imperatives of combining cultural strengths in an interconnected world.

In a commentary on the need for theoretical guidance to address the complexities of interdependence among cultures and nations, S. Gordon Redding examines the determinant literature of Child's 1981 publication, *Contingency, Culture and Capitalism*. According to Redding, Child's proposal that cultural issues and effects are more powerful in the matters of authority, style, conduct, participation and attitudes than formal structure and strategy is a valuable model to re-state the culturalist perspective and define the conditions under which research progress might be made. Beginning with a review of the problems associated with the use of culture in the cross-national study of organizations, Child identified five primary problems associated with the use of culture in the cross-national study of organizations, namely: (1) the lack of a clear definition of culture; (2) the discrepancy between cultural boundaries and national boundaries, with the misperception that they are identical; (3) the failure to consider cultural variables in an historical or functional context; (4) the lack of specificity of components which are relevant to organizations and which aspects of organizational behavior are influenced; and (5) measurement difficulties. (Child, 1981, cited in Redding, 1994, 326-327)

Much like the Hofstede research, above, Child's work stimulated volumes of subsequent analysis. His sophisticated model of the interconnections between contingency, culture, and capitalism defines the conditions under which research progress can be made in order to determine the factors of organizing human action. Child contended that progress in developing the study of organizations principally necessitates a consideration of the societal understanding of the meanings of authority and cooperation, and a recognition that cultural effects will be most powerful in the processes of organization relating to authority, style, conduct, participation and attitudes, but less powerful in formal structuring and overall strategy. (Child, cited in Redding, 328)

Cross-cultural inquiry has generated an incalculable array of training methods such as seminars, management techniques, and consulting exercises to instruct in how one may cross the culture gap and secure the best from each set of cultural biases. Global organizations are no longer able to retreat into the advantages or limitations of one cultural orientation. "With an appreciation for the complexity and diversity of human cultures, it is possible to get the best from those who are best at it." (Hoecklin, 77)

In 1982, for example, Moran and Harris proposed a theory of cultural synergy in organization systems, to incorporate the diversity of cultures and the stages of social and economic development in international commerce. Neither a cultural dominance nor native model, cultural synergy is an attempt to mold the different perspectives of cultures into a synergistic, or win-win situation for both parent organization and the culture within which it is operating. (Moran and Harris, 1982) Building on that earlier work on cultural synergy, Moran *et al* point out in a study a decade later that the forces of international competition and globalization of the marketplace, trade imbalances, and the impact of the transition from an industrial economy and way of life, along with an explosion of literature attesting to the influence of culture on trade, management, organization, business, and the professions are compelling organizations to address the cross-cultural challenge. (Moran *et al*, 1993, 8-9)

Carol Kinsey Goman warns that corporations who ignore the intercultural factor put their profits, as well as their customer relations, at risk. While she acknowledges the importance of functional skills, she proposes that ". . . without a proper understanding of cultural norms, even the most skilled technician may make social blunders which can jeopardize business opportunities." (Goman, 1994, 86) Not only does she advise that cultures differ as to their individual or collective nature, she lists a variety of specific cross-cultural differences that can potentially undermine corporations embarking on foreign ventures. These value assumptions describe how different cultures perceive behavioral attitudes such as confrontation and consensus; concepts of time and space; bases for decision-making and problem-solving; evaluations of oral and written contracts and agreements; interpersonal relationships and acceptable levels of formality and informality; symbols of power, status and deference; and loyalty, authority, and autonomy. (Goman, 92-94)

Companies based in North America, Europe, and Japan have severally begun to develop programs designed to create highly skilled and versatile international executives—what Moynihan calls a "cultural hybrid," who do not bear a home-office stamp and who serve both strategic business goals and broader political realities. Fewer and fewer multinational corporations continue to nurture executive talent solely within their home country; most now use local nationals as well as third-country nationals whenever possible abroad and increasingly, at their headquarters. (M. Moynihan, 1993, 3-12)

Frank Mueller, though, points to the need to exercise caution in making cross-cultural generalizations, arguing that traditional contrasts between countries may be over-emphasized. He suggests that aspects of work organization, government policies, training arrangements, and the influence of multinational companies have effectively diffused certain organizational and globalization effects across cultures that may complement or even counteract the societal effect. His argument makes the case that societal effects may not always be dominant. Mueller's argument rests on an assumption of layers of cultural convergence between major industrialized economies; in his reasoning, analysis of organizational culture opens the perspective for cross-border influences of culture, making certain structures and processes in different countries more similar. (Mueller, 1994, 407-409) It also turns our attention to the next section's discussion of how corporate cultures can vary irrespective of national context.

CORPORATE CULTURE SETS

Business corporations are not institutions in the same sense as a church, a state, a religious or political affiliation, or total institutions in the sense of prisons or mental institutions; they are, however, crucial institutions of civil society, built on constitutionally recognized rights of association and property, economic associations which serve the common good of the community in diverse ways. While they are dependent on the rule of law and a political regime favorable to their existence, they also possess their own moral ethos. (Novak, 1996)

The private business corporation is an extraordinary social institution with specific and limited economic and social responsibilities. It is independent of the state, enjoying transgenerational legal existence, it goes on even when its progenitors die. Its members are all voluntary; as such they pursue their own affairs, accomplish their own purposes, and in favorable political arrangements, reap their own financial rewards. The private business corporation is a prime model of public association, common motivation, and mutual dedication. Profit may be the regulator of the life of a business, but it is not the only one. In the long term, other human and moral factors are at least equally important in the life of a business. (Novak, 134-138)

The notion of "good business" is more than profit; it implies a certain moral duty to satisfy its customers with goods and services of real value, to make a reasonable return to its investors, and to create new wealth and new jobs, but it also insinuates certain social and moral accoutrements, among them the moral responsibility to reward the efforts of work rather than class and to promote the greater capacity of human beings as inventors, discoverers, and entrepreneurs. "Good business" is not a stamp one would apply to the images of the 1980s, when greed and avidity fueled a gluttonous chase for monetary returns and the accumulation of riches. The economic diversity of "good" private businesses acts is a force for political and social diversity; in an important sense, this diversity is crucial to preventing the tyranny of a majority. (Novak, 139-145)

Myths, Rituals, and Symbols

Corporate cultures are clearly analogous to social structures. The rites and rituals of corporate organizations spell out the way things are done; they are the unique characteristics of the corporate culture. (Deal and Kennedy, 1982, 64) Each organization has its own set of rituals with respect to rewards, frivolity, trivia, ceremonial expressions (such as retirement parties and gifts), and play, which may have no real purpose and few rules, yet bonds people together, reducing conflict, and creating new visions and cultural values. Bonding and other rituals help mediate and resolve conflicts and misunderstandings that threaten cultural harmony. (Deal and Kennedy, 61-66)

Much as the broader social culture is sustained by its traditions and superstitions, so corporate cultures are nourished by images, symbols, heroes, rites and rituals. While this corporate protocol may well exist in the formal structure, it is also embedded in the unspoken values and historical ethos that guide an organization. These values can both support and undermine formal statements of company philosophy; in reality there are often many different and competing value systems that compose the mosaic of organizational realities. (Morgan, 1986, 124-127)

While economic organizations may well be simply miniatures of society, they are also vested with distinguishing characteristics of structure, expectations, and goals. Employees, members of the organization, are expected to contribute to the organization in return for certain rewards. The structure of the economic organization, and the manner in which economic goals are interpreted and pursued, then, becomes a conscious and subconscious framework within which the physical and intellectual energy of human beings is directed toward a common goal. Ideally, this framework is socially and psychologically healthy for its participants, its culture dignifying rather than demeaning, possessing sound ethical effects which overflow into the larger society in a positive, enriching sense.

As argued in the previous section, business organizations are clearly affected by national cultural and social contexts. Yet, research also shows that corporate cultures vary substantially within nations as well in response to such factors as their business environment and individual leadership style. Intrigued by ideas generated at meetings conducted at McKinsey & Company with Tom Peters and Roland Mann, among others, and at Harvard's Graduate School of Education and Stanford, Deal and Kennedy framed a working hypothesis that outstanding companies who registered impressive track records in the marketplace had some sort of superordinate goal. Discussions centered around the absence of relationships among variables that organization theory said should be related. They were led to investigate the notion that organization structure and strategy might be more symbolic than substantive, and that there was something else at work. They would later conduct an informal survey by interviewing McKinsey consultants on the presence or absence of some set of visible beliefs in companies or organizations of which they had firsthand knowledge. Over a period of about six months, they developed profiles of nearly eighty companies. They discovered that of all the companies surveyed, only twenty-five had clearly articulated beliefs. But of this number, eighteen had qualitative beliefs or values, while the remaining companies had financially-oriented goals. What they discovered was that of the eighteen companies with qualitative beliefs, all were uniformly outstanding performers; they would characterize these consistently high performers as strong culture companies. While they acknowledged that the survey was far from scientific, they "did have evidence that the impact of values and beliefs on company performance was indeed real." (Deal and Kennedy, 7)

Deal and Kennedy decided to follow up their findings with an investigation of how the values got there, and how they were transmitted through the corporations. Their approach is based on their belief that a corporate culture is a contextual corollary to its environment; their categories are provoked by market realities, with the corporations assuming a certain culture in order to survive within their own environment. According to Deal and Kennedy, the environment comes first, and then the culture; but to the larger extent, the corporation chooses its own environment. (Deal and Kennedy, 13-14)

The Deal and Kennedy study, which included such companies as Caterpillar Tractor, General Electric, DuPont, Price Waterhouse & Co., 3M, Jefferson-Smurfit, Digital Equipment Corporation, Procter & Gamble, Hewlett-Packard, and Johnson & Johnson, among others, sought to discover what made these companies not merely organizations, but successful human institutions. The strong culture, the corporate values, the system of informal rules that spells out how people are to behave, enables people to feel better about what they do, so they are more likely to work harder, according to their analysis. (Deal and Kennedy, 3-16)

Weak cultures, on the other hand, either have no clear values or beliefs about how to proceed in their business, or they may be in disagreement as to values. Their heroes are destructive or disruptive, they do not build up, they tear down. The rituals of the company have no coherence: "The rituals of day-to-day life are either disorganized—with everybody doing their own thing—or downright contradictory—with the left hand and the right hand working at cross purposes." (Deal and Kennedy, 136) Such a culture becomes too inwardly focused, and too short-term oriented, to respond to the realities of either the marketplace or its own flaws. Deal and Kennedy's analysis showed that when workers are chronically unhappy, when morale is low and turnover is high, a weak culture feeds on its own distress. They warn that when a culture is weak or in trouble, workers get frightened; they become discontented, angry, emotional, and their personal lives become disjointed, even destructive. Such a situation allows the subgroups that form within the larger culture (natural social groupings based on age, gender, or other commonalities or task groupings and other natural groups based on commonalities) to become competitive rather than cooperative; they turn inward; they undermine each other; they substitute subgroup values for shared values, becoming destructive rather than constructive; and the culture literally disintegrates. (Deal and Kennedy, 136-138)

A weak corporate culture is in a precarious state. Such cultures lack some, perhaps all, of the characteristics that define strong corporate cultures—vision, shared values, enlightened leadership, employee loyalty, open door management policies and organizational flexibility, and the heroes, rituals and ceremonies which Deal and Kennedy found to characterize consistently high performers.

Deal and Kennedy's first culture is what they call the Tough-Guy, Macho Culture, an organization of individualists who willingly take high risks, but who also get quick feedback on whether their actions and decisions were right or wrong. They argue that this is the most arduous of all business cultures because the stakes are excessively high, in terms of both financial success or failure, as well as, in the case of police departments and medicine, literally matters of life and death.

They describe this culture as young, high risk, strenuous, and rigorous. Into this culture they would place construction companies, cosmetic firms, management consultants, venture capitalists, advertising companies, and the entire entertainment industry. The financial stakes are high, and the feedback is quick. Internally, this culture is as tough and unforgiving as its environment seems to be. Relationships among employees are very aggressive, opportunistic, "can't take the heat-get out of the kitchen" type. This is a world of gamblers, risk-takers, and self-confident individualists; in no sense is there a team concept in this culture—everyone wants to be a star.

Deal and Kennedy contend that these tough-guy cultures enable companies to function in high-risk, quick-return environments, often taking the chances necessary to move industries ahead. But it is this strength that is the source of the culture's basic weakness—there is no value placed on long-term persistence. The consequences of a short-term orientation short-circuit cooperation and collaboration; there is no room, or time, to learn from one's mistakes, to mature either as organization or individual. (Deal and Kennedy, 107-113)

The second of Deal and Kennedy's categories is the Work Hard/Play Hard Culture, which they label as the "benign and hyperactive world of sales organizations," and manufacturing, where risks are smaller and fewer, but the feedback is quick and intense. In the sense of sales, one either gets an order or one does not; in manufacturing, something either works or it does not. In this category activity is everything; persistence, repetition, day-after-day activity is expected to lead to success. The primary values are centered on the needs of the customers. "If the tough guy culture is built on `find a mountain and climb it,' then work hard/play hard rests on `find a need and fill it.'" (Deal and Kennedy, 113) There are a number of keys to success in this category—the customer service tradition of IBM; the quality-service-cleanliness-value mystique of McDonald's; the "try it; fix it; do it" ethic of Hewlett-Packard, Intel, and others. Generally the rationale is that in a dynamic environment, corporations must perform consistently, and continuously; there is a high demand for activity and initiative, where success is measured in volume. There is a sense of teamwork and team incentive because the team effort represents greater volume.

Contrary to any other of the Deal and Kennedy categories, this culture delights in game-playing, contests, promotions, conventions, motivation seminars, clubs and rallies. And this culture is very productive; it can make and move things quickly. As a culture it makes available the mass-produced goods the market seeks, perhaps better than any other. But its disadvantages are to be found in its lack of attention to detail, its sense of emphasis on quantity rather than quality that may only be ephemeral success. Like the tough-guy cultures, their perspective may be short-term, and their ability to discern reasons for failures blinded by their desire for quick-fix solutions. Not surprisingly, the success of these cultures is also frustrated by its own high-energy enthusiasm. The zeal of the young in these cultures frequently drives them to continue to seek the rush of success, depleting the organization of a mature core of employees which can provide the stability and constancy necessary for it to survive. (Deal and Kennedy, 113-116)

The third culture is a high-risk, slow feedback type of organization which Deal and Kennedy call the Bet-Your-Company Culture. These are the cultures where the stakes are high, but feedback is years down the line. They include in this culture capital-goods companies, the mining industry, large-systems businesses, oil companies, investment banks, architectural firms, computer-design companies, the military—these giants invest millions in development, refining, and testing before there is any significant indication of success.

These organizations are characterized by a deliberateness born of a need to make the right decisions; the world of this culture is more properly spoken of in months and years, not days and weeks. The core value is the future and the importance of investing in it; those who succeed within this culture must have the character and confidence to carry them through ambiguity and the miasma of the unknown. These organizations cannot afford mistakes; they are sustained by the technical competence, patience, and perseverance of their leadership. There is less a sense of internal competition, and more sense of sharing, dependency, mentoring, and respect; experience is a valuable commodity in this culture.

This category particularly illustrates the correlation between culture and environment. These company cultures are invaluable, but they are also incredibly slow-moving; they do not produce on a mass scale, nor act quickly or decisively. Therefore, again their strengths become their weaknesses in that these companies are extremely vulnerable to short-term fluctuations in the economy, cash flow problems, and unexpected change. (Deal and Kennedy, 116-119)

The fourth of Deal and Kennedy's categories is the Process Culture, the low-risk, slow-feedback world of banks, insurance companies, financial-service organizations, government activities, utilities, and heavily regulated industries. The financial stakes are low, in that no one transaction is going to make or break the company, and there is virtually no feedback. Consequently, employees in these cultures begin to focus more on how they do a job than what they do, developing artificial organizational identities, blowing things out of proportion, and creating an internal environment of personal distrust and paranoia. Such attitudes create workers who are orderly, detail-oriented, neat, and bound tightly to procedures and rules. Such organizations are essentially process cultures, where identifiable success is illusory. These organizations find great satisfaction in exercises in reorganization, which often become a corporate ritual. These corporate cultures serve as a scapegoat for much that is wrong with business organizations; maligned as depersonalizing, callous, obdurate, implacable, inflexible, intractable, and unwarranted, nevertheless the notions of efficiency and redtape are a response to certain circumstances and trends. (Deal and Kennedy, 119-123)

Organizational cultures are also largely reliant on the type and style of the leader or leaders who drive, direct, and, ultimately, are responsible for the success or failure of the corporate enterprise. The cultures of work thus have a psychodynamic context in that they are shaped by the personality, the expectations, and the demands of leadership, which may be neither coherent nor consistent, expressed or exact; nonetheless, the vitality, vigor, and strength of the corporate culture may well rest in the philosophy and vision of one individual. (Deal and Kennedy, 37)

In 1985 Michael Diamond and Seth Allcorn outlned six personality types which they then examined as leadership personalities: The narcissistic, perfectionist, arrogant-vindictive, self-effacing, resigned, and intentional. Each of these types will expect something different from the organizations they lead; each will create an authoritarian structure that reflects largely their own character and disposition. For example, Diamond tells us that the narcissist will require grandiosity and admiration, and the perfectionist will demand that everyone measure up to her superior expectations and standards. The arrogant-vindictive individual insists on winning at any cost in a largely zero-sum context where for her to win, somebody else must lose; but the self-effacing type seeks little glory in victory, although winning is expected and may be orchestrated. The resigned character simply wants to be left alone, while the intentionalist requires mutually shared personal responsibility and collaboration. Of these categories, only the last is not consumed by stress and anxiety, pre-occupied by notions of power. (Diamond, 1993, 65) Leaders send a message throughout organizations; their personalities and sense of purpose cannot be overlooked as significant factors of corporate culture. While formal leaders do not have a monopoly on the creation of an organizational culture, their power gives them a special advantage in developing value systems and codes of behavior which have a significant impact on the ethos and value system that infuse the entire organization. (Morgan, 126)

GLOBAL CHANGE AND THE CORPORATE CULTURE

From the globalist perspective, an organization has its own culture, yet it may operate in a different culture, obtain support from yet another culture, and be expected to compete in a global culture. These are multiple communities of action, all of which are dynamic, and each of which may contradict the other. Cultures are social organisms; they may be alternately hospitable and haughty, frightening and comforting, familiar and aloof; nonetheless, they are the social cement that binds a people together and gives them the strength and the spirit with which they are identified.

The microcultures of organizations are malleable; leaders can redirect them; society can demand more of them; workers can expect more from them. But at the end of the day, the microculture must be of sound enough character to respond with vigor to the demands put upon it and persist in the face of internal and external threats.

Echoing Deal and Kennedy's analysis, Hampden-Turner and Trompenaars define strong corporate cultures as discovered in those combinations of characteristics that allow organizations to successfully originate and bring to the marketplace products and services in a manner in which all groups who share in these processes work together energetically and effectively. But Hampden-Turner and Trompenaars tighten the linkage between the corporate culture and its product, contending that products and services are symbols of the corporation that supplies them and that products and services can never be better than the human valuing that goes into them. (Hampden-Turner, 6)

But strong value systems, and the products and services they represent, do not emerge full-grown in and from an organization; sustainability requires the visible hand of management to make sure that self-interest and concerns for customers, workers, and society are mutually reinforcing. And in a world where more and more products and services are created and furnished by cross-national teams, joint ventures, partnerships, and by foreign subsidiaries, effective wealth creation demands that corporations learn and combine the cultural strengths of various nations into strong corporate cultures where values are integrated into day-to-day business. (Hampden-Turner and Trompenaars, 16)

How to preserve the integrity of the corporate culture, therefore, becomes a problem of management. Can the combined strengths of many cultures be fused with the corporate culture in some manner which takes from each their best, yet sustains the economic purpose and the social responsibility of all? There is no one way any longer; corporations are faced daily with choices hitherto unimagined. Technology is always both liberating and confining; in the effort to cope with interdependent economic systems and open borders, the forces of communication and technology in the Information Age become the drivers of both cultural sustenance and devastation. The modern organization can either give meaning to people's lives, or it can drain them of meaning. Responding to the cultural contingencies of interlocked economic ventures in a era of declining state significance may well be modern management's most crucial responsibility.

Economic interdependence and information technology have allowed, indeed compelled, the interpenetration of cultures. In a headlong rush to participate in newly expanded markets and take advantage of investment opportunities, organizations have spread about the globe, carrying their own sets of values, rites, and rituals into unfamiliar cultural environments. Organizations present their own traditions, endorse specific behavior, expect certain results; they are indeed corporate tribes with distinct cultural properties.

These corporate tribes have become the conduit of change for many societies; they represent new ways of doing things, enabling linkages and opportunities hitherto unknown to many peoples of the world. And newly open societies are no longer just consumers; they are discovering their own commercial capabilities, propelled into production of goods and services, yoked unevenly with mature democracies and economies in cross-border business alliances, networked organizations, mergers, acquisitions, joint ventures, and corporate arrangements which form an interwoven big global jumble of individuals, communities, and corporations.

The transformed nature of the twentieth century economy, and the uncertain challenges of the twenty-first, suggest that the defining corporate culture of the Industrial Age must also be altered. Mass production techniques which stress hierarchy, rigidity, division of labor, and machination—a process which indisputably created great wealth, a myriad of products, and millions of jobs—may not be the most effective way to do business. Such a system, in which the job is defined by the machine, rather than the worker, and where there is almost no capability to respond quickly to rapid change in consumer demand, is too inflexible to deal with a global economy where new actors, incentives, and technology are writing new economic rules of behavior. Managers in some of the most labor-intensive industries, where assembly line arrangements have persisted for many years, where products have been carried by conveyer systems from worker-to-worker for limited and partial motion, are finding that procedures which break down those systems into sets of activites and allow workers to do multiple tasks and regulate the speed at which they work, are not only productive, they are also more easily adapted to changing demands of the customers. Experimenting with manufacturing matrix systems—pods of activities grouped together—or training single workers to monitor and manage several high technology production machines autonomously establish greater worker responsibility as well as increasing flexibility and product development.

Fordism, specialization, and the assembly line represent the corporate culture of the Industrial Age; indeed, mass production became society, as the "one way" notion of Taylor mirrored the efficiency and replicability needs of the Industrial Age, and society searched for satisfaction in rationality and reason. Current conditions mandate significant organizational change; the rigidity of the mass production paradigm is no longer seemly: For economic reasons, it is unsuitable for the quick response and redeployment of resources required by truncated product cycles and fragmented markets. But there is a larger incongruity which suggests that the entire panoply of the social nature of the Industrial Age is dissolving in the uncertainties, re-orientations, and accelerated motility of the Information Age.

Robert Denhardt tells us that the way we work makes a difference in the way we act, and represents as well the way we seek meaning and continuity in our lives. The rational biases of industrial productivity and the impact of bureaucracy on the social structure have created certain societal assumptions about objectivity and order that define society. For

Denhardt, and numbers of other scholars from the fields of psychology and administration, it is not so much the relationship between individuals and particular organizations as it is the ethic of organization and its power to prejudice the way we see the world that provides a metaphor for living:

> The interest of science and organization in regulation and control has been applied to human relationships as well as to physical objects. Moreover, science and organization have become models for human behavior, making it more structured, more directed, and more impersonal. Over the years, therefore, our efforts to control nature have become intertwined with our efforts to control one another, to the point that Horkheimer has written, "The history of man's efforts to subjugate nature is also the history of man's subjugation by man." (Denhardt, 1981, 41-42 citing Horkheimer, 1974, 105)

Herbert Simon's advice on the search for rationality in decision making argues that "Human rationality . . . gets its higher goals and integrations from the institutional setting in which it operates and by which it is molded." (Simon, 1976, 101) In *Administrative Behavior*, his "how-to" book for understanding organizations in terms of their decision processes, Simon claims that: "The behavior patterns which we call organizations are fundamental, then, to the achievement of human rationality in any broad sense. The rational individual is, and must be, an organized and institutionalized individual." (Simon, 102) But Simon's interpretation of rationality as efficiency falls far short of a comprehensive view of reason, as Horkheimer argues:

> [E]ntire philosophical systems have been built on a notion of rationality as existing in the world, not simply as a relationship between means and ends, but as a criterion against which to judge the reasonableness of various ideas and proposals. This mode of reason, in its best expressions, focuses on "the idea of the greatest good, on the problem of human destiny, and on the way of realization of ultimate goals." (Denhardt, 23, citing Horkheimer, 1974, 4-5)

Simon admits that "Since these institutions largely determine the mental sets of the participants, they set the conditions for the exercise of docility, and hence of rationality in human society." (Simon, 101) Earlier philosophical critiques of scientific management, building on the Freudian argument that human behavior was the product of the interplay of unconscious forces with the external world, emphasized the failure of the rational model:

> Man is not viewed as acting on a reasoned and logical basis, rather he is, in Freudian terms, the unwitting product of his emotions. Further, the values a man professes are no more determined by rational or logical thought processes than is his behavior. (Simmons and Dvorin, 1977, 219)

In *Psychopathology and Politics* (1930) Harold Lasswell claimed that the Weberian-Wilsonian-Scientific Management assumptions of predictable behavior within organizations were extraordinarily unscientific because they ignored the significance of self-knowledge:

> Formal patterns of organization as described by organization charts are unrealistic as human dispositions may be unpredictable. Further, the "setting" of an organization is not determined by preconceived logical-rational design but by the reactions of differing personality types to each other and to the overall "social setting." (Simmons and Dvorin, 221, citing Lasswell, 1930)

The Hawthorne studies, accumulated over a period of several years, revealed a number of significant conclusions regarding human behavior in organizations, not the least of which was the revelation that "the logic of technical organization was undercut and had failed . . . organizations must take into account `nonlogical social routines.'" (Simmons and Dvorin, 223, citing Henderson, Whitehead, and Mayo in Gulick and Urwick, 1937, 158)

This proposition would be echoed by Chester Barnard in 1938 in *Functions of the Executive*, which advanced the thesis that formal and informal organizations were co-dependent. (Simmons and Dvorin, 223, citing Barnard, 1938)

Daniel Bell's predictions in 1962 in *The Coming of Post-Industrial Society* pointed out the consequences of the increasing bureaucratization of mankind, a condition he believed would be exacerbated by scientific managers and the domination of methodology and the technical elite:

For Bell man is, by nature, an intuitive creature whose behavior and emotions cannot be reduced to mathematical formulas, abstract economic constructs or "bits" of information punched onto computer tapes. Man, being expressive, seeks maximum freedom for that expression toward his own self-fulfillment. (Simmons and Dvorin, 236, citing Bell, 1962)

If the way we work is both defined by and defines society, the organizations within which we work are indeed powerful agents for social change, an idea which forces us to consider those organizations as more than the machines of commerce and greed, unless we are content with a society whose defining quality is self-interest.

It therefore seems to be a propitious time to reconsider the internal nature of our economic organizations in which assumptions about objectivity and order mirror the historic rationality-based assumptions of organization. Naisbitt and Aburdene contend that this is one of those rare times in history when the two crucial elements for social change are present: new values and economic necessity:

You must have *both*. Neither force is powerful enough to produce social change on its own. There must be a confluence of both changing values and economic necessity. And that is precisely what we have now: new humanistic values and global economic imperatives. (Naisbitt and Aburdene, 1985, 2)

Organizations may be well served by divorcing themselves from a reliance on science and mathematical measurement as guides for organizational choices. The philosophical perspective of existential phenomenology holds that rationalized schemes are misguided, focusing unwisely on the vertical direction of human relationships:

Despite the advances of science and physics, the universe is not "ordered." Therefore, no matter of fact can be stated as absolute truth, for any relationship between things is subject to change at any moment. Man's existence is not capable of exhaustive description in scientific terms. Much that science posits as truth is therefore illusory. Phenomena—the subject of phenomenology—are not describable as empirically verifiable facts; however, this does not affect their truthfulness or falsity. (Simmons and Dvorin, 239-240)

The existentialist critique maintains that organization forms based on the intellectual-rationalization of the head and constrained by notions of "one best" form of organization are inappropriate to the conditions of human existence: "Existential man exists in a universe of random unfolding so that rationalized schemes for controlling it are doomed to futility. Existence cannot be reasoned or contained within any conceptual scheme." (Simmons and Dvorin, 241) To the contrary, existential phenomenology claims that the "nonrational subjective factors in any situation are irreducible truths insofar as they are integral parts of the whole situation." (Simmons and Dvorin, 241)

The existential phenomenological perspective may have real impact on the design of organization theories to respond to the consequences of globalization in that it directs organizations to decentralize and proportion themselves to the needs of the situation. It also reflects an "administrative optimism based on a future of manifold and unbounded possibilities in contrast to the administrative pessimism that has dominated much of traditional administrative thought." (Simmons and Dvorin, 243)

On the one hand, the uncertainty and market fragmentation of globalization dictates radical restructuring of organization forms that are cumbersome, bulky, and tedious; on the other hand, communication and information technology allow innovation and modernization techniques inconceivable as recent as five years past. Further, the social and economic consequences of the Industrial Age are not uniformly auspicious.

The latter assumption is not new; thirty years ago Robert L. Heilbroner pled for business to adopt a new ideology, abandoning its traditional philosophy of superiority and certitude for the recognition of a new reality characterized by professional responsibilities and human values. (Heilbroner, 1964, 1-36) In the 1970s Erwin Schell suggested the development of a participatory theory of management to assuage the deepest desires of human beings to be their own masters, believing this to be the natural next level for organizations to assume in their role as social institutions. (Schell, 1979)

Perhaps the Age of Information is the enabler of the natural next level of organizational change. In an industrial society, the strategic resource may be capital, but in the new information society, the key resource is redefined as information, knowledge, and creativity—and the only place where the corporation can recover these resources is from its employees. And these employees are likely to exhibit values quite different from those of the time of mass production. In 1990, the baby-boom generation, those born between 1946 and 1964, accounted for 54 per cent of all workers; (Naisbitt and Aburdene, 7) and they seem to be unwilling to be content with the society created by industrialization.

> If you have ever asked yourself what happened to civility, why work isn't fulfilling anymore, what—if anything—of lasting value you've done to make things better, or simply why you have hundreds of acquaintances but few really close friends, you are part of the trend, regardless of your age. (Zemke, 1996, 26)

Much is made of the discontent and dissatisfaction of the American worker. The naysayers abound; they read the economy as alternatively booming, declining and contracting; they consider real income to be either stagnant or declining, at the same time that GDP and corporate wealth are rising. In any event, most workers do not feel in control of their own work situation, hence their lives. There is a broad cynicism that seems to have captured the spirit of the American worker, which drives her to spend an inordinate amount of time worrying about the future the pundits ordain. Charles Handy captures this rather lonely state of affairs in *The Hungry Spirit*:

> ... it is clear that the psychological contract between employers and employees has changed. The smart jargon now talks of guaranteeing "employability" not "employment," which, being interpreted, means don't count on us, count on yourself, but we'll try to help if we can. No longer can anyone expect to be able to hand over their lives to an organization for more than something like six years. After that you are on your own again, either by your initiative or theirs, and can only hope that you are, indeed, as employable as was promised. We are, in effect, all mercenaries now, on hire to the highest bidder, and useful as long as, and only as long as, we can perform. (Handy, 64-65)

But others see a different side to the conditions that prompt this type of litany. Economist Robert J. Samuelson argues that in the last fifty years Americans have achieved unprecedented prosperity and personal freedom, accompanied by shorter work weeks, better health, and longer lives; but he admits that "The paradox of our times is that we are feeling bad about doing well." (Zemke, 26)

> Whether we are doing badly and know it, or doing well and don't appreciate it, the result is the same. We—meaning a large number of working, thinking North Americans—are questioning the means and ends of many of the organizations we work in or depend on. (Zemke, 26)

Robert Wright proposes that the modern world can be an uncomfortable, unfulfilling place to live, in that it makes us behave in ways that are contrary to the natural patterns of human behavior. (Wright, 1995, 50) Some evolutionary psychologists are predicting the creation of a new field called "mismatch theory," to study the maladies resulting from contradictions between the modern environment and the environment for which human beings were psychologically, emotionally, and physically equipped. These scientists point to rates of depression that have been doubling in some industrialized countries roughly every ten years, to the high rates of suicide among young adults, to growing numbers of clinical anxiety disorders, and to the pathological alienation that is a hallmark of our time. (Wright, 52)

It appears that it is not unrealistic to expect that the cultures of our economic organizations are among the greatest sources of influence on our private lives and sense of well-being, or, as suggested by the evolutionary psychologists, as a force for misery and despondency. And according to Deal and Kennedy, and others, restructuring the corporate culture is a powerful means by which to reshape personal lives and attitudes: "In fact, corporations may be among the last institutions in America that can effectively take on the role of shaping values," (Deal and Kennedy, 16) and in the process, securethe means for productivity and profitability in an uncertain environment.

According to Deal and Kennedy, corporations are just collections of individuals, human institutions whose real existence lies in the hearts and minds of their employees. For an organization to succeed, rather than fail, the corporate culture must both capture and reflect the hearts and minds of employees, managers, and customers. The corporate culture is more than just the way things are done, it is a powerful influence throughout the organization and affects practically every event within it. (Deal and Kennedy, 3-19)

Denhardt tells us that organizations play such a large part in our lives, the way we construct reality is guided by the experiences and training of our organizational life. This is a heavy responsibility, but one which organizations have historically embraced—creating and extending the corporate image; encouraging the maturation of the company man; applauding and rewarding technical competence; extolling the virtues of practicality, objectivity, and impersonality; and concentrating on the bureaucratic usefulness of a project rather than on its broader impact, suspending moral judgment in favor of organizational decree. (Denhardt, 1981) In all stages of history, organizations have been indicted for the prostitution of their purpose as a means by which human beings seek to order their affairs. Families, tribes, churches, and states have all been accused as betraying the social contract, transcending the eminence of the people who erect and seek to live by them. (Wicker, 1975, cited in Denhardt, 6)

But in an age of declining loyalties to political institutions and proliferating economic activity, the development of fealty and self-identification within the working group is of considerable importance. Peter Drucker argues that "Increasingly it is in his work that the citizen of a modern industrial society looks for the satisfaction of his creative drive and instinct, for those satisfactions which go beyond the economic, for his pride, his self-respect, his self-esteem." (Drucker, 1954, cited in Denhardt, 9) If humanity is seized by its organizations, then it well behooves organizations to reconcile their economic and social goals to human goals—these contexts can no longer be estranged.

CHAPTER III
The Individualist Model: American Organizational Culture

THE ATOMIZED SOCIETY

The research of Hofstede, VanMaanen and Laurent, Hoecklin, Goodman, and a host of other sociologists and anthropologists presents compelling evidence of substantial differences among societies and the cultures represented in those societies. But of all the cultural distinctions, that which signals the role of the individual is the most significant, because it carries with it not only the most basic theoretical conceptualizations of the origins of society and its institutions, but it also establishes the manner in which members of that society interact among themselves and with members of cultures whose nature is alien to their own.

American society is pridefully, indeed mythically, committed to the presumption of society as an aggregate of unrelated wants and wills whose nucleus is the single human being. This individualistic conception, with ancient philosophical roots in the Sophist's notion of society and the state as artificial constructs, decrees that human beings are not innately social creatures, and are not naturally concerned with any greater social good; to the contrary, human beings are individual egotists who are originally and ultimately concerned with their own self-interest. This individualistic and egotistical psychology of human theory, or radical individualism, implies self-sufficiency, selfishness, greed, and the struggle for personal power. It is the interior experience of human beings that is all-important; social reality is nothing more than mind-set and self will. (Parenti, 1994, 18)

As a cultural identifier, individualism justifies priorities in people's lives and goals. In individualistic societies people are socialized by the strength of custom, tradition, and convention to pursue their own goals; to be true to oneself and one's own interests is the energy of social interaction. Society and the state are but unnatural arrangements created for limited purpose. Individualist societies encourage and advocate self-reliance, self-worth, the development of personal skills and expertise, and a utilitarian approach to the use of time and energy. Individualism is analogous with competition and merit; it is largely contrary to authority and trust of authority figures. Commonly individualists are interested in pursuing a varied life, with little sense of loyalty to one's associations or companions. (Brislin, 1994, 78-79)

Geert Hofstede's seminal multinational survey of value dimensions in 1980 found the United States to be the world's most individualistic nation, accompanied by, at a lesser degree, Australia, Great Britain, Canada, The Netherlands, and New Zealand. (Hofstede, 1980 cited in Brislin, 77-78)

Ward reminds us that Tocqueville defined the American social ethic as individualism, a tendency for the American to look to himself alone, a fundamental aspect of American society that bears an aura of the ideal ultimate reality. In an essentialist context, this element enabled the acceleration of the energies of acquisition and entrepreneurship and the growth of the American economic system. The litany to the self-made man Ward likens to a sense of nationalistic congratulation; the fact that it was a credo rather than the social reality does not diminish its importance as an American cultural convention. (Ward, 1964, 37-76) With Ward, Parenti argues that the myth of individualism is a legitimating force, diffused into the culture as common sense and correctness, so woven into language and practice as to appear almost sacred. (Parenti, 98-99)

The venerable quality of the American myth of individualism is perhaps her deepest cultural identity; it is beautifully expressed by a quote from Bellah's *Habits of the Heart*:

> We believe in the dignity, indeed the sacredness of the individual. Anything that would violate our right to think for ourselves, judge for ourselves, make our own decisions, live our lives as we see fit, is not only morally wrong, it is sacrilegious. Our highest and noblest aspirations, not only for ourselves, but for those we care about, for

society and for the world, are closely linked to our individualism. (Bellah *et al*, 1985, cited in Hampden-Turner and Trompenaars, 47)

The American culture celebrates the lone individual who endures against great odds; they are the Lone Rangers, the Lone Eagles, and the caped crusader with the heroic selflessness to defend society without really joining it. "The value of American heroes to their society is that they stand alone, not needing others, not depending on their judgment, and not submitting to their wishes." (Hampden-Turner and Trompenaars, 51) Indeed, American culture is celebrated for its self-made, and continually self-making quality:

> Our literature, from the Leatherstocking tales and *Moby-Dick* to *The Great Gatsby* and *Catch-22*, is full of stories about ad hoc societies in which people feel free to invent new rules, backgrounds, and identities for themselves . . . . Most of our national myths are about the people who won't listen to others and end up doing what supposedly can't be done. Benjamin Franklin moves to Philadelphia and succeeds; Abraham Lincoln is elected after countless defeats; the American colonies throw off the British. Chuck Yeager bent the army's admission rules to get his chance to fly; Lee Iacocca made Chrysler profitable . . . . (Fallows, 1989, 60)

American Political Individualism

Philosophically, individualism is considered one of the leading elements of well-being in a democratic society. It is generally considered the core concept of classical liberalism, the font of psychological integrity, civility, and the ability to reason. (Etzioni, 1995, 16) "Liberal ideology is characterized by a commitment to individualism, the belief in the supreme importance of the human individual, implying strong support for individual freedom. From the liberal viewpoint, individuals are rational creatures who are entitled to the greatest possible freedom consistent with freedom for fellow citizens." (Heywood, 1994, 8)

The peculiarly American-style individualism originated in Puritan ethics; while we can identify its earliest philosophical roots in the Greek Sophists, it was controverted by Platonic and Aristotelian thought, which regarded human beings as essentially members of a community, not as individuals; in fact, Plato's *Republic* is not concerned with describing the good individual, it is focused to the contrary on defining the good community.

Sartori reminds us that Aristotle's definition of man was socially constructed. Aristotle perceived of man as a political animal, embedded in his society; he never envisioned man as a private self, entitled to being himself. "The Greek *idion* (private), in contrast to *koinon* (the common element), conveys the sense of privation and lack . . . . Correspondingly, *idiotes* was a pejorative term, meaning he who was not *polites*—a non-citizen and therefore a vulgar, unworthy, ignorant man who was concerned only with himself." (Sartori, 285) To the Greeks, the notion of the individual was negative. Quoting Jellinek's 1921 translation of *Dottrina Generale dello Stato*: "In ancient times man was never definitely recognized as a person . . . . Only the nineteenth century has scored a general victory with the principle: `man is a person.'" (Cited in Sartori, 285)

By the period of the rule of Alexander, individualism had become nothing more than the philosophical refuge of the Cynics and the Stoics, and later that of the earliest Christians, who argued that a man could live a good life no matter the social circumstances. As time passed, although numbers of mystics struggled to keep the ethic of individualism alive, it was more-or-less manipulated to its own ends by the Catholic Church, who claimed the right to interpret what was true and what was good. (Russell, 1945/1972, 598) The conception of a private self entitled to respect came first with Christianity, but cultivated by the Renaissance, Protestantism, and the modern notions of natural law, it took on a new meaning distinct from its medieval connotations. (Sartori, 285; 294n)

The first conclusive breach in the "organicism" of man was not to come until Protestantism and the reform movement of Martin Luther, whose belief in the abstract right of autonomy, self-direction, and the supreme worth of man built a moral foundation for individual freedom of thought and the pursuit of political and economic freedom of action. Although Luther's domain was the Church and its failure to provide full personal or intellectual satisfaction, his argument that no one had a right to impose an obligation upon a Christian man without his own consent, along with his contention that faith alone was the source of individual salvation, are clearly linked to ideas of self-help, and political and economic freedom. The Protestant belief in individual salvation and its stress on the moral value of personal striving and hard work—the Protestant Ethic—is clearly explicated in the American culture. (Dillenberger, 1961; Sartori, 294n)

With Luther, the determination of truth became an individual enterprise, but the result was strife, because different individuals reached different conclusions of truth. In the end, it became obvious that there must be some way to reconcile intellectual and ethical individualism with the notion of social order. Early liberalism became individualistic in intellectual, political, and economic matters. It was this philosophy that guided the American Revolution, inspired the French encyclopedists, and animated the theories of Jeremy Bentham; it was to find its greatest success in America, untempered by feudalism and a State Church. (Russell, 599-600)

> Since it was necessary, upon the intellectual side, to find justification for the movements of revolt, and since established authority was upon the side of institutional life, the natural recourse was appeal to some inalienable sacred authority resident in the protesting individuals. Thus "individualism" was born, a theory which endowed singular persons in isolation from any associations, except those which they deliberately formed for their own ends, with native or natural rights. The revolt against old and limited associations was converted, intellectually, into the doctrine of independence of any and all associations. (Dewey, 1927; 1954, 86)

Believers in Luther's, and later John Calvin's assertion of the possibility of a direct relationship between the individual and God, were to become the emigrants from Europe to the New World. Their determination to create a new society was largely based on their sense of individual autonomy, responsibility, opportunity, and personal choice. Independence was the political legacy of this spiritual presumption. "Individualism worked for Americans so well that the culture is indelibly marked by its success." (Hampden-Turner and Trompenaars, 50)

Individualism is firmly bound to the American political system through the concept of individual rights as a limitation on government. The individualist notion defines and grants to each individual an identity which may not be abrogated by government. (Lowi and Ginsberg, 1994, 39) To speak of American individuals is to reference them as autonomous, unique, and independent. To see American society in these terms is to understand human beings in personal terms who are judged according to qualities of moral worth, such as character, personality, talents, and skills, rather than by social background, race, religion, gender, or any other accident of birth. (Heywood, 326-327) There is a certain social looseness in American society that releases individuals to their own devices; but it also makes American society less hierarchical and less class-bound than others. (Fallows, 60)

While the American political culture has changed somewhat over the years, there has been a remarkable durability to many of the core values and beliefs to which Americans have traditionally turned as defining and distinctive, among them none more enduring than the claim that America is a nation dedicated to the freedom of individuals who value life, liberty, property, and the pursuit of happiness. These are the values that reflect the way many people think about living, and the role of government. This emphasis on individual freedom and government as the insurer of that freedom is much more apparent in the American political culture than in other major western democracies. A poll conducted by the Times Mirror Center for the People and the Press in 1990-1991 measured citizen responses in five nations to the proposition that "Success in life is pretty much determined by forces outside our control." Results of the research indicated that Americans are much more likely to take responsibility for their own individual success, as well as failure. Fifty-seven percent of Americans polled disagreed with the statement, as compared to 42 percent in the United Kingdom, 36 percent in France, 33 percent in Germany, and 31 percent in Italy. (Cited in Bennett, 1994, 11) Of course, individualism as a cultural theme in the American political ethos may well be disputed and contradicted in specific behavior and particular policies; nevertheless, it is an energy that drives the convolutions of a system of institutions which at times seem baffling to the rest of the world. (Bennett, 10-15)

The American Constitution emerged from colonial dissent, not so much over separation from England, but over cultural concerns about order and individual liberty:

> For some, the idea of liberty involved freedoms of thought and action. For others, liberty meant separation from the old system of monarchy and the creation of a new ideal of popular sovereignty. For still others, liberty had economic aspects like private property and free enterprise, which required enough government order to protect property from those who might threaten it. (Bennett, 15)

The unique mix of culture and institutions served to create a system first and foremost to allow individuals the freedom to pursue their own causes. The founders sought stability, but they sought freedom first, conformed to the notion that government is best which governs least. Over time, even though the complexities of a large, industrialized society have seemed overwhelming, there is little evidence that individualism as a tenet of the American creed has lost its power. (Bennett, 15-16)

It is no surprise, then, that the classical traditions of the American "Madisonian democracy," became linked with individualistic atomism and the anti-statist defense of market capitalism during the nineteenth century. Individualism in the modern doctrinal translation regarded social organization as simply the means by which to protect the inalienable rights of the individual. If property was, as Locke asserted, an extension of the individual, then it followed that government was consequently bound to the protection of property rights also. In his argument over judicial compensation in *Federalist 79* Hamilton charges that "a power over a man's subsistence amounts to a power over his will." (Hamilton, 1952 ed., 233) The American experiment with social contract theory became not only a political statement of the individual moral worth of man, it linked liberalism with the notion of a possessive market society. (Heywood, 327-328; Sartori, 377-378)

Individualism and Capitalism

Capitalism is perceived to be the historical economic legacy of individualism. Developing first in eighteenth century Britain and later transferred to northwestern Europe and North America, the fundamental principles of democratic capitalism—private ownership of property, non-limited accumulation of property, the free market, the profit motive, and profit as the measure of efficiency—are articulated in the *laissez faire* manifesto of Adam Smith, which became the justification for American economic liberty. Smith's notions of self interest and its implications became the byword for American entrepreneurship and the universalist dispensation of the redemption of self-interest in the public good. (Sargent, 82; Hampden-Turner and Trompenaars, 53-54)

Intellectual individualism fits nicely with economic self-interest. "In economic terms, this means that individuals should be free (the free market) to pursue their interests (profit). The result should be the most efficient economic system, and everyone will benefit." (Sargent, 82) The fundamental link between capitalism and democracy is self-interest and the individualist ethic: capitalism supports democratic freedom; freedom is based on private property; capitalism creates economic freedom; economic freedom enables political liberty. (Sargent, 84-85) C. B. Macpherson uses the term "possessive individualism," to describe "the conception of the individual as essentially the proprietor of his own person or capacities, owing nothing to society for them." (Heywood, 328, citing Macpherson, 1973, 199) Economic individualism is thus clearly united with political and social individualism; the right to acquire, use, and dispose of private property according to individual choice is the fundamental principle of *laissez-faire* and other forms of capitalism. (Heywood, 328)

The basic premise is that capitalism allows more freedom for the individual than does any other economic system. And the historical record is clear: Modern democracy has developed exclusively in states practicing free markets in the production and exchange of goods. The realities of life insinuate a certain value of physical goods; one must be fed, clothed, sheltered, and educated in order to accomplish almost anything. While the mere possession of material goods does not guarantee a fruitful life, there is no question but that capitalism allows greater accumulations of wealth than any other system. "Capitalism appears to be the only economic system that, quite literally, can deliver the goods. Certainly no other system has experienced anywhere near its success over a sustained period of time in maximizing economic output." (Ebenstein, et al, 1994, 47)

There is also an idealized affinity between the self that earns money and owns property and the cultivated, learned, resourceful self; in this sense, capitalism is an expression of the democratic ethic. Capitalism in theory is built on individual initiative, and the deeper tie between capitalism and democracy is not exclusively economic productivity, but the values it engenders and sustains. (Ebenstein, et al, 47) According to Ralph Waldo Emerson:

> Freedom's secret wilt thou know?
> Counsel not with flesh and blood
> Loiter not for cloak or food.
> Right thou feelest, rush to do!
>
> (Emerson, "Freedom", cited by Hampden-Turner and Trompenaars, 50)

More than any other of the myriad variables that compose the American ethos, the individualistic bias dominates. "The individual is considered prior to any relationship formed or feelings expressed. It follows that self-interest is `basic,' while benevolence is `nothing but' an expression of that individual. (Hampden-Turner and Trompenaars, 53)

Twentieth Century American Liberalism

Until the 1930s, classical liberalism and a market-capitalist economy were considered the inborn attitude of a normal civilized Westerner toward life, a mental pattern and political morality deeply rooted in the American experience. Generally symbolized by the principles of equality, liberty, individualism, belief in private property, limited government, and popular sovereignty, the 19th century age of classical liberalism represents the perfection of the Lockean-Smith political and economic liberalism.

But in the 20th century, despite continued ideological affinity on a number of significant concepts, the classical Lockean/Smith legacy of economic liberalism and commitment to the concepts of negative freedom and the minimal state were diminished in the name of a new reading of the social contract. Post-New Deal liberalism remains firmly constructed upon social contract theory, but while the ideological elements remain, the terms of the contract have been profoundly altered.

Nineteenth century liberalism was established on the principles of individual sovereignty, a meritocratic society, and the conviction that human beings should be self-sufficient as far as possible for their own lives and circumstances. Nineteenth century liberalism was typified by a general skepticism and distrust of government, especially the remote national government. While the 19th century allegiance to private property persists in the post-New Deal era, in a number of significant ways post-New Deal ideology has attenuated its classical legacy.

Until 1929, America's national government remained limited in size, scope, and influence, while states provided most of the important functions of government. By 1933, however, the influence of government expanded to address the economic and social chaos in the wake of the Great Depression. During the Roosevelt presidency, the late 19th century utilitarian movement toward theoretical redefinition became a coherent shift from classical liberalism to "mainstream" American liberalism, divided from its philosophical tradition over the principal issues of limited government and the purpose of government. Identified with the capitalist economics of Adam Smith, classical liberalism rested on the free market theory; it doctrinally branded government intervention in economic and social life as always misguided and usually counter-productive. Post-New Deal mainstream American liberalism rejects the idea of an unrestrained free market and the minimal state; it is based essentially on freedom from want. Turning from economic freedom to social justice, post-New Deal liberalism is identified with the expectation of government intervention to secure general prosperity and social stability by means of welfare provision and the management of the broader economy. This ideological bifurcation has created the modern welfare state, with an expectation of protection of all members of society from the vagaries and circumstances of life. Associated with big government, public assistance, government regulation of all forms of commerce, and the Keynesian economics of deficit spending, this latent form of liberalism endorses a host of social engineering programs, income redistribution schemes, and preferential policies specifically disavowed by the limited government standards of classical liberalism. (Baradat, 1994; Heywood, 1994; Lowi and Ginsberg, 1994)

John Rawls describes this development as a consequence of the tension between the inequalities of a capitalist economy and the principles of justice in a democratic society; but he denies that the welfare state resolves their philosophical dissonance. Welfare state capitalism accepts as a given substantial inequality in the initial distribution of property and endowment of skills, but then seeks to redistribute income ex post. (Rawls, 1971) Sartori, furthermore, argues that it is philosophically inappropriate to reduce liberalism to economic premises and presuppositions. He believes that property conceived in the sense of security has little in common with capitalism as an economic ideology. According to Sartori, liberalism is not a by-product of a market economy; rather, liberalism and its consort individualism can only survive in the absence of concentration of political and economic power. While the economy pervades society, it does not necessarily shape the polity or the vertical dimension of politics. On the contrary, political liberalism and economic "liberism," (the Italian translation of the economic doctrine of laissez faire) are separate ideologies that are assumed to be connected from a past experience, but not because the former is a by-product of the latter. (Sartori, 378-379)

INDIVIDUALISM AND CORPORATE CULTURES

The Triumphant Individual

Individualism advocates a defining world view with respect to how members of society interact with one another, therefore it seems reasonable to expect the organizations of an individualistic society to reflect an equally individualistic perspective. Just as members of individualist societies work together in informal and formal organizations in ways that exhibit their atomist nature, American organizations and the theories upon which they are structured, have traditionally reflected the American notion of the individualist/atomized society. As would be expected, this is especially true of business corporations which generally resisted the post-New Deal redefinition of liberalism in America.

Philosophically, the circular pattern of self-interest to common good in the organizations of atomized societies would therefore mean that if one concentrates on one's own self-interest, then one will automatically serve her customers and society better, which in turn will allow one to again concentrate on her own self-interest. But such generalities are much too banal to reflect the significance of the individualist orientation in organizations. American organizations represent American culture just as surely as organizations of other cultures depict their particular traditions, customs, and social perceptions.

American corporate practices are significantly individualistic. From the earliest notions of the artisan-craftsman and the entrepreneur, the posture of American economic achievement has been fixed to the individualistic standard, where one is assumed to be rewarded according to one's performance in a contract into which one freely entered. In an individualistic culture where the individual is noble, independent, courageous, and supreme, there is little room for the contribution of the collectivity.

> The problem, then, with American individualism is that it scorns its own origins in the supportive community. The dauntless entrepreneur is a self-made man. This may be a good political argument for

keeping the money you have accumulated, but it is a very dubious claim in reality and one that sells short the many who sustained you. (Hampden-Turner and Trompenaars, 59)

There is no greater disparity between Eastern and Western cultures in organizations than that which elevates the inner-directed person over the other-directed. Represented by the pioneer, the gold miner, the farmer who staked out his patch of land, the inventor, the industrialist and the financial wizard, American organizations are an exercise in obeisance to the Bells, the Edisons, the Carnegies, the Fords, the Rockefellers, and other captains of industry who are assumed to have created the industrial dynamic. (Marshall, 1995, 18-19)

While the team player may be valued, individual creativity is venerated as a particularly American proclivity. Conventional wisdom contends that while Germans may be particularly good at building infrastructure, and the Japanese may excel at innovation, Americans prevail at invention and dreaming up new products. (Hampden-Turner and Trompenaars, 3)

This sense of creativity is bonded with the historical American work ethic, which was reinvigorated by the American economic success of World War II, where victory for the right depended importantly on America's capacity to outproduce the harbingers of wrong, Germany and Japan. (L. Harrison, 1992, 226) Ego-driven, individualistic entrepreneurism is archtypically American. The American entrepreneurial spirit is legendary; (Kotkin and Kishimoto, 1988, 216) it is inextricably tied to intellectual individualism and classical liberalism and perhaps not separable as simply an organizational typology or theory.

Hoecklin contends that the deeply rooted cultural norm of individualism influences organizations in three essential ways: (1) In the relationships between the individual and the work group; (2) In the significance of informal, intuitive mutual obligations to decisionmaking; and (3) In the importance of networked relationships and alliances between organizations with common interests. (Hoecklin, 71)

In organization behavior, then, persons prejudiced by individualism would be expected to remain essentially and primarily calculative with others, with no expectation that employment carries with it any obligations on the part of employer to protect the worker for her lifetime, nor commitment on the part of employee. Individualist organizations have only moderate influence on the well-being of their members, as those members, or employees, are expected to defend their own interests. With welfare responsibility vested in the state, the individual member of an individualist organization does not feel that the organization is her source of stability or long-term security. Promotion choices in the individualist organization are based largely on market value; there is no fundamental principle which calls for internal grooming and promotion, as opposed to bringing in outsiders. Management in the individualist company is expected to express contemporary and professional norms, with policies and practices applied to all members of the organization equally. Decisionmaking is largely independent; leaders are expected to conform to heightened levels of individual initiative and achievement. In individualist organizations everyone has a right to a private life, and an opinion; there is little evidence of mutuality or a shared experience. (Hoecklin, 36)

Individualism in organizations is clearly a consequence of how the members of the organization perceive of themselves. Hoecklin claims that it is of utmost importance to determine whether a person regards himself or herself primarily as an individual or primarily as part of a group because such attitudes have obvious implications for organization management choices:

> Practices such as promotion for recognized achievements and pay-for-performance, for example, assume that individuals seek to be distinguished within the group and that their colleagues approve of this happening. They also rest on the assumption that the contribution of any one member to a common task is easily distinguishable and that no problems arise from singling them out for praise. None of this may be true in more collectivist cultures. (Hoecklin, 42)

The individualist component of American organizational style creates an autonomous employee/worker who is directed by personal goals, rather than those she might hold in common with her fellows. While there may be a degree of informal groupings even in individualist organizations, the formal structure of the individualist organization is an endorsement of the larger society's predilection to "focus on individuals so that they can contribute to society as and if they wish . . . ." (Hoecklin, 42) There is the presumption that fixated individualism creates an aversion to sharing; if my success is predicated on my singular behavior and achievement, then to share my thoughts or ideas or abilities is to diminish my own personal chances for reward and remuneration. After all, there is no protective covenant between the individual and the individualist organization, therefore there is little surety that one's job will not be taken by another. The individualist organization is not conceived in terms of benevolence, or even generosity; in many cases, there is an adversarial, rather than cooperative spirit which is exacerbated in the presence of organized labor. Yet company unions are forbidden by American law. The cultural and legal relationship between worker and employer in the American individualist organization is antagonistic, a circumstance exacerbated by laws which stipulate minimum wages and union contracts which compel wage rates, jurisdictional, and seniority arrangements that inflate individual rights at the sacrifice of individual responsibilities. The flow of responsibility-merit-reward is interrupted in the individualist model by the force of the individualist ethic and the framework of law and custom which protects it.

Competition and Capitalism

Jon Alston describes the American competitive spirit as a feature of all organizations in American society, wedded to the concept of the distribution of goods and rewards, imposed even when there is little rationale for its use. In both impersonal and personal competition, Alston believes that the tendency of American organizations to nurture competition between individuals rather than against any certain standards, diminishes performance to simply the goal of winning, suggesting its ruthlessness in a quotation from Ray Kroc:

> This [the food industry] is a rat eat rat, dog eat dog. I'll kill 'em, and I'm going to kill 'em before they kill me. You're talking about the American way of survival of the fittest. (Alston, 1986, 77 citing Boas and Chain, 1976, 20)

Alston further believes that this exaggerated sense of competition leads to the development of a disabling pride, where one believes that to ask for aid is to acknowledge one's own inferiority or to incur a personal obligation that is egoistically unacceptable. (Alston, 1986)

Weick also speaks to the self-fulfilling nature of competition, where one tends to adopt a competitive stance because she believes others to be competitive, even when they are not. (Weick, 1979, 162) Citing a study by Kelley and Stahelski (1970) of differences in the style of interaction between cooperative and competitive individuals, Weick argues that "a competitive person's anticipations of how other people will behave tend to have a self-fulfilling aura that transforms those other individuals, regardless of their preference for cooperation, into competitors." (Weick, 162) Weick's theory of organizing as natural selection describes the active role of members of organizations as a form of progressive enactment, where one's behavior is largely determined by direct engagement with one's environment and the reaction from that environment. According to Weick, organizing then proceeds through the process of selection and retention in order to reduce equivocality, not unlike the description of Clifford Geertz that "man is an animal suspended in webs of significance he himself has spun." (Weick, 135, citing Geertz, 1973)

Morgan follows Weick to describe organizations as the enactment of a shared reality; in his estimation it is the ethic of competitive individualism that stands out most clearly in the United States cultural context. Morgan argues that the American perspective of economic and industrial performance is akin to the competition of a game: "And the general orientation in many organizations is to play the game for all it's worth: set objectives, clarify accountability, and `kick ass' or reward success lavishly and conspicuously." (Morgan, 119)

There seem to be two major elements in considering competition as a defining cultural identifier in organizations; on the one hand there is the game itself, but the game is inexorably tied with the reward if won, and the penalty, if lost. Quoting a 1940s study by anthropologist Gregory Bateson, Morgan describes the American competitive spirit as a deeply embedded cultural practice, nurtured from childhood, sustained by child-rearing customs which encourage boastful and exhibitionistic behavior. Bateson believed that such American traditions created independence and strength, and according to Morgan, the competitive spirit not only establishes the American organizational practice of opening up opportunities for achievement to subordinates, but also is used to justify excessive rewards for those in superior positions. (Morgan, 119)

There is a good deal of evidence of this idiosyncrasy in American economic organizations; most successful American organizations have some sort of reward procedure for motivating their employees to see themselves as winners. At Rubbermaid the reward system is linked to new product development, with managers' compensation tied in part to new product introductions. Indeed, production at Rubbermaid is essentially a competition to achieve targets and goals. (Waterman, 1994, 179-181)

The current state of downsizing, outsourcing, and contracting out is to a large extent the result of free market conditions within organizations. Dartmouth professor James Brian Quinn argues that companies should constantly ask if each part of the organization is the best it can possibly be. Smaller units, whether they be divisional or operational, administrative, developmental, or staff, must compete for excellence; and, according to Quinn, if they cannot measure up, then the activity should be farmed out.

> Do we have one of the best human resources departments in the world? Best accounting department in the world? Purchasing? Research? . . . This threat alone may bring a laggard function up to snuff. If not, better to look to an outside, more competitive resource. (Waterman, 171 citing Quinn)

At Levi Strauss, rewards and recognition are part of a creative peer-recognition program; in some cases recognition and reward actually take on the guise of team sports:

> The womenswear division began with what it called a "Run for the Roses" built around a set of goals sketched on a colorful race track motif covering three walls. Anyone who felt a co-worker went an extra mile toward overcoming a hurdle could award the person a rose. From the race track, the division graduated to a "Bank of Aspirations," a system under which employees had a "checkbook" of coupons they could give out, and then finally to an aspiration "Olympics" that was kicked off with an outdoor ceremony in a park. (Waterman, 147)

The Levi model is interesting in the fact that rewards are oftentimes trivial; in the grand scheme of things, they seem insignificant. But they represent recognition, which is the ultimate reward. (Waterman, 147) The ceremony, the ritual, the hoopla is the value of recognition; indeed, some rewards and recognitions are just plain silly—literally void of objective value, but chock-full of subjective value. Morgan relates a colorful example of the intrinsic

The Individualist Model: American Organizational Culture 77

worth of recognition which he discovered in the research of Peters and Waterman (1982) into the Foxboro Corporation. Foxboro was desperate for some means to advance technologically in order for it to survive. Morgan tells the story:

> Late one evening, a scientist rushed into the president's office with a working prototype. Dumbfounded at the elegance of the solution, and bemused about how to reward it, the president rummaged through the drawers in his desk, found something, and leaning towards the scientist said "Here!" In his hand was a banana, the only reward he could immediately put his hands on. As Peters and Waterman report, from that day on a small "gold banana" pin has been the highest accolade for scientific achievement at Foxboro. (Morgan, 120)

James Fallows believes that the competitive spirit is America's greatest potential strength in that it allows people to invent new roles for themselves. He claims that it should be obvious that in a rapidly changing world, inventing new roles for corporations generally is a prudent organizational response. He calls this spirit a talent for dealing with disorder, which arises out of the real prospect for winning, for changing one's fortunes, identity, and role in life. He calls this a peculiarly American tradition to take risks, knowing that if one fails, there will always be another chance to compete. (Fallows, 48-50)

But how much of this competition is of American orientation and how much is due to the competitive nature of capitalism, if indeed these two concepts can be differentiated, remains at issue. A capitalist market is a competitive system; Thurow tells us that "'Survival of the fittest' and inequalities in purchasing power are what capitalistic efficiency is all about." (Thurow, 1996, 242) It is not surprising that internal organizational traditions have developed in likeness and similarity to the system itself. Companies, as well as countries, are always seeking competitive advantage in economic competition. There seems to be some sort of inherent venality to capitalism that declares it the duty of the economically fit to drive the unfit out of business. (Thurow, 1996, 243) Tradition and order may well represent a jaded stability stodgy in the face of relentless competition from both known and unknown sources. It is likely to be a question of who controls the rules of the game, rather than taking the competition out of the game entirely. (Fallows, 49; 56)

The here-and-now crisis of competitiveness that American corporations face today is not the result of a temporary economic downturn or of a low point in the business cycle. Indeed, we can no longer even count on a predictable business cycle—prosperity, followed by recession, followed by renewed prosperity—as we once did. In today's environment, nothing is constant or predictable—not market growth, customer demand, product life cycles, the rate of technological change, or the nature of competition. Adam Smith's world and its way of doing business are yesterday's paradigm. (Hammer and Champy, 1993, 17)

Joseph Schumpeter's theory of creative destruction is built around the inherent unpredictability and capacity for disruption built into capitalist life: businesses start and fail; products are invented, become popular, and fade into obsolescence; people train for one job and migrate into others. The long term benefits of capitalism—more wealth, more jobs, and more leisure time—are as much a product of competition and change as they could possibly be. (Fallows, 52-55) Ian Jamieson contends that American culture is integrated with capitalism, and relatively unbridled by other social restraints or contradictory values. (Jamieson, 1980, 190-191)

Scientific Management

American emphasis upon the entrepreneur as a "Triumphant Individual" also promoted an organizational revolution based upon the introduction and implementation of "Scientific Management Techniques." In a philosophical sense, the passion for scientific management in organizations is an attempt to divorce the rational from the irrational; in a social context, scientific knowledge became an integral part of Western culture during the seventeenth and eighteenth centuries. Anchored by the 1543 publication by Copernicus of *On the Revolution of the Heavenly Orbs* and the 1687 publication of Newton's *Principia*, the science that was to become such an integral part of American culture rested on certain philosophical and mathematical innovations which were eventually found to be capable of direct application to industrial and technological needs and control of the natural environment. (Jacob, 1980, 3-4)

In fact, the entire process of industrialization seems in large part a consequence of the acquisition of scientific knowledge and its subsequent application to the processes of production; to understand nature mechanically was to be armed with a new and compelling kind of knowledge, (Jacob, 221) which was to be organizationally articulated by Adam Smith's prototypical pin factory described in *The Wealth of Nations* in 1776.

By the turn of another century, Frederick Taylor's theory of scientific management would emerge full-blown. Over time, American companies became the best in the world at translating Taylorism's efficiency principles of division of labor, specialization, and standardization into working business organizations. With the refinement of the assembly line concept of Fordism, the mass production management practices of Alfred Sloan, and the diversification model of Harold Geneen, the organizational model for the United States was more-or-less complete. (Naisbitt and Aburdene, 1985; Hammer and Champy, 1993; Piore and Sabel, 1984)

For more than a hundred years American entrepreneurs set the pace for the rest of the industrializing world in product development, production, and distribution; the American corporate model became the organizational paradigm. American corporations afforded the technological advances that changed the way her people, and many other peoples, lived, producing the highest standard of living the world had ever known.

The American corporate style became an easily recognizable pyramid, and it was well-suited to a high-growth environment because it was endlessly scalable; ideally suited for control and planning; demanded little attention to training; and lent itself well to increasingly simplified, repeatable tasks, which could also be mechanized or automated. But managing such a process became burdensome in two very important aspects. While fragmenting work into smaller and smaller units required growing numbers of functional or middle managers, the more critical dilemma was the growing remoteness between management and the customer or user. In the 1950s and 1960s the chief operational concern of company executives was capacity, or keeping up with an unrelenting and ever-increasing demand for goods and services from customers who were rarely selective as to quality and service. "Any house, any car, any refrigerator were infinitely better than none at all." (Hammer and Champy, 16) Customers were essentially simply faceless numbers that rose up through the corporate layers. (Hammer and Champy, 13-17)

According to Piore and Sabel, the affinity between the factors of mass production and the organizations created to match them did indeed generate material success and enormous gains in productivity, profits, wages, numbers of products, and lower prices. Automated machines, one more technically sophisticated after the other; billions of dollars invested in specialized equipment; standardized commodities; and unskilled operators are but a reflection of rigid, specialized, mechanized nature of mass production. And the corporate structure that evolved to manage this colossus of the Industrial Age bore its own set of standards: hierarchical control; line and staff composition; rules and regulations; efficiency and rationality; labor adversarialism; fragmented knowledge; and functional differentiation. In this system skill became superfluous, because the product defined the worker, rather than the worker leaving her stamp upon her creation. The combination of assembly line production with corporate management style became an effective riposte to the demands of mass markets and inflated expectations of returns on investment. (Piore and Sabel, 1984)

But Piore and Sabel also argue that mass production industrialization and the corporate organization model are economically and socially deleterious, the precursors of deteriorating economic performance in all advanced capitalist countries and progenitors of social decay. "Machines are as much a mirror as the motor of social development." (Piore and Sabel, 5)

Morgan describes the use of scientific management theories as a reflection of the consideration of organizations as machines. Explicated in the work of Frank and Lillian Gilbreth, Taylorism became as much a tool for controlling the workplace as it was a means to generate profits. Non ideologically-specific, the principles of scientific management have crossed many ideological borders, having been used extensively in the former Soviet Union, as well as in capitalist countries; its only ideology is power. (Morgan, 32)

The strength of the scientific management metaphor in American organizations is immense; in most cases, it is almost instinctive to organize structurally, with clearly defined lines of command, communication, coordination, and control. In practice, the mechanistic approach to organization has worked well under conditions where machines would work well: when tasks are straightforward and simple; when the environment is stable; when products produced are appropriate to demand; when repetition is desired; when the human cogs of the machine are compliant and acquiescent. But the model also

The Individualist Model: American Organizational Culture

has its limitations, which have become more and more apparent in the current period of rapid change, global competition, and market uncertainty. The model is rigid; its organizational forms often have great difficulty responding to changing circumstances. Such organizations surrender their personality to conformity, submerging the goals of the organization to rote and routine. (Morgan, 34-35)

A clue to the link between Taylorism and Fordism and the larger society is offered by Denhardt, using Habermas:

> "It is the singular achievement of this ideology to detach society's self-understanding from the frame of reference of communicative action and from the concepts of symbolic interaction and replace it with a scientific model." Accordingly, the institutional framework of society is absorbed by the subsystems of purposive-rational action, and the consciousness of the people is re-ordered to accommodate this shift. (Denhardt, 72, citing Habermas, 1970)

Exercising this analogy, then, we would be forced to describe American society in the same terminology of her economic organizations: Individualistic, competitive, structured, insensitive, efficiency-oriented, achievement-driven, opportunistic, and temporal.

Domination

Organizations are a means of arranging human interaction; economic organizations assume a certain centrality—a product or service—which is the reason for organizing. But organizations have always been associated with the processes of social domination, where one individual or group imposes their will on others. Economic organizations cannot escape this social trap; indeed, they are particularly vulnerable to this charge, in that uneven financial gain is always involved. As indicated in the previous section, the combination of American individualism and enthusiasm for scientific management resulted in huge corporations under authoritarian management.

The ancient roots of organizations reveal a clear relationship between achievement and exploitation. "Whether we are talking about the building of the pyramids, the running of an army, a multinational corporation, or even a family business, we find asymmetrical power relations that result in the majority working in the interests of the few."

(Morgan, 275) In this context, organization is by necessity a process of domination and the use of power.

Power and domination are inextricably linked to exploitation and achievement in organizations. Understanding the rational motivations of exploitation, or asymmetrical power relations that result in the majority working in the interests of the few, exploitation and domination through power in organizations is a complicated theoretical exercise because exploitation is an intrinsically paradoxical strategy of interaction. It may be reasonable to assume that in some cases one agent must be able to dominate another, and it may also be reasonable to see some forms of domination legitimized as normal, socially acceptable power relations. However, there is also an ethical content to the process of domination which considers exploitation a violation of rights and therefore intrinsically immoral. (Morgan, 275-276; Airaksinen, 1988, 3-26)

Paradoxically, therefore, the individualism which provides the philosophical foundation for capitalism in the United States has seemingly been transformed to justify the subordination (i.e., denial of individualism) of most of the work force. And such a conundrum is the subject of much reflection. Institutions, i.e., organizations, were the chains of man's will, according to Rousseau. Weber investigated the ways in which domination is perceived as a right. He identified three types of social domination that could be considered legitimate forms of authority, which he called charismatic, traditional, and rational-legal. And Weber was convinced that bureaucratization, that American corporate style of organizations so favored by scientific management theorists, was a "special mode of social domination, and [he] was interested in the role of bureaucratic organizations in creating and sustaining structures of domination." (Morgan, 276) Indeed, for Weber, the whole process upon which bureaucratization is built, rationalization, is itself a mode of domination. "As we become increasingly subject to administration through rules and engage in strict calculations relating means and ends and costs and benefits, we become increasingly dominated by the process itself. Impersonal principles and the quest for efficiency tend to become our new slave drivers." (Morgan, 278 citing Weber)

It is in this aspect of organizations that we encounter much of the ethical debate. The liberal compassion for the disenfranchised and the oppressed is aroused by the vision of impersonality and greed of economic organizations, their potential to consume and exploit both employees and the environment, taking for themselves what they will, milking it for its objective value, and throwing the rest away. (Morgan, 280)

Morgan tells us that organizations have always been class-based, with distinctions between owners, managers, and workers the source of stratification in the larger society. Moreover, economic globalization appears to be exacerbating such trends. The search for control of the work force and the reduction of labor costs is a tendency examined by Harrison as a characteristic of the 1990s corporate style. According to Harrison, chronic uncertainty, market fragmentation, and accelerating product cycles have driven large American corporations and their partners to increasingly pursue policies of sweating labor by downsizing, outsourcing, subcontracting, and moving jobs "South," all in an effort to secure a certain return on investment for stockholders at the expense of the workers. Calling this syndrome the "low road to company profitability," (B. Harrison, 213) Harrison contends that the tendency of American managers to compete by cutting wages rather than by upgrading technology and skills is largely to blame for the exacerbation of economic and social dualism. (Harrison, 190-213)

In the case of women, the concept of male dominance and the Western stereotype of masculinity in American organizations arises out of the general theory of male superiority, a cultural creation of not only America's Western European historical roots but identified in most other cultures as well. Hymowitz and Weissman are convinced that the Western version, whether based on the Eve theory of original sin or its paradoxical converse, the Virgin Mary theory of innate goodness, has a profound impact in the workplace. (Hymowitz and Weissman, 1978) The Lundins maintain that the workplace is a fortress of male domination, in which there is as much male domination of other men as there is male domination of women. (Lundin and Lundin, 1993) Cynthia Enloe addresses the issue of domination in organizations as articulated in gendered decision-making. Enloe is convinced that gendered decision-making is more than a cultural norm—it is a masculine/feminine dichotomy based on power relationships, compulsorily structured to achieve certain ends. (Enloe, 1990)

Domination is also at the heart of sexual harassment and racial discrimination in American organizations. Patriarchy and hierarchy are epistemological cousins; both have had a decisive influence on opportunity structures in society, both creating and perpetuating stereotypical assumptions, and class consciousness and divisiveness.

While American employment law has worked to mitigate against the most egregious violations of individual rights in the workplace, regardless of gender and ethnicity, the stubborn survival of patriarchy and hierarchy is like a willful weed in the organizational garden.

The market system seems to inevitably reinforce a power structure that

> ... encourages people with certain attributes while disadvantaging others. And in developing differential patterns of control for employees from different sectors,they produce patterns of favor and privilege that symbolize, and hence reinforce underlying socioeconomic divisions. (Morgan, 287-288)

"TURBOCAPITALISM" AND THE NEW ECONOMIC ORDER

The American model is one of political and economic leadership. Politically it has served as the ideological engine which has propelled the rest of the world into capitalism and a global economy; but the organizations of that economy exhibit certain defining characteristics and unintended consequences which may neither be transferable nor tolerable outside the American experience. The American experience has revealed certain weaknesses in its own paradigm, defects which accompanied uncontrollable federal budget deficits, loss of competitiveness, changing labor markets, and general economic malaise, job insecurity, and depressed notions of America's economic health and productivity during the 1980s.

In the first three decades after World War II America grew rapidly, and fueled a world economy which grew even more rapidly. Clearly, mass production techniques based on an ethic of individualistic capitalism were working well and helped greatly increase the material standard of living through the United States and most of the developed world. But beginning in the mid 1970s, the American economic engine gradually began to slow. Peter Drucker argues that a series of economic events from the mid 1970s to 1990 defied the prediction or explanation of economic theory. A chain of perfectly logical, sound economic decisions by both Democratic and Republican presidents designed to promote American exports and create jobs first resulted in stagflation—persistent inflation and unemployment at the same time—then dangerously high interest rates. The reasons for this policy failure are probably attributable to changes in the international economic environment. First, the oil price shocks of the 1970s sent an unprecedented inflationary surge through the industrial world. Second, by the 1980s the process of globalization meant that much of the mass production of standardized goods could be moved "off shore" to developing nations with their low wage work forces. (Drucker, 1989) But the American economy has shown amazing resilience. In fact, the performance of the American economy remains singularly vigorous when compared with the economies of other nations in the Group of Seven industrial countries—Japan, Germany, Britain, France, Italy, and Canada. 1998 marks the eighth consecutive year of sustained growth:

> Everything that should be up is up—GDP, capital spending, incomes, the stock market, employment, exports, consumer and business confidence. Everything that should be down is down— unemployment, inflation, interest rates. (Zuckerman, 1998, 18)

The American economy has churned along through the latter half of the 1990s with an inexorable strength, according to many economists. The once uncontrollable federal budget deficits which fantasized economic pundits has largely disappeared, leaving the American Congress in an enviable position of whether to save or spend. The elimination of what at one time was a federal deficit of $290 billion gives a boost to savings, sustains lower interest rates, and enables noninflationary fiscal and monetary policies for the future. The mid-1998 unemployment rate hovers around an innocuous four per cent and is still falling, and inflation could well be statistically zero. Job opportunities, as well as beginning salaries for new college graduates are spectacular after years of empty campus career development offices which drove undergraduates back into the sheltered halls of ivy rather than face an uncertain future with impending student loan debt.

Consider the general conditions of the American economy: 73 million new private sector jobs created since 1980; 64 per cent of the American adult population employed; GDP growth of close to 4 percent; inflation at a 30-year low which has preserved lower interest rates allowing for greater capital investment, rising productivity, and astounding corporate profits. Recovery and energy in the general economy has been matched by equally amazing innovation and growth in the world of investment and finance capital. The American stock market, which in April 1998 closed above 9000 for the first time, has surprised and confounded its critics and supporters alike. Booming corporate profits and diverse investment outlets have allowed for billions of dollars in capital investment, much of it in long-term, risky ventures; real spending for plant and equipment, new orders for capital goods, and manufacturing capacity have all risen dramatically since 1990. (Zuckerman, 19-26)

By some estimates, American businesses have successfully traversed the perilous transition from Industrial Age to the Information Age and economic globalization. The uniquely American policy trends to deregulation and cautious fiscal and monetary policy, coupled with broader market participation, and technological and logistical innovation and job creation would seem to indicate a strong and vibrant American economy and an optimistic future. (Zuckerman, 28-3)

Paul Krugman warns, however, that it is presumptuous to assume that "traditional limits to economic expansion are no longer relevant." (Krugman, 1998, 33) He argues that it is too early to exhibit an unbridled optimism with respect to the American economy, even though the times are undeniably good. He argues that the economy's long-run growth has not accelerated; rather, the economy has simply gotten better at making use of its capacity without overheating.

> We have had a favorable turn in the business cycle, abetted by some temporary factors that have helped keep inflation down, and probably also by shifts in the labor market that have reduced the bargaining power of workers and therefore allowed fuller employment without accelerating wage increases . . . . Things could be worse, but nothing fundamental has changed—the amount of good news is not enough to justify the triumphant rhetoric one now hears so often. (Krugman, 40)

Krugman also suggests that the American economy looks good because other economies have not attained their own predicted/expected growth rates for the 1990s. He argues that there has been no revolutionary improvement in the American economic performance, that its real gains are mediocre. even though it is structurally and fundamentally sound: "[T]he current sense that the United States is on top of the world is based on a huge exaggeration of the implications of a few good years here and a few bad years elsewhere." (Kruger, 45)

Edward Luttwak warns that while it may be economic orthodoxy to praise "turbo-capitalism . . . accelerated change fueled by global free trade and domestic deregulation . . . as the only way to run an

economy," (Luttwak, 1996, 21) there is a downside to such economic dogma which is manifested in personal economic insecurity for millions of American workers. (Luttwak, 1996)
There is little doubt that the restructuring and downsizing undertaken by American industry have left the American worker in a state of perpetual anxiety with respect to job security:

> American workers understand that their employment today depends far more on the global competitiveness of their industry or plant than on the phase of the business cycle. Even in good times, workers and management are constantly conscious of waves of downsizing and restructuring and the need to cut costs. Those who survive restructuring always fret that they may not next time. In 1996, 46 percent of workers in large firms feared being laid off—twice the 1991 level, despite five years of economic expansion and a sharply lower unemployment rate. (Zuckerman, 30)

We are left with the image of an American economy which is almost certainly strong and vibrant, but with the impression that the American worker is plagued by insecurities and instabilities. The economy may have created 8.5 million net new jobs since the beginning of 1993, but it is the numbers of jobs lost to downsizing that dominates. Downsizing is frightening, coming in massive numbers to the biggest companies, such as AT&T, BellSouth, and Kmart; and it is often perceived as unfair in light of swollen corporate profits. ("Why more looks like less," April 27, 1996, 26) Jim Hoagland agrees, contending that it is difficult for people to accept that they will lose their jobs while their companies reap huge profits. Economic insecurities that appear inexplicable and uncontrollable, that threaten jobs and careers, and jeopardize the future economic prospects of their children are a pervasive and real political force in today's industrialized democracies, "whether the national employment and industrial production statistics are ghastly—as in France and Germany—or on the robust side as in England and America." (Hoagland, 1996, 28)

Downsizing in American businesses struck not just at workers whose jobs were lost to lower-wage localities, the rush for the lean organization decimated the traditional American-style ranks of middle managers. But in April 1998 Tim Smart of the *Washington Post* reported that

... downsized, de-layered and re-engineered themselves to the bone throughout the early 1990s—[American corporations] have found they cannot run their businesses with a few executives at the top, the worker bees at the bottom and nobody in between. And so these companies again have started rebuilding the middle layers of their organizations. (Smart, 1998, 19)

While increased job offerings in categories of managers, administrators, and executives is auspicious, there may be a variety of reasons behind it, i.e.: a robust economy that creates overall job growth; corporate realization that organizations have certain needs that can only be met at the mid-level; newly generated complexities of the globalization and technological development. Ironically, some of the bigger corporations who led the rush to downsizing are now refilling many of those empty slots. In addition, in some cases former managers are finding themselves marketable as consultants to do essentially their old jobs. It is apparent, however, that managers are doing old jobs in new ways, becoming risk takers, innovators, and team builders. (Smart, 19-20) The job pruning of the 1980s and 1990s has stimulated new growth, largely because the environment is more demanding, more complex, and more competitive. It is probably prudent to remember, however, that the sound economy is the enabler. American corporations whose driving force is return on investment are typically innovative and creative; rehiring may be simply the other side of the downsizing coin.

Both the British and American experience with early forms of organization were to transform society from one of self-employed persons to that of wage-earners. The system of wage labor led the capitalist to place primary emphasis on the efficiency of labor time and the labor process, and to design organizations and management techniques which are balanced on expenditure on labor as the main variable item. "... there was a great incentive for organizations to develop a system that would allow labor to bear the vagaries of the business cycle and other changing circumstances by adjusting the size and cost of the work force to suit the organizations' immediate needs." (Morgan, 284)

Another critical factor in judging economic success or failure and its impacts on American workers lies in the area of inequality, which is clearly increasing in the United States. The United States Census Bureau declares that between 1968 and 1994 the bottom 80 percent of American households lost ground in income, with the biggest income gains going to the top 5 percent. While chief executive compensation in 1995 was up 23 percent, wages remained flat; even with greater expenditures on social spending, the gap between the rich and poor held fast. There is some commentary that claims that inequality is endemic to a capitalist economy, and that the only remedy is broader ownership of property. However, inequality in the concentration of wealth in America is even more extreme than the maldistribution of income. The value of the stock market has increased more than threefold in less than a decade, but according to the Brooking Institution, the top 5 percent of households own 77 percent of all stock holdings, while the bottom 80 percent own less than 2 percent. (Kuttner, 1996, 5) While this depiction of the concentration of wealth is somewhat altered when indirect stock ownership via mutual funds, annuities, variable insurance policies and pension funds is factored in, inequality in holdings is still very large.

Clay Chandler reiterates Kuttner's observations:

> The millions of American investors who climbed aboard the Starship Dow before its takeoff in the 1990s have watched their net worth soar to dizzying heights. But many more have missed the ride . . . . The most recent data suggest that six of every 10 households still do not own stocks—and thus have reaped no direct benefit from the current boom in share prices. (Chandler, 1998, 18)

According to the Federal Reserve's Survey of Consumer Finances, for the year 1995, 41 per cent of American families were stockowners, which is indeed an increase from the 1992 figure of 37 per cent and 32 per cent in 1989. But there is a vast disparity in stock ownership by income group, according to statistics quoted by Chandler: 84 per cent of households earning more than $100,000 a year held stocks, median value of $91,000. But of households reporting earnings of between $25,000 and $50,000, only 48 per cent are stockholders, and their median value stood at $8,000.

When such figures are considered along with Congressional Budget Office figures which reflect an increase of 72 per cent in the average after-tax income of the wealthiest one per cent of Americans, a stagnate after-tax income growth figure for the middle fifth of the population, and a 16 per cent loss for the poorest 20 per cent of families in the years 1977 to 1994, there appears to be a growing disproportion between the haves and the have-nots. (Chandler, 18)

Most Americans would like to believe they can be rich one day. The "embourgeoisement" phenomena suggests that even though they envy the rich, and rebuke policies perceived to favor them, most people would like to emulate the rich, if they had the chance. And in some important economic ways, Americans, even median income Americans, still savor the taste of the good life. Although average household cash income has risen only slightly, families are smaller, and non-wage compensation has also increased in real terms. While this may not mean cash in hand, it does represent positive, rather than negative, income figures. The problem lies in the numbers of workers who are poor. According to *The Economist*, 5.9% of workers were poor in 1977, but by 1993 that figure had risen to 7.4%. ("Up, down . . . , 33)

Again, there may be multiple causal factors, as social and economic change appear to be highly interconnected. There are more single-parent households; the average hourly wage for the lowest-paid workers has fallen in real terms; and the less-educated are finding well-paid jobs harder to come by. And the middle class is not immune. The ladder from poverty to middle class is still there, but it appears to take longer to climb it; and once one reaches one's goal, the top rung on the ladder may break, sending one sliding swiftly back down to the bottom. For many workers, the energy to both begin and continue the quest may be exhausted. In fact, it may well be that education is the biggest factor in worker anxiety. The premium on education widens income distribution, feeds blue-collar uneasiness, and fuels middle-manager apprehensions. Corporate downsizing injected a sense of insecurity into the ranks of middle managers, many of whom were older, unskilled and untrained in Information Age technology, obliged to take a pay cut or seek retraining and re-education to re-enter the market. ("Up, down . . . 33) In an Information Age society, lack of the intellectual tools to compete in a technological, computerized marketplace is perilous to economic security. Even more threatening is the notion that some companies have no use for many employees, no matter how well educated.

> But what most working people in the United States, as in Europe, now want is not the possibility of better jobs or higher incomes through growth. They rightly suspect that their earnings will not increase with more turbo-capitalism. Rather they want security for the jobs and incomes they already have—which are threatened as much by growth, as by a lack of it. (Luttwak, 1996, 21)

It is obvious that despite its foibles, America's individualist capitalism remains dynamic. According to Economist Robert J. Samuelson, conventional wisdom insinuates that Americans are slothful, overconsumptive, profligate, self-indulgent, shallow, and short-sighted. But he argues that neither of the other leading economic models comes anywhere close to outperforming the American economic model. The American system may be more open and chaotic, with sharper ambitions and insecurities, but it is also a more responsive model which reveals and corrects mistakes more rapidly than others. (Samuelson, 1996, 56) According to Samuelson, the American economic culture favors growth:

> America still embraces the market culture: its obsession with growth; its striving for wealth (and tolerance of inequality); its acceptance of change. Europe is less enthralled and more inclined to reshape market culture through government. The lesson is not that government is bad ... But too much government or misguided government can subvert economic growth .... To work well, government needs to be used with restraint. To work well, capitalism needs to retain its central features—including the freedoms to fail and to get rich. (Samuelson, 49)

Zuckerman agrees. He contends that American economic achievement is a product of its culture, which "... nourishes its mavericks, cherishes its young, welcomes newcomers, and dramatically opens to energy and talent rising from the bottom up." (Zuckerman, 22)

Contradictory trends that exhibit enormous corporate earnings, downsizing, re-hiring, high employment, and increased income inequality imply that there is a greater lesson to be learned. There is no doubt but that the conditions for a great many of American workers have changed, but there are certain mutualities and responsibilities inherent at every organizational level, beginning at the level of worker. As companies must become more competitive, so must the worker. My research convinces me that the work force, which Bennett Harrison depicts as rather passive, reactive, and victimized, can be aroused out of its illogical expectations, but only when its individual members start accepting a certain measure of responsibility for their own fate. It is apparent that the turbo-capitalized workplace has opportunities for those members of the work force who are willing to upgrade their skills, accept transfers, work long hours, and make personal sacrifices—in other words, who understand the concept of "work." I am not convinced that the system is so inherently unfair and exploitive that effort is not rewarded; the work ethic still matters, but it is indeed an ethic of work and responsibility, not one of easy money, over-inflated wage concessions, cushy middle-management paper-pushers, jurisdictional demands, unearned security, and resting on one's laurels. As companies are different, so is the society from which emerges the American worker. Uneducated, lazy, self-centered, and uncooperative workers will never be able to compete with trained, energetic, interested, caring, self-starters who consider responsibilities before rights.

The American capitalist system is an exacting one; its organizations are endlessly adaptive and curiously intriguing. The literature alludes to the cultural unsuitability of the traditional orientation of American organizations in meeting the challenges of global competition and economic interdependence, yet some observers argue that "America's economy is even better suited for today's rapidly changing knowledge-based economy than it was for the mass production, industrial economy of earlier times. (Zuckerman, 23) Ward proposes that the ultimate challenge to the American theory of individualism is to create sufficient individual character to control the realities of society. (Ward, 37-76) And Lester Thurow proposes that a new theory of teamwork, which may be antithetical to the American myth of individualism, is in order. He suggests, as does Ward, that when the myth is more important than the reality, economic success will suffer. (Thurow, 1996, 320-323)

The American business style offers wealth, but that wealth is uneven and comes only with commensurate sacrifice. Doing business American-style is simply not acceptable in many cultures. Americans are perceived to be unnecessarily frenetic, disrespectful of authority, pragmatic, loquacious, uninhibited, generous but wasteful, loud, rude, boastful, immature, over-confident, hard-working, and both egalitarian and prejudiced. These characteristics do not necessarily travel well.

There is likely a middle ground between the individual and the collective, between science and values, between competition and collaboration, and between domination and interaction. Profit and loss may go hand-in-hand; the market system may be unforgiving; but the constraints of values and obligations will not be ignored. The powerful American organizations that excelled at mass marketing and mass manufacture are equally capable of excelling in a new age, but not without metamorphosis. There is a balance to be sought, the achievement of which will likely affirm or deny American political and economic success and leadership. There is no valor in false humility, but neither is there strength in specious perseverance. An organization must be equally complex with its environment if it is to prosper; if it does not prosper, neither do its participants. Uniting pride in accomplishment with the ability and willingness to correct one's shortcomings may offer the solution for American organizations whose purpose can never be fulfilled with the bounty of greed alone.

The times seem to demand a new American organizational paradigm; the examination of the atomist/individualist conceptualization provides one data set; an examination of the collectivist conceptualization serves as its philosophical polar opposite. Somewhere in between the two lies a workable foundation to ease the natural inequalities of capitalism as well as to provide a positive model for socioeconomic growth and stability in virtual globalization. Settlement lies somewhere between lucre and loss.

CHAPTER IV
The Organic Model: The Japanese Organizational Paradigm

COLLECTIVISM AND THE ORGANIC SOCIETY

Detected in not only the most ancient tribal societies, but in Greek classical political thought, and in the social philosophy of the Chinese sage Confucius, collectivism is a social philosophy with rich and multiple cultural and historical origins. The philosophical counterpoint to individualism, collectivism bears with it the belief in society as an organic, natural phenomenon, in substance and meaning antithetical to the atomist viewpoint of society as artificial and contrived. As an ideological construct, the presumption of society as natural to the human condition describes one of the deepest contrasts between East and West. While it is not inappropriate to consider America as the model for individualistic societies and Japan as a model of collectivist societies, on a broader scale the individualistic-collectivist duality describes a bifurcation between the majority and minority of the world's peoples. The majority of the world's population live in societies where the interests of the group antecede the interests of the individual. (Hoecklin, 35-71) There are few cultures in which there is greater sensitivity to matters of status, gradations of hierarchy, and an abhorrence of individualism. In the collectivist society, the ultimate sin is selfishness; there is little room for the respect of individual rights. But there is also an expectation of respect and decency to be accorded to all those who fulfil the conventional duties of their roles in the social order.

The affirmation of an organic society arises out of the belief that society is a natural institution, and human beings social animals, not egotistical individualists. (Nelson, 5-21) Society in this context is the affirmation of the social context of one's existence, it is a teleological notion of association in that the value of the collective enterprise transcends that of the unattached individual. This distinction between nature and convention is among the most important philosophical dichotomies in the history of political thought. It is not surprising, therefore, that it lies at the center of the debate between individualist and collectivist interactions.

In collectivist societies feelings of self-worth are linked to the approval of the group; therefore there is a greater willingness to share one's own talents and material resources to support the group and conform to the views of others. While members of collective societies certainly have private opinions, they are likely to keep them to themselves if they feel that their opinion might disrupt the solidarity of the group. The concept of *face*, meaning the respect and affection of oneself and others, is inherent in the collectivist spirit; in such societies one would avoid any embarrassing encounter that might cause others in their collective to feel that they have lost status, affection, or respect. (Brislin, 79-80)

In the sociohistorical context, the organic society is affirmed by the Vygotskyan paradigm of psycholinguistics, which regards control by others to be fundamental to human nature. For Vygotsky, participation in social activity is the starting point in explaining the development of human consciousness, establishing a socioculturally defined way of looking at the world on the basis of a set of principles clearly antithetic to the notion of an egocentric individual who later becomes social. (McCreary, 1986, 7-10)

The Confucian roots of collectivism and the organic society are fundamental to its Eastern explication. Revered first in the Eastern world by the Chinese as editor and compiler of the Five Classics—a miscellaneous collection of poems, annals, histories, and handbooks of divination and of manners—Confucius was the progenitor of a strong and influential dispersed Eastern culture of decorum, a vision of a society in which everyone knew one's place and kept it. The Confucian philosophy combined and reaffirmed the importance of both family and empire, the principal foundations of all Eastern societies.

The good life, for Confucius, could be led only in society, by fulfilling exactly and graciously the roles that fell to each individual human being, day by day, hour by hour, and even minute by minute, throughout life. (McNeill, 1990, 153)

Confucian collectivism is ideally expressed in a united country in which everyone behaves properly, virtually automatically in every human relationship. Indeed, Confucianism assumes that human nature is basically good, and that the good, ethical life can be assured by order, harmony, moderation, good manners, and a Confucian formulation of the Golden Rule: "Do not unto others what you would not have others do unto you." (Harrison, L., 82) Its five relationships—father/teacher and son; ruler and subject; husband and wife; older brother and younger brother; and friend and friend—represent the building blocks of an aristocratic, authoritarian, and static society. It glorifies education, achievement, and virtue. The central point of Confucianism is the refusal to make distinctions between the virtues required in public life and the virtues of private life. The relationships of society are no different from that of family, only more complex; the essentials of good order are the same, with the state simply being the family writ large. (McNeill, 152-153)

COLLECTIVISM AND JAPANESE SOCIETY

The Japanese interpretation of the organic society and the collectivist thesis symbolizes the most significant difference between Japanese and Americans, or Westerners in general. With philosophical roots in the Eastern reverence for Confucian thought, the Japanese notion of society and the role of the individual are as mythically compelling as their American counterpart.

The Historical Record

The Japanese Confucian acculturation is a complex concoction of borrowed finery and native rituals. Between the sixth and the ninth centuries the Japanese, who had in earlier times been somewhat of a "Johnny-come-lately" in comparison to the rest of the peoples of northern Europe, and less sophisticated than their Chinese neighbors, consciously set out to avail themselves of the educated order and civility of Chinese society. But the clan organization of Japanese society resisted many of the Confucian rituals. The earliest civilization in the islands of Japan were tribal groups of warlike clans who fought among themselves, and the realities of the tribal tradition prohibited Japan from absorbing wholesale the imperious nature and refinement of Chinese culture.

The upshot of this tension was the development of a system in which Confucianism was the formal way of life for the emperor, but with the bulk of effective authority vested in warrior clansmen who embraced Buddhism, a religion which arose roughly at about the same time as Confucian thought, and whose spiritual and ethical force was far more accommodating to discipline and the *samurai* way of life. For the most part the warrior clansmen continued to obey their emperor out of respect for the legacy of chiefdom, but the clans, not the emperor, controlled the majority of the Japanese population. The influence of the virtual serenity of the Confucian way of thought was thus controverted by the allegiance of the warriors to Buddhism, the monastic sanction of the warrior tradition, and the land, wealth, and strength of the monastic communities. (McNeill, 254-257)

In the seventeenth century, during the time of shogunate-enforced total isolation from the rest of the world, a Japanese variant of Confucianism was declared the official system of learning; it fit well into Japanese culture of the period, with its emphasis on deference toward superiors and feudal loyalty. And with all Christians and foreigners expelled, and foreign travel forbidden under threat of exile, the Japanese culture remained curiously colored by Chinese models, but in diverse ways that were not always true to the Chinese heritage. (McNeill, 413-416)

Confronted with the superior technology of the West, the Japanese first attempted to adopt Western science but stick to Eastern Ethics, a concept largely pursued by other Asian peoples. But the Japanese leadership shortly realized that there was no clear dividing line between techniques, institutions, and values. This realization, and the eagerness to learn without feeling culturally threatened, enabled the Japanese to take the social steps necessary which would liberate their society from strict class barriers, and eventually discard the entire feudal system. (Reischauer, 1981, 127-129) With the seizure of power from the shogun Tokugawa in 1868, the Meiji Restoration started Japan on a path which would transform its society in only one or two generations from one in which status was primarily determined by heredity to one in which status depended largely on education and achievement. Its government was modeled largely on nineteenth-century Western,

The Organic Model: The Japanese Organizational Paradigm

mostly French and German, regimes, at the same time that it remained true to Japanese social realities. The Japanese sent students abroad to acquire new skills, and hired Western experts to come to Japan to share their technical knowledge. Highly selective as to the models and experts they chose, the Japanese experiment was well launched into modernity by the turn of the new century. (Reischauer, 1981, 82-84)

Japan's uncanny ability to borrow from other civilizations while retaining its innate cultural vitality sustains an incredibly complex society whose sometimes confounding characteristics are a testament to pragmatism and practicality. It is an ancient tribal civilization with a Confucian intellectual lineage, enlightened by the civility of ancient Chinese virtues and the Buddhist and Shinto spiritual traditions, energized by Western technology, and politically arrayed in the French and German institutional style. The Japanese historical pattern of acculturation has given rise to the stigmatization that it is nothing more than an uncreative nation of borrowers; nevertheless, the potency and resilience of its composite culture cannot be denied. (Reischauer, 1981, 41; 123-126) The Japanese are a very distinctive people, whether one considers their culture indigenous or improvised; indeed, Japanese improvisation in the face of changing realities may survive the threats of globalization more wholly than societies that stubbornly confront change head-on. On the other hand, it may be so tightly linked to the Confucian notion of a benevolent state that it is unable to conform to changed realities.

The Individual and the Group in Japanese Society

Reischauer tells us that the Japanese version of the organic society is its most profound cultural identifier, so esteemed beyond the bounds of reality as to affect the interpretation of everything in terms of "personal factional alignments . . . interrelationships . . . and personal patronage and recommendations. They like to insist that what counts is not one's abilities but one's *kone*, an abbreviation of the English word `connections.'" (Reischauer, 1981, 127-128) While the leaders of the Meiji Restoration recognized the necessity of putting more emphasis on the individual, and individual rights were written into the 1889 constitution, nonetheless, there is a vast difference between Western perceptions of the group and the individual and Japanese attitudes. (Reischauer, 1981, 128-129)

Hampden-Turner and Trompenaars contend that in the quandary between "self and other" cultural assumptions, American and Japanese cultures are like ships that pass in the night:

> Inscribed on the hull of each ship is the dominant cultural value. Repressed in the water beneath each opposite ship is the subordinate cultural consequence. No sooner do relationships break down than each streams off in the opposite direction—obviously mad! (Hampden-Turner and Trompenaars, 16)

But it would be intellectually and analytically stultifying to be delimited by generalities and "either-or's." The Japanese are neither complete aesthetes nor are they rule-bound samurai, brutal militarists nor single-minded fanatics. They have changed as much over time as any of the peoples of the world, considerably more than many:

> Though a homogeneous people culturally, the roughly 115 million Japanese display great variations of attitudes and ways of life by age group and according to their diverse roles in society. A teenager and an octogenarian, a day laborer and a corporation executive, a bank clerk and an artist show about as much diversity in attitudes as their counterparts would in any Western country. Almost anything that might be said about Japanese in general would not be true of many and might be flatly contradicted by some. (Reischauer, 1981, 124)

It would be wrongheaded to assume that Japan is a nation of impassive, imperturbable robots who endlessly, patiently conform to the needs of others and to the politically and socially correct mandates of a collective society. Just as Americans will express their individualistic nature through an oftentimes over exuberant interest in athletic team competition and achievement, the Japanese preserve a strong sense of self-identity and desire for self-expression. But even in social rebellion, the Japanese will tend to seek comrades in arms; there is little evidence of a lone operator or individual eccentric. (Reischauer, 1981, 146-147)

The group orientation remains a marked Japanese cultural attribute. Not surprisingly, the Japanese have learned to cultivate their own individuality in socially acceptable ways within a cloyingly compact society—through the love of nature, through prose and poetry, through art, music, and dance. While such pursuits might be considered hobbies to Americans, to the Japanese they are *shumi*, or "tastes," which enable them to express their identity. (Reischauer, 1981, 146-151)

The deference toward the group is more understandable when it is put within the framework of the myths of Japanese racial unity, purity, and uniqueness. From notions of physiological differences to the assumption that non-Japanese are physically, culturally defective, and mentally incapable of speaking Japanese, the Japanese bias against foreigners is a profoundly unifying social force. Nevertheless, Japanese mutual trust is facilitated by its sense of one-ness; with the same orthodox family patterns, the same virtues, the same emphasis on consensus and conventional wisdom, and the same abundance of steady, high-average performers, Japan's unity permits its meritocratic style to work as well as it does. (Fallows, 32-35)

Japanese Collectivism and Democracy

According to Fallows, "Japan is nowhere near as 'democratic' as America, either politically or socially." (Fallows, 34) The social stratification of its medieval feudal society has survived. There is a strong system of honor and hierarchy in Japanese society: "Women defer to men, the young defer to the old, everyone fits in above and below someone on the national chain of command . . . . the system of honorifics . . . [decrees] the different titles and entirely different vocabularies from which you select words according to whether the person you are addressing stands above you or below." (Fallows, 35)

There is a cherished tradition of master and disciple in Japanese society that is connected to the Buddhist ethic of self-control and self-discipline; proficiency and skill is more a matter of inner strength than technique or muscle. This same spiritualism and dedication to self-restraint and will power infuses the larger society. ". . . social conformity to the Japanese is no sign of weakness but rather the proud, tempered product of inner strength." (Reischauer, 1981, 152) This strength is crucial to the Japanese perception of the proper response to the demands of duty to family, associates, and the greater society. This sense of duty, or *gimu*, is clearly a remnant of earlier times; nonetheless, it is a powerful expression of cultivated, purposeful self-discipline. (Reischauer, 1981, 152)

Powerfully influenced by the exigencies of the Meiji Restoration, despite constitutional injunction, the Japanese State during the prewar period rested on the principles of political centralization and the

citizen's duty to the state, rather than on such democratic principles as popular sovereignty, local autonomy, checks and balances, or individual rights. (Pempel, 1982, 12-14)
During the postwar period, however, important democratic reforms were introduced under a totally new constitution, which was generally reflective of the American and British systems. Popular sovereignty was introduced; the emperor was reduced in standing from absolute sovereign to symbolic head of state; both houses of the Diet (parliament) were made elective and empowered; the cabinet was made responsible to parliament, along British lines; an independent judiciary was established, in the American tradition; and the legal rights of citizens and the powers of local governments were significantly enlarged. While in these important ways, government was made more accountable to the people, over the period of the Occupation, the power of the Japanese state was only minimally reduced. Despite fluctuations in its power, a prevailing sense of the need for strong central direction and wide-ranging authority, worked toward national cohesion, consensus, and centralization. (Pempel, 15-16)

The Japanese democratic model rests on both personal and institutional centralization: ". . . numerous centripetal forces pull Japanese political actors toward one another." (Pempel, 16) The success of the parliament is based on party solidarity; rarely will an individual vote against his party. The cabinet is profoundly powerful in its institutional authority to oversee the bulk of parliamentary activity and draw up and present most of the legislation; it is extremely rare for either nongovernment bills to pass or government bills to fail. The system of advisory councils, study groups, and research committees attached to government agencies, whose members are appointed by the ministry with which they are affiliated, possess broad authority to investigate and present unified proposals for action to the government. Differences within the government are essentially negotiated away by a group of senior civil servants on the Conference of Vice-Ministers, much in the same manner in which cabinet cooperation is expedited through ad hoc and permanent cross-ministerial councils, whose purpose is to provide the guidelines to direct ministerial actions.

Overall, the Japanese state, which in absolute numbers is one of the smallest in the industrialized world, is a force for cohesion rather than diversity, and obedience rather than dissent. (Pempel, 20)

Likewise, the party model in the Japanese state has, since 1955, exhibited an equally authoritative force for consensus and unity. After the collapse of several multiparty coalitions in the early postwar years, the Liberal Democratic Party (LDP), a vague and amorphous amalgam of conservative economic and cultural values supported both electorally and financially by key elements of business and organized agriculture, exercised one-party control of Japanese politics for almost forty years. Until the elections of the summer of 1993, the LDP had successfully managed to viscerate attempts by other parties to unseat it. Indeed, from 1955 until 1993, the LDP dominated both parliament and the cabinet, frustrating all party opposition and forging a formidable conservative coalition. (Pempel, 35)

The elections of July 1993 may well have killed Japan's post-war hegemonic party system, but the practice of leaving overall policymaking largely in the hands of an unelected and self-appointed group of bureaucrats survives. Calling the absence of a center of political accountability Japan's major political flaw, vanWolferen argues that Japanese ministries "come closer to being states unto themselves than any other government institutions in the industrialized world." (vanWolferen, 1993, 58) Fingleton explicates this argument, contending that the real power in the Japanese state, the arbiter of all legislation, policy, and decision-making, remains the Ministry of Finance, the capstone of a Confucian system of power whose essential control over taxing, spending, and defense policies is unbalanced by any politically accountable unit. (Fingleton, 1995, 69-72)

> As a Confucian society, Japan is avowedly paternalistic, and there is little sympathy for the essentially alien view that supreme power is rightfully the prerogative of elected representatives. Thus the bureaucrats do not have to apologize for overruling populist tendencies. As ever in Japan, politicians reign and bureaucrats rule. (Fingleton, 85)

But Pempel remarks that the Japanese model of bureaucratic sovereignty and one-party control, however centralized and conservative it may be, is not necessarily anti-democratic. To the contrary, he argues that the LDP has been responsive over the years to the public will. (Pempel, 312-313)

Japanese Collectivism and Capitalism

According to Hampden-Turner and Trompenaars, Hofstede's 1991 study revealed a clear connection between collective values and economic development. According to his research, the belief in the need to serve the group rather than self is a necessary, although non-sufficient, condition for the economic growth which he found in praxis in Japan, Singapore, Hong Kong, and Taiwan. Echoing the studies of Harvard professors George Lodge and Ezra Vogel, Hofstede found that collectivism correlates highly with growth and investment rates in a relationship which seems to be anchored in the collective belief that "whole organizations, societies, and economies can learn to act coherently to nurture higher rates of economic development." (Hampden-Turner and Trompenaars, 163-164 citing Hofstede, 1991 and Harvard Business Press, 1986)

Contending that an outer-directed collectivism, with socially attributed status, as in the case of Japan, serves customers rather than extracts profits, Hampden-Turner and Trompenaars make a powerful case for an analogy between the ancient Japanese tradition of resilience and adaptation and Japan's economic achievement. (Hampden-Turner and Trompenaars, 164-169) But a variety of historically conditioned institutions, seemingly embodying what Hampden-Turner and Trompenaars identify as communitarian ethics, proved extremely functional for promoting industrialization in Japan.

The origins of the modern Japanese version of capitalism are paradoxically to be identified in the Meiji Restoration of the nineteenth century. Habits of economic growth fostered by a combination of government and private enterprise developed during the Meiji era were easily transformed into the economic miracle of postwar Japan. Reischauer argues that capitalism was far advanced in late feudal Japan, with a landed class legally recognized by the Meiji government who were anxious to abolish all feudal claims and create a uniform and simple system of land ownership. Because of the development of capitalistic moneylenders, national markets, trade and production monopolies, and nascent financial management experiments, "Japan, and the economy, despite the feudal facade, was in many ways an early capitalistic economy, not unlike that of Western Europe in early modern times." (Reischauer, 1965, 64; 182)

The Meiji government established a pattern of government economic behavior that would prove remarkably similar to the modern

The Organic Model: The Japanese Organizational Paradigm

Japanese political economy. Providing a secure political condition and reliable financial framework for the country, it sponsored and also supported early developments in some industries, while leaving to the private sector the responsibility for major industrial development; indeed, among the economic measures of the Meiji Restoration was the sale to private buyers of factories and enterprises that had originally been financed by the government. (Morton, 1994, 158-159; 172-173)

But there is no question that the Occupation following World War II brought Japan into the modern capitalist fold, albeit on its own terms. Stimulated by the severe retrenchment policies of the Occupation and the procurement policies for the 1950s war in Korea, the Japanese economy moved forward at a dizzying pace; by the mid-1950s the Japanese had recaptured their prewar per capita production levels, and by the late 1950s the Japanese economy raced along at a rate hitherto unheard of among the industrialized societies of the world. (Reischauer, 1981, 115) But the same international forces which have revealed the weaknesses of the American model have also exposed cracks in the historic economic armor of post-war Japan, bringing into question many of the practices which are rooted in its cultural collectivism.

There are important differences between the collectivist approach to capitalism and the individualist strategy. In individualist societies and in Western economic theory, capitalism is based on MacPherson's notion of possessive individualism and the self-interest-orientation of the philosophies of Adam Smith. But according to Thurow, in the Japanese collective society, profit maximization and self-interest are subsumed in a larger, extended enterprise to participate in the building of an economic empire without parallel: Their goal is market-share maximization (strategic conquest) and value-added maximization (a measure that includes profits and wages), not simple profit maximization. (Thurow, 1993, 118)

Being part of a powerful group transcends pure self-interest and gain in the Japanese capitalist model. It is the difference between self-interested consumer and other-interested producer economics that explains in part the collective version of capitalism. "In the Anglo-Saxon world the business firm exists to provide income-earning opportunities—no more, no less." (Thurow, 1993, 122) But in Japanese terms, consumption and leisure are not substitutes for power. In an intriguing analogy to the animal world, Thurow likens individual and collective capitalist behavior to the instincts of solitary and herd species. The Japanese explication of capitalism taps into the drives of the pack, using it to generate solidarity and a willingness to sacrifice for the welfare of the group. (Thurow, 1993, 119-122) Further, the Japanese version of producer economics is not threatened by direct government intervention into the economy. Collective societies are clearly comfortable with, indeed expect, government to take an active role in economic growth:

> In Japan industry representatives working with the Ministry of International Trade and Industry present "visions" of where the economy should be going. In the past these visions served as guides to the allocation of scarce foreign exchange or capital flows. Today they are used to guide R&D funding. Key industries are targeted. What the Japanese know as "administrative guidance" is a way of life. (Thurow, 1993, 37)

In the Japanese experience, government intervention in the economy is an obligation of responsible leadership. Unlike developments in the early industrializing nations of Britain and the United States, Japan seemed destined for greater government direction and economic nationalism. Economic policies were always a joint, rather than exclusive, affair of government and big business, what Pempel calls "state-led capitalism." (Pempel, 46-52) The Ministry of International Trade and Industry (MITI) administers Japanese economic policy, formulating policies of capital assistance, advising on the reorganization of target industries, encouraging mergers and affiliations, and overseeing ad hoc arrangements between industries and other agencies. With the power to coordinate industrial energy use and to facilitate arrangements to strengthen some industries and hold the line on others, set quotas, approve and reject joint ventures, direct Japanese environmental affairs, and adjust employment levels, MITI is vested with formidable economic power. (Pempel, 1982; Morton, 1994) Morton claims that MITI's greatest contribution to Japanese capitalism is in its ability to secure consensus among government, labor, and management on the problems and direction of industrial development. Such cooperation may be the chief form of Japanese solidarity: ". . . when an outside element—virtually any outside element—poses the mildest threat to Japan, government, management, and labor close ranks to face the foreign world, with the tacit agreement to settle their own differences later." (Morton, 217)

THE JAPANESE ORGANIZATIONAL PARADIGM

In all societies, strength depends very much on the way ordinary people behave in ordinary situations. But response to guidance and direction is largely determined by the cultural inclinations of a society; it is the collectivist nature of the Japanese culture that enables its organizations to adopt procedures that tap into the willingness on the part of individual Japanese workers to supplant individual self-interest with the collective good, resulting in a theory of organizational behavior and management style contradictory to the individualist American paradigm. Cultural assumptions are the psychological cement of organizations; the tendency to suppress self-interest in favor of group solidarity, and the anticipation of benefits in exchange for loyalty and conformity cannot be ignored as key components of theoretical responses to cultural integration in organizations. (Fallows, 14; Hampden-Turner and Trompenaars, 14)

The profound differences between the atomist/organic notion of the norms of society and the individualist/collectivist attitude of the members of society have led to the creation of organization cultures approached from diametrically opposed perspectives. But in comparing what Hoecklin calls an East/West dichotomy in organizational theory, she reminds us that "What is true or who is right is less important than what works, and how the efforts of individuals with different thinking patterns can be coordinated toward a common goal." (Hofstede and Bond, 1988, cited in Hoecklin, 75)

Characteristics of the Japanese Organizational Paradigm

Hampden-Turner and Trompenaars suggest that the Japanese concept of social order as a harmonious pattern of particulars animates Japanese organization theory: "For them, the particular relationships of *honne*, a spirit of intimacy between persons, is the moral cement of society, and to the extent that such relationships are trusting, harmonious, and aesthetic, rules of wider generality can be derived from them." (Hampden-Turner and Trompenaars, 105) Fallows calls this element the radius of trust, which arises quite logically out of a society where there is a strong sense of racial purity and uniqueness. He adds the Japanese notions of social order, tribal consciousness, and a belief in the ultimate importance of effort as significant sources of Japan's strength. (Fallows, 28-43) Norton suggests the Japanese preference for indirectness as an explanation for its unique organizational style.

(Morton, 2-3) Thurow includes cultural predilections for academic achievement and the acquisition of skills as key components of the Japanese organizational paradigm. (Thurow, 1993, 113-122) Drucker cites the tradition of community which has been translated into institutions of employment not unlike the feudal clan, or *han*, as representative of modern Japanese business enterprise. (Drucker, 206) This characteristic is associated with a number of typically-Japanese organization qualities at both the macro- and micro-level. In large Japanese companies it is clearly articulated in the Japanese custom of life-time employment, as well as in the economic groupings or *keiretsu*, which are based on the traditional trading companies, and *zaibatsu*, the legacy of the mercantilist stage of Japan's economic development. Companies in a *keiretsu* are committed to reciprocal and complementary interaction; they buy and sell from one another; they own parts of each other; they demand that price and quality remain competitive; and they are a formidable collective economic force in international economic trade practices. These groups provide their own research agencies, set their own standards, encourage quality, and are willing to forego immediate profit for the integrity of *keiretsu* as a whole. (Hampden-Turner and Trompenaars, 190-192; Reischauer, 1981, 181) While the interdependence among banking, shipping, and trading associations is impressive, the personal loyalties among the executives in the groups are inextricably intertwined. Interlocking directorships are common, and affiliates customarily are socially and professionally interactive. (Reischauer, 1981, 182) According to Bennett Harrison, the Japanese *keiretsu* represent the consummate example of networked production systems.

Bennett Harrison, quoting estimates from Charles Ferguson and Marie Anchordoguy, contends that more than one-half of Japan's largest companies are members of six intermarket *keiretsu,* three of which evolved out of pre-World War II family-owned *zaibatsu*.

> Virtually all of Japan's top city banks, trust banks, insurance companies, and computer, telecommunications, and semiconductor makers are group members. In the late 1980s, these six keiretsu earned some 18 percent of the total net profits of all Japanese business [and] had nearly 17 percent of total sales. (B. Harrison, 153)

A second type of supply *keiretsu* have formed in the automotive and consumer electronics and machinery industries where numerous

The Organic Model: The Japanese Organizational Paradigm

suppliers provide components for final assemblers. These firms are related both vertically and horizontally, if not formally, then by agreements or other types of strategic alliances. These arrangements are so complex and pervasive as to require a ministerial department to monitor them. Their most important feature is the degree of reciprocity expected and extended among members and affiliates, a reciprocity naturally sustained by in-common ownership, with an estimate that fifteen-to-thirty per cent of stock is held by other members of the group.

> The cross-holding of equity among the members of a Japanese *keiretsu* has become an extraordinary source of institutional stability. Such cross-holding frees corporate managers to a significant extent from concerns about the availability of investment capital and encourages them to adopt a longer-term planning horizon than that which characterizes especially British and American corporations. (B. Harrison, 159)

The same Japanese sense of unity and reciprocity is illustrated in the cooperative nature of the private/public relationship. Recognizing the interdependencies of technologies, and pursuing the logic of community over rivalry, the Japanese government is an active partner, rather than adversary, of Japanese industry. (Hampden-Turner and Trompenaars, 192-193) Like all the other governments of East Asia, the political institutions in Japan are structured to enhance informed and flexible economic policies to stimulate certain industries and diffuse growth and development across the spectrum of the economy. The public and private sectors are intertwined and integrated in complex interrelationships which put a premium on flexibility and foresight. These consensual and reciprocal relationships between the business community and the Japanese government are critical contributors to Japan's rapid economic growth. (Clark, 1993; Reischauer, 1981)

> The relationship in Japan between government and business is not that of mutually suspicious adversaries, as in the United States, but of close collaborators. The contrast is so great that Americans have frequently exaggerated it, mistakenly claiming that government and business in Japan form a single entity—"Japan, Inc."—in which either the government is said to control business completely or conversely a mysteriously unified big business world is said to control the government. (Reischauer, 1981, 191)

Much of this cooperation is facilitated by the government Ministry of International Trade and Industry, which sets industrial goals, controls foreign exchange and the licensing of foreign technology, encourages/discourages mergers, and provides a high level of administrative guidance to the Japanese business community, which welcomes its intervention because of the community's overall confidence in the honesty and excellence of its advice. (Reischauer, 1981, 190-194)

Lawrence Harrison uses Lucian Pye's analysis of vertical and horizontal relationships to describe the paradoxical Japanese organizational style that emphasizes both authoritarianism and consensus:

> [T]he Japanese must learn early to balance their vertical ties with superiors . . . against their horizontal ties with peers, who for their part define the boundaries of the group, organization, or company that will become the basis for the individual's identity. The security of the individual thus involves having the combination of a nurturing authority figure and a collectivity to which loyalty is owed in return for the self esteem it provides . . . . (L. Harrison, 140)

Much of the literature thus makes the judgment that Japanese organization theory is culture-based and nurtured by social norms which demand team effort, respect for authority, discipline, homogeneity, and conformity. Kelley and Worthley illustrate the more-or-less cultural determinism theory in their analysis of the role of culture in management attitudes. Their research was overwhelmingly supportive of a congruence between the basic elements of Japanese management attitudes and crucial cultural variables. They found not only a significant relationship, but their research enabled them to draw certain conclusions about the relationship between Japanese management standards such as team effort, respect for authority, self-development, group appraisal, nepotism, and long-term employment and characteristics of the larger culture, such as respect for authority, desire for achievement, an orientation toward the future, values, social orientation, and personal behavior. (Kelley and Worthley, 1982, 50-51)

The Theory of the Cooperative Japanese

Jon Alston is convinced that Japanese organization style is based on the notion of the cooperative Japanese, proposing that modern Japanese organization theory is a contemporary interpretation of the *bushido*, or warrior's moral code, which elicits a continuing lifelong and unlimited employee/employer relationships based upon self-sacrifice, total loyalty, self-effacement, and humility. He proposes that Japanese organization theory is in essence an expression of a worker-management partnership, where there is a chain of benefit from worker to company to nation. This is in general the idea of *kokka*, or the large family, that became official policy during the Meiji Restoration. He cites the Japanese use of the term *uchiwa*, which means "all-in-the-family-economy," as suggesting that the cooperative effort is more important than individual rewards. (Alston, 31-33)

Cooperation is a traditional Japanese virtue; it sustains both the company and future generations; it assures the survival of Japanese society in the face of external economic and political threat. Alston's theory of the cooperative Japanese incorporates the principles of group membership and the traditional Japanese social system and concern for group harmony, a social norm which he attributes to the cooperative ethic of Buddhism and Confucianism. He makes the point that there is no classical Japanese word for the Western term "competition," proposing that the only respectable use of the word in Japanese culture is for group-to-group competition for survival or prestige, or in a narrow application to athletic contests. (Alston, 31-49) Alston's perception of Japanese organization theory is a clear analogy to the collective nature of its larger culture, and what he defines as the Japanese Helping Ethic, or *Wa*, a cultural predisposition to help each other. (Alston, 95)

In somewhat of a reiteration of Alston's point, Pegels proposes that it is Japanese attitude and philosophy, rather than technique, which distinguishes Japanese organizations from other management styles. His 1984 research focused on the Japanese work force itself, which he also links to the traditional Japanese cultural concept of *Wa* and its implications for harmony, unity, and cooperation in Japanese organizations. (Pegels, 1984, 67-72)

Wa is the conceptual framework that distinguishes Japanese culture and provides the ethical basis for proper conduct in all human relationships. Strengthened by nurturing, upbringing, and education, the

Japanese are taught from birth that non-conformity leads to social disorder, and one must not strive for his/her own interests, but should always act in the interest of the group. While *Wa* is significant as a Japanese world view, Pegels claims that it gives rise to an organization model that is not culture-specific, which he illustrates with the "Eleven-C Circular Model" featuring eleven qualities of organizations built on the Japanese cultural style. Centered on the hub of culture, Pegels arranges ten other key words on equidistant radii in a wheel-like pattern which describe his perception of the requirements of a successful Japanese-style management system: Communication, concept, concentration, competitiveness, cooperation, consensus, coalition, concern, control, and circles (derived from Total Quality Management). (Pegels, 1984) As a management model, Pegels' Eleven-C concept is too simplistic to be of comprehensive value; but as a means of viewing organization theory as culturally-centered, it is extremely worthwhile. Even its non-hierarchical pattern is revealing of the sociological perspectives of organization theory. While the vast majority of Western organization thought would be focused on economic perspectives, the Pegels model attempts to describe an ideographic approach that is concerned with cultural meanings and interpretations in organizational behavior.

Hampden-Turner and Trompenaars consider the Japanese concern with harmony and cooperation from another perspective, however, focusing upon the Japanese tendency to harmonize the emotional, responsive, dynamic, aesthetic, and relational particulars in their organizations, a practice which has led Western observers to accuse the Japanese of being amoral. The Japanese do not seem to work from universal principles, but rather from an arrangement of propitious elements: "If a certain kind of behavior is appropriate in one setting, then it's entirely natural to the Japanese that another kind of behavior is appropriate for another setting ... But where was the moral core?" (Hampden-Turner and Trompenaars, 109)

In *The Enigma of Japanese Power*, Karel van Wolferen charges:

> The malleability, relativity and negotiability of truth in Japan; the claimed superfluity of logic; the absence of a strong intellectual tradition; the subservience to the administrators of law; and the acceptance, even the celebration of amorality; these are, of course, all causally intertwined. All extant civilizations who have developed religions and system of thought acknowledge the existence of a truth

transcending socio-political concerns. Neither Shintoism nor Buddhism has been of assistance here. (Hampden-Turner and Trompenaars, 110, citing van Wolferen, 1989)

In a correlative appraisal, Hampden-Turner and Trompenaars borrow from Magorah Maruyama the hypothesis that Japan is a "polyocular" culture, which leads them to take the position that "all phenomena can be seen from multiple points of view, and that the additional angles make reality more whole and comprehensive." (Hampden-Turner and Trompenaars, 113) They make the point that objectivity is a Western notion, for which there was no Japanese translation prior to the country's penetration by the West. In Japanese, the word now used is *kyakkanteki*, which literally translated means "the guest's point of view," with *shukanteki*, or subjectivity, the host's point of view. The implication of these two viewpoints is that the guest's view is only partial; it may be sharp, but it is decidedly superficial. To the contrary, the host's view is a perception of depth and wholeness which derives from the whole truth. In an organizational application, the "problem with `objectivity' is that those who claim to have it believe they need to look no further, need listen to no one else, and never alter their convictions. They have `the data,' or `givens.' But those pursuing polyocular knowledge will never be satisfied, never know enough." (Hampden-Turner and Trompenaars, 114-115) Legalistic, rational, cerebral, detached, instrumental organizational theories of objectivity disallow the intimacy, affection, brotherhood, and rootedness of the polyocularism and subjectivity of Japanese organization theory, and prevent the organistic engagement of all human resources and aspirations. (Hampden-Turner and Trompenaars, 115-133)

Lawrence Harrison's observations speak to this same issue. Quoting the work of Ruth Benedict, he proposes that the Confucian nature of the Japanese ethical system reflects an assumption that human nature is naturally good and trustworthy, so "[t]he Japanese have no need of overall ethical commandments." (L. Harrison, 137) In the secularism of the Buddhist and Shinto tradition, the operative ethical code is the legacy of Confucius' five sets of reciprocal relationships, and behavior is driven more by shame and a fear of negative reaction by others than by guilt and conscience. (L. Harrison, 137)

Koji Matsumoto's comments on *kigyoism* describe a similar viewpoint. According to Matsumoto, *kigyoism* is the true essence of

Japanese organization theory, in that it facilitates participation rather than authority and coercion. *Kigyoism* expresses the mutual responsibilities that extend from the president of a firm down to its lowest ranking employee. (Matsumoto, 1991, 202-213) This sense of shared responsibility has a great deal in common with the highly valued Confucian relationship of *sempai-kohai*, or elder brother to younger brother, and the veneration of generational cycles where the old pass along wisdom and knowledge to the young. (Hampden-Turner and Trompenaars, 132-136) In a culture which honors and respects its elders, an organizational tradition which supports the same notions of fealty and deference is to be expected. Japanese organizations act much as a family, with the same cultural sense of veneration and familial bonds; *kigyoism* clearly expresses this kinship.

Human Capitalism

Robert Ozaki's review of the "human enterprise system" presents a Japanese organizational model based on what he calls "human capitalism," an egalitarian economic system which differs so distinctly from the traditional capitalist model as to be a discrete economic orientation on its own merits:

> While the bulk of the nation's output is produced through a private, free, fiercely competitive market, looking more closely we observe that the usual behavior of representative Japanese firms . . . deviates from the norm of capitalism to such an extent that it becomes misleading or even inaccurate to describe Japan as capitalistic. (Ozaki, 1991, 7)

Defined in terms of mutuality, cooperation, and integration, Ozaki insists that human capitalism as a broad economic theory enables companies to incorporate principles of sharing and cooperation which are ideologically unacceptable in the American corporate model. He argues that at its most basic, human capitalism is oriented toward people, while traditional capitalism is oriented toward profit. This conceptual difference alone is of a magnitude powerful enough to divert primary attention away from owners and stockholders to those who actually produce the product or service. The work force is not primarily a means of profit-making; rather, the firm, much like Japanese society, is an "organic group of thinking and feeling beings

The Organic Model: The Japanese Organizational Paradigm

working together for long-term prosperity and security. Workers are seen as the vital asset (human capital) generating values for the firm, instead of faceless inputs whose costs are to be minimized in pursuit of maximum profits." (Ozaki, 12)

But Ozaki insists that to assess the merits of human capitalism as a cultural aberration is nothing more than to accept a tautological argument which explains both everything and nothing. He discounts the national character argument as a distortion of the enormous diversities among members of a society and contradicted by historical fact. To the contrary, he makes the argument that human capitalism is a deliberate institutional innovation designed to mobilize the productive energies of ordinary workers under specific conditions. (Ozaki, 80-95)

The theory of human capitalism both departs from and sustains portions of the cultural argument. Ozaki posits that because Japan is a non-ideological society, whose every context is ephemeral, it has been peculiarly responsive to the tides of change:

> Ideology, or its absence, is a double-edged sword. A strong belief can move a mountain, stir human emotions, and mobilize millions toward a common cause. It may become the solid foundation of a great civilization and accomplish many worthy goals. The danger of ideology is that it may degenerate into a dogma that induces tunnel vision, a biased view instead of an enlightened grasp of the whole truth . . . Hence, ideology encourages a confrontational stance in dealing with life's problems. (Ozaki, 75)

According to Ozaki, it is Japan's non-ideological culture that allows it to "seize the moment," or grasp whatever works and makes sense in reality, rather than seeking some contextual or historical relevance to presupposed principles as social and economic truth. (Ozaki, 75) Paradoxically, however, Japanese organizations seem to be much more humanistic than their Western counterparts, more attuned to the basic values of sharing, participation, cooperation, and more cognizant of basic human needs for recognition and self-worth within the social structure. With no commitment to either capitalism or democracy as a disciplining ideology, a "humanistic enterprise system slowly evolved and assumed its shape out of the pragmatism of both management and workers." (Ozaki, 76)

Ozaki contends that the humanistic organization is simply the model which corresponds most realistically to Japan's economic system, much like the American mass production model was designed to correspond to capitalism of the nineteenth and twentieth centuries. And, as we have found in earlier arguments, he reiterates the point that such a system evolved in Japan because of peculiar cultural elements. Like Sartori, Ozaki is asking us to look at capitalism apart from liberalism, contending that the unhealthy aspects of American organizations are not an inevitable consequence of American culture, but rooted in Western capitalism itself. He describes human capitalism as a parable on Aristotelian logic:

> According to the logic business transactions take place *either* through market *or* within organizations, the firms *either* compete *or* cooperate with each other, and people are *either* individualistic *or* group oriented. Human capitalism reveals that business can be efficiently executed through organized market, competitive cooperation can enhance productivity of the firms, and the same rational people may be individualistic and group oriented, depending on circumstances. (Ozaki, 182-183)

Theory Z

William Ouchi's Theory Z, the culmination of many years of research into the management patterns of large American and Japanese corporations, is as much a review of cultural norms as it is organization theory. Both philosophical and functional, Ouchi articulates specific Theory Z management practices in American corporations which seem to illustrate clearly a Japanese organizational paradigm quite distinct from the American model and quite intimately related to the generalized nature of the Japanese culture.

The Theory Z lexicon is an important analysis of organization theory, but it perhaps goes beyond theory to assume the form of a cultural philosophy with a distinct set of values and relationships. It is clearly predicated on the ability to create and sustain a certain distinct humanist orientation in organizations; as a description of a corporate culture, it exhibits the same cultural dimensions of Japanese society. But it is significant that Theory Z is not an organizational paradigm for Japanese organizations; it is a hybrid American model, derived from qualitative analysis into the management styles of large Japanese and American organizations. (Ouchi, 1981, 165-177)

The Organic Model: The Japanese Organizational Paradigm

Finding that there was little structural difference in the approach of typical Japanese and American companies operating in both countries, Ouchi turned his attention to the intricacies of the Japanese management style that had escaped earlier analysis. His interviews revealed profound differences between Japanese and American styles of management, a divergence he proposes rests on significant deviations between corporate philosophies of values and beliefs, and means and ends—essentially ideologically disparate corporate cultures.

Ouchi's research is significant to our purpose in that it leads us to consider the origins and impact of the corporate culture, its affinity or aversion to the social forces that shape them, and the possibilities for convergence in an interdependent world. With Ouchi, we have proposed that corporate cultures have distinct personalities and well-defined corporate norms which direct corporate behavior. These corporate cultures exhibit their own unique beliefs, attitudes, objectives, and habits which arise, in large part, from the social and historical traditions of the societies that spawn and sustain them. Ouchi's argument for Theory Z builds on this more-or-less ecological view of organizations, proposing that the search for theoretical guidelines for American (Western) organizations is simply a process of matching the culture of the organization with its environment.

Neither purely Japanese (Type J) nor American (Type A) organizations, and with a management style based neither on Theory X or Theory Y as proposed by Douglas McGregor, Ouchi distinguished a set of Theory Z organizations which developed naturally in the United States and were conspicuously successful in Japan, distilling from them a set of characteristics that illustrate a distinctive and especial corporate personality. This syndrome becomes the essence of Theory Z for organizations.

Ouchi's comparison of Japanese and American corporate characteristics proceed from his comparative analysis in seven categories: length of employment, process of evaluation and promotion, career path, type of control mechanisms, centers of decision making and responsibility, and degree of concern for employees.

Ouchi interviewed managers from a great variety of industries, asking them to name any American companies that possessed the Japanese version of these characteristics, i.e., lifetime employment, slow process of evaluation and promotion, non-specialized career paths, implicit control mechanisms, collective decision making and responsibility and wholistic concern for all members of the enterprise.

To his surprise, Ouchi found that a number of companies were named repeatedly as possessing the same characteristics as Japanese companies, all of which were commonly considered among the world's best-managed. He includes in this group IBM, Procter & Gamble, Hewlett-Packard, and Eastman Kodak. His analysis prompted him to make the claim that the fundamental properties of the Japanese form of organization are non-cultural specific. To this point he recalls the reaction of an IBM vice president during the research period comparing Japanese with American companies: "Do you realize that this form that you have been describing as Japanese is exactly what IBM is? Let me point out that IBM has developed to this form in its own way—we have not copied the Japanese!" (Ouchi, 57)

Ouchi found that the lifetime employment tradition of Japanese firms was modified in the Z organization, but not to the extent that it became the short-term employment custom of the American model. While lifetime employment is "the rubric under which many facets of Japanese life and work are integrated." (Ouchi, 15) employment in the Type Z companies tended to be long-term in practice, while not formalized in policy, arising out of the desire of companies to retain employees in whom they have invested. In like manner, these companies had slower evaluative and promotion cycles than in the usual American model, though not as slow as in the Japanese model.

The non-specialized nature of career paths in Japanese organizations is also thus echoed, but not copied in the Z organization. By the time an employee of a Japanese company reaches the pinnacle of his career with his company, he is likely to be an expert in every function, every specialty, and every office. Since it may take as long as ten years for a man to receive his first major promotion, over that period of time, he is increasing his expertise and knowledge, as well as building an intimate relationship with the company; the negative, of course, is that such an employee is endowed with company-specific skills, a somewhat non-professional development that is not necessarily transferable to other companies. To a large degree, long-term employment and company career paths are linked together, and while some of their features may be malleable, some would prove entirely distasteful to the American worker accustomed to periodic performance reviews and systematic pay increases.

In the case of control mechanisms, Ouchi argues that Type Z organizations have reached somewhat of a balance between the implicit nature of Japanese-style organizations and the explicit character of their

The Organic Model: The Japanese Organizational Paradigm

American counterpart. He claims that while Type Z companies are replete with the trappings of modern information and accounting systems, nevertheless, these mechanisms rarely dominate in major decisions. Unlike the typical Western management style which favors the rational over the non-rational, the objective over the subjective, the quantitative over the non-quantitative, and quantitative analysis over personal judgments in decision making, Z organizations seemed to weight the analytical evidence with understanding. He explains:

> Let me not seem to imply that Company Z is unconcerned with profitability. The record is clear. Company Z is among the fastest-growing, most profitable of major American firms. Every manager knows that projects survive only as long as they produce profits well above what other companies demand. But at Company Z, profits are regarded not as an end in itself nor as the method of "keeping score" in the competitive process. Rather, profits are the reward to the firm if it continues to provide true value to its customers, to help its employees to grow, and to behave responsibly as a corporate citizen. (Ouchi, 63-64)

Type Z organizations appear to use analysis and formal control mechanisms in order to realize their own peculiar set of corporate values and beliefs. The profitability standard seems to be appended to a larger philosophy, in that stated profits are a very inexact measure of the unknowable true profits. The subtle and implicit goals are supported by the explicit and rational, but neither is assumed to exist without the other.

Type Z companies have also assumed a more Japanese orientation in matters of decisionmaking and the determination of centers of responsibility. In a somewhat democratic decisionmaking process, Type Z organizations generally draw more people into the shaping of important decisions, which serves a number of significant purposes: (1) It disperses information throughout the organization; (2) It defines and reinforces corporate values; (3) It demonstrates a commitment to cooperation; and, (4) It develops individual skills. But this is not purely the collectivist style of Japanese management; decision making may be collective, but the ultimate responsibility still rests in one individual, a testament to the Western craving for individual responsibility. Ouchi admits that it is difficult to merge the two techniques, because the combination of collective decision making with individual responsibility demands an atmosphere of trust which is only achievable when all the members of the group hold basically compatible goals and no one of the group is engaged in self-serving behavior:

> When a group engages in consensual decision making, members are effectively being asked to place their fate to some extent in the hands of others. Not a common fate but a set of individual fates is being dealt with. Each person will come from the meeting with the responsibility for some individual targets set collectively by the group. The consensual process . . . is one in which members of the group may be asked to accept responsibility for a decision that they do not prefer, but that the group, in an open and complete discussion, has settled upon. (Ouchi, 66-67)

As to matters of the wholistic concern of Japanese organizations versus the segmented concern of American organizations, the Type Z organization is neither fish nor fowl. Similar to the Japanese orientation which is so broadly inclusive as to be both quasi-familial and patriarchal, the wholistic orientation assumed by Type Z companies is more committed to creating a work environment where there is a broad degree of concern for the welfare of subordinates and co-workers as part of the working relationship, but absent the almost kinship bonds of the Japanese organization. Relationships tend to be informal, personal, and open, with little of the dehumanizing techniques and authoritarianism of the American model, or the cloying familiarity and goal congruence of the Japanese model. Like in the decision making context, there is a strong connection between an egalitarian style of management and a robust level of mutual trust. Type Z organizations do exercise hierarchical modes of control, but they are tempered by self-direction and symbolic efforts to encourage an egalitarian attitude, mutual trust and a wholistic bond between employees: "It is a consent culture, a community of equals who cooperate with one another to reach common goals. Rather than relying exclusively upon hierarchy and monitoring to direct behavior, it relies also upon commitment and trust." (Ouchi, 70)

In general, the Type Z organization is more like a clan than a bureaucracy, whose employees have attained a sense of personal autonomy and freedom much like that of employees of the Japanese firms who frequently work with so much more enthusiasm than their counterparts in many Western firms. Highly dependent on mutual trust

The Organic Model: The Japanese Organizational Paradigm

and the organistic approach to social relationships, however, the Type Z organization is profoundly shaped by a social environment which encourages commitment, goal congruence, and community. Ouchi calls the Type Z organization a "consent culture, a community of equals who cooperate with one another to reach common goals." (Ouchi, 70)

Ouchi suggests another important parallel between Japanese management and the spirit of Theory Z: The Quality Control Circle program which was initiated by W. E. Deming in Japan after World War II. The attachment of Deming and J. M. Juran's measurement techniques to the Japanese concern with the human side of organizations, created a framework within which workers could share actively in matters of quality and productivity. The program serves three fundamental purposes: To contribute to the improvement and development of the enterprise; to respect humanity and build a happy, bright workshop which is meaningful to work in; and to display human capabilities fully, and eventually draw out infinite possibilities. (Ouchi, 226)

In Japan a Quality-Control Circle typically consists of from two to ten permanently-assigned employees who create a natural working group in which everyone's work is related in some way to the work of the others. These circles are tasked with the job of studying any problems of production or service that might fall within the scope of their work. At an appointed time of the year, usually November, conventions are held where the circle's efforts are studied and recognition is given:

> [I]f it is a particularly innovative or important solution, it will be nominated for a company, industry, or even national award. The company will report to its employees the collective impact of all the implemented suggestions, so that everyone will see the relationship between their successful work and the profits of the company and the size of their bonuses. (Ouchi, 225)

Ouchi contends that the greatest contribution of the Quality-Control Circle program is its endorsement of humanitarian values: "People spend much of their lifetime at their working place. It would be much more desirable to work in a pleasant place where humanity is paid due respect and where people feel their work has some real meaning. That is what Q-C Circle aims to achieve . . . ." (Ouchi, 227) It is Ouchi's belief that the Quality-Control Circle program fits well within the Theory Z organization; but it is unclear whether it is a management technique that could be discretely applied without the rest of the Theory Z organizational accouterments, which seems to be a fault consistent with some of the other weaknesses of the model.

Despite what Ouchi calls its "remarkable properties," the clannish Type Z organization manifests several potentially crippling flaws. While inclusivity is supportive, it can also lead to a disabling xenophobia, or such an extreme level of fear of outsiders and strangers as to limit the ability to bring in managers and executives from outside the company. The organization may become so close that it literally throws out the baby with bath water, unable to accept innovations because they threaten the consistency and order. The Theory Z culture is staid, steady, and consistent, so much so that it is highly resistance to change. Theory Z is not just an organization paradigm, it is a corporate culture whose values are deeply integrated into a consonant network of beliefs that works against change and maintains the status quo, which may well be disastrous in an environment of constant change. The Theory Z organization is also plagued with a loss of professionalism, likely due to the culture's emphasis on the team, rather than on individual performance, and on the internal nature of the career path of Theory Z employees. We might label this tendency one of complacency, which may breed contentment and self-satisfaction, but retards professional growth and development.

One of the most serious weaknesses of the Theory Z organization is its tendency to be both sexist and racist. Type Z managers tend to be homogeneous to a fault; this becomes a significant barrier to gender and racial diversity. Ouchi describes a common Z-type top management team as "wholesome, disciplined, hard-working, and honest, but unremittingly white, male, and middle class." (Ouchi, 77) This is fully in congruence with the Japanese organization syndrome: "Probably no form of organization is more sexist or racist than the Japanese corporation." (Ouchi, 78)

Jared Taylor in *Shadows of the Rising Sun* (1983) describes a profoundly male-oriented work environment in Japan organizations:

> When a major corporation hires a woman, it is not hiring a worker. It is hiring a potential wife. The company expects to squeeze a lot of quality work from its brides-to-be, but beauty and culture are important hiring criteria. Many companies are quite open about the qualities they are looking for. Some, for example, will not hire a

woman unless she lives at home with her parents. There is no telling what manner of mischief an unsupervised woman might be up to, and a woman with a past does not make a fit wife for a future executive. (Eberts and Eberts, 1995, 11n citing Taylor, 1983)

Although American Z-type organizations may well have affirmative action plans in place, the uncertainty encountered when diversity is introduced into the homogeneous culture mitigates against meaningful application. Not unlike the outrageous sexist attitudes of Japanese organizations, it is unreasonable to expect a Theory Z organization to deal forthrightly with an American work force which is more than forty percent female and in which female professionals fully expect to be treated equally with males. The presence of these attitudes in both Japanese and Theory Z organizations, as well as in other managerial styles, suggests that the role of women and minorities as full partners in the workplace, as well as in society, remains problematical in many cultures.

On the whole, the Theory Z organization is a flawed model, with respect to American expectations of equality and fairness in economic opportunity. While the essence of Theory Z may be more generally humanistic, its success as a guide for organizations is undermined by its tendencies to sanction policies that reflect paternalism, patriarchy, and bigotry, using race and gender to justify the denial of full participation in the economic enterprise. There is much too great an expectation of homogeneity in Z-type firms to fit the diversity of American society. As Ouchi admits, the intimacy, subtlety, and mutual trust so intrinsic to Type Z organizations is a product of "a long period of cultural homogenization during which the people of a nation become accustomed to one another and come to espouse a common body of values and beliefs." (Ouchi, 79) America is a very young nation; its society is heterogeneous, without the social symmetry and synchronization of thousands of years of common experiences, without which the spirit of Theory Z becomes fouled in the rigging of legalistic remedies and half-hearted, cosmetic solutions.

CHALLENGES TO THE JAPANESE MODEL

The modern Japanese economy is defined by the swiftness and magnitude of its economic maturation. Arising out of American policy in the post-World War II period, inspired to move beyond mere recovery to rapid growth, succored by a wave of American military buying in the early 1950s, and encouraged by its U.S. mentors and occupation forces to strive for quality and high productivity, the Japanese economy doubled its GNP in less than a decade. The Japanese economic power elite, which includes business, bureaucracy, agriculture, and for forty-eight years the leadership of the Liberal Democratic party, coordinates its efforts to produce economic growth and development while protecting its industries from excessive competition, its companies from failure, and its workers from unemployment. (Bronfenbrenner, 932-934; Luttwak, 1993, 66)

Japanese development in the post-World War II period was based on imported science and improving the technology developed by others; it became export-led, with high quality goods produced by low-wage but highly trained labor. By pursuing infant-industry protection along with low-wage labor exports, the Japanese reaped the high prices and high profits of a protected home market, as well as establishing themselves as competitive exporters in a world market. (Drucker, 148-152) Japan's spectacular economic success from the 1950s until the 1990s was based on a growth strategy essentially controlled by the government, first channeling funds into heavy industries with high value-added per worker properties, and away from traditional labor-intensive industries to encourage industries believed to reflect Japan's future comparative advantage. During the 1970s Japan's industrial policy was aimed at encouraging new, knowledge-intensive and high technology industries through a combination of research and development subsidies and joint government-industry research projects aimed at developing new technologies. Coupled with direct and indirect barriers designed to protect their own manufacturers at the expense of non-Japanese firms, Japan's economy enjoyed spectacular growth. (Krugman and Obstfeld, 1991, 273-274) From 1979 until 1989, Japan's average industrial growth rate was 4.6 per cent per annum, the highest of any of the Western democracies. (Thurow, 1993, 72)

Although Japan carries a trade surplus with every major nation in the world, it tenaciously resists pressures to open up its economy. The protectionist nature of its industrial policy renders Japanese trade practices distasteful to Westerners, particularly the United States. Committed to the preservation of their home markets, which may have been logical policy in the immediate postwar years, and focusing government and enterprise energies on those markets they can capture by improving on existing technologies, the Japanese have obtained market control, or at least predominance in automobiles, steel, consumer electronics, photography, and optics, and changed the basic rules of trade, challenging existing, historical, traditional economic and trade assumptions. (Drucker, 130-131)

But the economic engines of Japan and an activist industrial policy have not been entirely successful in protecting its economy. In 1993, Japan's gross domestic product increased by 0.1 percent; in 1994, the figure was 1.0 percent; but in 1995, its 0.3 percent rise was by far the lowest rate of growth among all industrial nations, a continuing trend in 1996. According to James Glassman, the Japanese economy fell victim to deflation in 1995, a decidedly unfamiliar economic antagonist to a country whose economic growth in the past has been the stuff of which legends are made. And legends without roots in reality, according to Glassman, is what they have been. (Glassman, 1995)

Calling Japan's economy a "bubble economy" based on 1980s government action to counteract the yen's rising value, citing David Asher, Glassman claims that reacting to monetary policy which encouraged borrowing to buy real estate, skyrocketing land prices created "a speculative bubble of a magnitude greater than previously experienced anywhere in the world . . . By 1988, the paper value of all Japanese property had risen to four times that of all land in the United States—a nation 25 times its size!" (Glassman, citing Asher) But by 1995, land values had fallen, dragging stock and consumer prices down with them, and presaging sagging retail sales. Between April 1995 and March 1996 the yen dropped by 22 percent, interest rates plummeted to almost zero, and the government appears to have infused almost nine trillion yen ($86 billion) into the economy. ("Half time," March 2, 1996, 38) In the fiscal year ending March 31, 1996, the six year run of Japanese budget surpluses was expected to be broken with a central and local government deficit of 7.7 percent of GDP, increasing the outstanding stock of public debt to the equivalent of 95 percent of GDP in 1996, a figure only exceeded by Belgium, Canada, and Italy. Even accounting for the assets of Japan's postal saving system and public-sector pension funds, the net debt figure has grown sharply. ("The Japanese numbers game," March 2, 1996, 71)

These economic problems, in turn, have significantly undermined the competitiveness of Japanese manufacturers, even in their home market:

As a result of the strong yen, and the bursting of the financial bubble that has raised the cost of capital in Japan, Japanese industry is moving a significant part of its production capacity offshore and often shipping products back home. Thus, Japan has become a net importer of television sets, VCRs and air conditioners, and Japanese auto companies are beginning to ship some autos from their U.S. assembly plants to dealers in Japan . . . this reexport phenomenon combined with the partial opening of the Japanese market . . . will continue to reduce the Japanese surplus and could even bring Japan's trade into balance in the 21st century. (Prestowitz, 1996, 20)

Japan's economic problems have proved persistent over the course of the 1990s. Despite pressure from the West to address in fundamental ways the financial issues that most observers believe lie at the heart of the Japanese economic dilemma, Japanese political leadership, facing national elections in July of 1998, has been cautionary. Despite the apprehension of financial and political leaders around the world who believe that breakdown in the Japanese economic model has a chilling effect on the rest of Asia, the political leadership of Japan has avoided taking what may necessarily be drastic steps to clear its heavy debt burden and shore up the falling yen. (Jordan, 1998, 13)

There is no question but that Japan's economic performance during the 1990s confounded its managers and exasperated international economic leaders. The bureaucrats and politicians who manage the Japanese economy, whom most observers blamed for the country's economic distress, are not likely to make systemic reform in the model. According to Edward J. Lincoln of the Brookings Institution, recovery in the Japanese economic system is blocked by barriers that are both endemic and contrived. Lincoln argues that the protestations and plans for broad deregulation of its financial markets is improbable, given the traditional resistance of the government and MITI to American-style financial arrangements. Lincoln also claims that deregulation would demand public disclosure of corporate financial information—a condition which Japanese corporations are likely to consider unacceptable. He is pessimistic: "Gimmicks and government capital infusions will probably stave off a serious financial collapse, but at the expense of the economy's long-term health." (Lincoln, 1998, 63)

Jim Hoagland's quote from a senior U.S. official who deals with Japan seems to support Lincoln's criticism: "This is about a system that can't change, and a national leadership that really has no intention of

The Organic Model: The Japanese Organizational Paradigm 127

trying to change it." (Hoagland, 1998, 5) With Lincoln, Hoagland observes that there are cultural factors involved in Japan's unwillingness to implement the draconian strategies that seem necessary for Japan's long-term growth. However, paradoxically, he notes that perhaps Japan is persisting in its rejection of advice to spend its way out of recovery precisely because it is thinking in the long-term of its rapidly aging population, which looms the largest in the industrial world. He concludes:

> Whatever risks he faces now from inaction, [Prime Minister] Hashimoto is convinced he and his nation would face even greater perils by depleting national savings and taking actions that would tie his successors' hands. In characteristic fashion, Japan gazes into the next century while the United States focuses on the immediate problems a global power cannot avoid. The grim reality is that Japan will offer no quick fix to the world's Asia problems. (Hoagland, 5)

It is clear that there is a cultural side to the economic problems that have distressed Japan, its Asian neighbors, and its international economic partners during the 1990s. Its leaders have made small steps, deemed insufficient by the international economic community, announcing a $127 billion economic stimulus plan of tax cuts and credits, public investment plans, and measures to relieve banking system debt. ("Changing the Way People Live," 1998, 20)

The economic slump and efforts to mend it have led to eclectic social change in Japan, as well as the rest of Asia. Declining land prices, in some cases by more than 50 per cent, has enabled demographic change. Less spendable income has reduced the ability of parents to afford the prestigious schools formerly favored for their children. Women, generally the victims of discrimination in the work force, have been moving into the part-time labor market in astounding numbers:

> "What is going on now is, companies are firing men and putting in part-time women," says Akiko Domoto, a leading member of parliament. The unemployment rate is the highest in 45 years, but 500,000 more women hold jobs than [1997] . . . albeit part-time. (Jordan, 1998, 20)

On the other hand, however, female college graduates are finding it harder to get jobs, and, as is generally the case in difficult economic times, women are often the first to lose their jobs; but this situation is somewhat mitigated by hiring practices of foreign companies located in Japan. Further, dispensing with the traditional life-time employment patterns and extravagant gift-giving customs between businesses are also changing lives—"the invisible Japanese dad is seen around the house more." (Jordan, 20) Ouchi calls lifetime employment the most important feature of the Japanese organization model. Affecting first numbers of new hires, the program which in the past has been routinely expected to absorb thousands of the best and brightest of Japan's universities in mass hirings each spring, (Ouchi, 15) is truncated by the unfamiliar and unwelcome phenomenon of unemployment. As reported by the Tokyo Student Employment Center, only a few people are being hired. (Butler, 67) And many of those already employed have been dubbed *madogiwazoku*, or "windowside employees," who are being paid to do almost nothing at all, and whose future employment is in doubt. "[A]mid a weak economy, the ranks of these so-called in-house unemployed are now estimated at 2 million strong and growing. Whether these workers stay by the window or are eventually shoved out the door will say much about the future Japanese economy." (Dentzer, 1995, 72) This is a crucial question, because it goes to the heart of the Japanese model.

Beck and Beck argue that the lifetime employment system of Japanese businesses has always been more fluid and adaptive than presumed by Western observers. Their analysis leads them to conclude that "Although they may modify the lifetime employment system, the Japanese are unlikely to abandon it. They will retain those parts of the system that still give them competitive advantage, while abandoning elements that are at odds with successful international economic competition." (Beck and Beck, 1994, 256)

The American capitalistic model has exhibited strong trends toward deregulation, intense competition, and downsizing to create a more flexible labor market; the question arises as to whether Japan can sustain its different model of "capitalism with a human face" and avoid the disruption of layoffs. (Dentzer, 72) The cultural trauma for Japan is profound: ". . . the dictum of Japan Inc. that no one can get hurt remains very much alive." (Sugawara, 1998, 19)

The unaccustomed and persistent economic slump has prompted calls for reinventing the Japanese government/private economic model, essentially taking the economy out of bureaucratic hands and letting the markets set prices. With unemployment unnaturally high for the Japanese model (3-4 percent in 1996), and with Japan's political leadership still reeling by the disintegration of the LDP and a series of scandals that put a revolving door on the Prime Minister's office, there is much commentary that the Japanese model of public/private economic control is losing its rosy reputation. But proposals to lift the ban on holding companies, to break up Nippon Telegraph and Telephone, to undertake massive deregulation, and even to introduce a winner-take-all electoral system have been met with a cool response from Japan's prime minister, Ryutaro Hashimoto, revealing an institutional sclerosis that has prevented the adaptation to changing economic realities. ("Half time, 38)

> After four years of recession and a shattering plunge in land prices, Japan's old economic and government system shows signs of a breakdown. Government agencies have passed the buck for three years as the disaster in Japan's banking system spilled slowly into international markets. Unemployment is creeping up . . . Japan's corporations are a generation behind in key areas of technology. Even if the economy begins to recover slowly, as some expect may happen next year, the days are over when Japan could serve as a model for America or Asia. (Butler, 1995, 62)

The human capitalism and human enterprise system described by Ozaki is expensive to maintain. So far large Japanese corporations have balked at American-style job cuts; lifetime employment and the perception of the corporation as *uchi*, or home, is a national ideal. Overstaffing, essentially internalizing unemployment within firms, consequently saddling companies with the whole cost, may have kept unemployment rates low, but heightened competition and falling prices have brought about stagnant manufacturing productivity in the last five years, a situation which has prompted some Japanese businessmen to dare to speak admiringly of downsizing and re-structuring. (Dentzer, 72)

Lincoln believes that entrenchment of the economic environment that was so successful during the 1950s and 1960s precludes real reform. To a large degree, the mechanics of the Japanese economic system, as well as its patterns of organizational behavior, are cultural in origin, arising out of the same characteristics that have historically controlled government and private behavior. The Japanese government does not trust the private market; banking institutions are able to shield their actions through a system of legal and illegal schemes; figures of bad debts as reported are specious at best as the system allows favored investors to continue to enjoy guaranteed returns on equity portfolios; personal relationships displace financial analysis; regulation which guarantees high profits to financial institutions also assures their acquiescence to government control; financially weak companies are not allowed to fail. (Lincoln, 57-66)

Ultimately, there will be some resolution; but Dentzer asks if Japan can create a new system, and if it cannot, is the present system acceptable:

> [H]ave U.S. firms, for better or worse, now set a high-productivity standard that their Japanese competitors will have no choice but to meet? And in the end, what's better for an economy or a society: to have people shunted into dead-end jobs, or to nudge them to new fields or to start up their own businesses even at the cost of disrupting their lives? (Dentzer, 72)

The same forces of changing international market competition and technological innovation that undermined America's mass production model, forcing American corporations to down-size, outsource, and contract out, have exacted a heavy economic toll on the phenomenal growth and productivity rates of Japan's families of organizations. It is unclear whether Japanese corporations can continue their commitment to their most cherished and distinctive conditions of employment, or whether the Asian model of government and corporate cooperation will survive. The Japanese model is facing an economic crisis which may inflict wounds upon it that are slow to respond to the normal healing process. Some of its most cherished and honored traditions may become insupportable relics of economic conditions that are forever past, a construct made vulnerable by the dynamics of both changing external challenges and internal credos that are unsustainable in the face of a re-energized global economy. It is advisable to remember, however, that while the government/private Japanese coalition is by nature and practice committed to certain organistic relational particulars, it is also an extremely malleable system, unashamedly willing to adapt to new contextual conditions while retaining a certain purity of mission. The harmony and cooperation, the fealty and deference, the paternalism and mutual dedication that characterize their corporate organizations are a part of their national character as well, but they are positive forces that are endowed with *shukanteki*, a subjective point of view with a depth and wholeness which derives from the whole truth. Reiterating Hampden-Turner and Trompenaars, objectivity is a Western notion.

CHAPTER V
The Communitarian Paradigm

The communitarian ethic represents a conceptual framework which respects both the unity and the diversity in an interdependent world community of unequal parts. It can be incorporated easily into the stream of organizational and institutional value systems which characterize the interactive assemblage of individuals, organizations and societies as components of an emerging transnational world economy. Weakened nation-states with parochial sovereign interests, transnational economic organizations with market interests, international organizations with interwoven interests, and human beings with personal interests are all a part of a gigantic web of relationships that exhibit both commonality and miscellany of pride and purpose.

As the communitarian ethic directs the individual to consider the source of her identity, at the international and transnational level, the communitarian ethic directs institutions and organizations to consider the source of their identity. Host and visitor cultures may be diverse, but if the community—the mix of the two—is constitutive, the members of each are expected to behave in ways that reflect the norms of this newly formed community. The global network is a jumble of cultures and civilizations; the communitarian ethic supports the validity of the global network as a web of relationships between multiple legitimate communities—institutions, nation-states, regions, organizations—whose common interest attenuates the individualist paradigm. The global network conforms closely to Etzioni's vision of "nested" communities, where the boundaries and scope of one community each rest within more encompassing ones. This concept of loyalty and commitment to multiple communities, while complicated, is not beyond the scope of human beings to attain institutionally, and it appears a valid process by which to protect local standards from the pressures of internationalism. (Etzioni, 1991; 1995) Global strategic political relationships may appear less volatile for the first time in fifty years; but appearances can deceive. Nationalism, cultural insolence, and religious pride, accompanied with resentment for any intrusion on indigenous societies, and the unintended consequences of democratization and modernization challenge peaceful coexistence. The communitarian ethic prescribes the recognition of the disparities of people who may have unique aspirations for their societies; it incorporates both the principles of free agency and collective unity, which suggests the enabling of a worldview of a society of mankind, void of the need for geostrategic alignment for preservation of state sovereignty. Self-direction and autonomy for nation-states need not be diminished by their global relationships, if both the nation-state and the global community recognize their mutualities and differences. The one is not threatened by the other if both are free of artificial assumptions of superiority/inferiority and fanatical xenophobia.

Indeed, globalism may prove the alembic which legitimizes the institutionalization of the communitarian ethic. Communitarianist theory may not replace the power structure paradigm which has historically dominated American organization theory, or the cloying collectivism of the Japanese model; however, it reveals possibilities for the consolidation of new theories incorporating the fundamentally humanistic principles advocated by an interdisciplinary field of thought in application to organizations.

THE COMMUNITARIAN ETHIC

Communitarianism is an ethic-based theory. It is the affirmation of the social context of one's existence, where both the individual and her community maintain separate moral standing in an attached, interdependent relationship, both shaping and shaped by the resultant community. (Etzioni and Lawrence, 1991) Communitarianism is an ageless expression of the reconciliation between the individual and the collective, insinuated in the wisdom of civilization's ancient tribal customs, conspicuous in Platonic and Aristotelian thought, and identified later in the contributions of Rousseau, Montesquieu, Burke, and Durkheim. Amitai Etzioni has articulated communitarian theory for over thirty years as an expression of a socially-responsible philosophy of individual rights.

As a social philosophy, communitarianism has a variety of interpretations. Quite often, and perhaps wrongfully, it is seen as a challenge to classical liberalism. Spragens makes a powerful argument for "communitarian liberalism," as the true essence of the moral roots of liberalism, claiming that the individual in classical liberalism enjoyed freedom only within the context of complementary obligations deriving from communal attachments and responsibilities, from the restraints of a valid moral order, and from the force of human sympathy. He argues that modern interpretations of liberalism are a departure from its moral roots, and have diminished important dimensions of the well-ordered society by attempting to superimpose modern thought on traditional moral doctrine. He directs attention to the third expectation in the French Revolution, the concept of "fraternity." According to Spragens, fraternity is the capstone of a liberal society, and the affirmation of the communitarian ethic. (Spragens, 1995) When communitarianism is thus approached as an ethical construct which enlarges, rather than displaces the concept of individual liberty, it serves as a theoretical remedy for the moral deprivation and social discontent of a society of radically isolated individuals, divided by their inalienable rights. (Walzer, 1995)

Michael Walzer argues that the pursuit of individualism creates an "asocial society" devoid of value, a Hobbesian world where society is reduced to the coexistence of isolated selves:

> [L]iberal rights . . . have more to do with "exit" than with "voice." They are concretely expressed in separation, divorce, withdrawal, solitude, privacy, and political apathy. (Walzer, 55)

Walzer contends that liberal theory misrepresents real life. "The world is not like that, nor could it be. Men and women cut loose from all social ties, literally unencumbered, each one the one and only inventor of his or her own life, with no criteria, no common standards, to guide the invention: these are mythical figures." (Walzer, 56)

While communitarianism is an effort to break through some of the logjams of contemporary social and political thinking, it is much more than simply an articulation of the natural theory of the sociality of human beings. The communitarian ethic suggests that while nature may give human beings sociability, it does not give them community—only the predisposition to it. Community requires cultivation; social relationships among human beings are more fragile than those among non-human animals, but they are also more capable of adaptation, transformation, and renewal. (Wolfe, 1995, 133)

If one seeks a link between social theory and natural theory—as has been pursued by just about every other major innovation in social theory—it is not difficult to argue that human behaviors have biological roots. But that observation alone tells us little about the kind of communities in which we might prefer to live. To what degree ought we to attribute what we do to the nature we have as human beings? The debate between "nature" and "nurture" may well be one of the most futile controversies in the history of social science. The most acceptable position is to consider human beings as a product of complex interactions between heredity and learning, rather than in terms of either-or:

> Biology may set the broad outlines and limits of our potential, but how or whether we use that potential depends on the environment in which we live. The key to understanding the interaction of "nature" and "nurture" is the process of socialization, where biology and culture meet and blend. (Robertson, 1989, 70)

For centuries scholars have pondered the question of what human beings would be like if raised in isolation from human society. Would they be brutes? Would they be perfect? Literally thousands of cases involving children raised in isolation or in institutions, and myths involving children alleged to have been raised by wild animals, have revealed a great deal about human nature. But the consensus seems to reveal that "children need close emotional attachments with at least one other person if they are to prosper." (Robertson, 71) The process of socialization, through which people acquire personality and learn the ways of life of their society, is the essential link between the individual and society. It is a link so vital that neither the individual nor her society can survive without it. (Robertson, 69)

Mayo, writing in 1945, proposed that there were two symptoms of social disruption in modern industrial society: unhappiness, and lack of cooperation between groups. (Adams, 1965, citing Mayo, 1945) He discounted the so-called "rabble" hypothesis, which proposed that there is a "rabble of persons all acting without regard for others," an hypothesis Adams identifies with David Ricardo's arguments for the self-interested individual in a natural society of unorganized individuals. (Adams, 374) The exigencies of industrial society, argues Adams, citing Durkheim, Wells, and LePlay, displaced the natural bonds of the society of mankind and disrupted the stability of the social order. As Mayo would discover, however, a "horde of solitaires can be transferred to a social group by someone interested in them." (Adams, 375, citing Mayo)

If we want a society which enables people to cultivate a sense of responsibility toward others, we will focus less on the nature of man and more on learning the skills of sociability. A human natural community may be sociable, but if such sociability is presumed to be achieved without the active participation of its members, it is a community not worth having. (Wolfe, 126-140) Wolfe tells us that numbers of social and political theorists have directed their attention to the same issues of individuals and groups in the last ten years as were being considered by Mayo, and cited by Adams. Considering publications by Bellah et al (*Habits of the Heart*, 1985 and *The Good Society*, 1991), Etzioni, Philip Selznick (*The Moral Commonwealth: Social Theory and the Promise of Community*, 1992), and James Q. Wilson (*The Moral Sense*, 1993), Wolfe comments:

> Concerned about a weakened sense of obligation in advanced industrial societies, these scholars argue that liberal political theory, as important and defensible as it may be, pays insufficient attention to the ties that hold individuals together. (Wolfe, 126)

Personal responsibility to one's group(s) is a significant element of the communitarian ethic. Indeed, the acts of an individual to accept and exercise her personal responsibilities are inseparable from the community which provides that opportunity. (Wolfe, 126-140)

Theory of the Embedded Self

For communitarians, the question of what sort of person we wish to be or become involves a deeper discovery process of finding out who we already are. Kymlicka's observations on the theory of the embedded self propose that the self is a product of a particular social identity; that freedom is situated; and that our selves are at least partly constituted by ends that we do not choose but discover in our shared social context. The communitarian social thesis argues that individual autonomy cannot exist without the social environment, because it is the environment that enables and supports individual choices and the capacity of the individual to choose. (Kymlicka, 1990)

The core of the communitarian ethic is the discovery of the self and its relationship to the community. The communitarian self is both an "I" and a "We"—a condition exhibiting both free agency and collective unity. This concept is best understood in juxtaposition to the Rawlsian concept of the unencumbered self, or, as "the self [which] is prior to the ends which are affirmed by it." (Rawls, 560) The essence of this view is that we can always review and revise any particular project through our own choices. "This is often called the `Kantian' view of the self, for Kant was one of the strongest defenders of the view that the self is prior to its socially given roles and relationships, and is free only if it is capable of holding these features of its social situation at a distance and judging them according to the dictates of reason." (Kymlicka, 207)

But the communitarian concept is one of an "embedded," rather than an "unencumbered" self:

[I]n deciding how to lead our lives we all approach our own circumstances as bearers of a particular social identity . . . Hence what is good for me has to be the good for one who inhabits these roles. Self-determination, therefore, is exercised within these social roles, rather than by standing outside of them. (MacIntyre, 1981 cited in Kymlicka, 207-208)

Elshtain argues that to consider individuals as wholly autonomous subjects whose freedom lies solely in the voluntaristic choices they make is much too thin a view of the self. To the contrary, asserts Elshtain, possessive individualism, which translates wants into rights, reduces human existence into an unnatural contractual framework whose institutions have neither binding obligations, deep commitments, or moral weight. On the other hand, the communitarian individual recognizes the individual as "a historical being who acknowledges that he or she has many debts and obligations and that one's history and the history of one's society frame one's own starting point." (Elshtain, 1995, 105) Elshtain makes a sharp distinction between the thin view of the social contract and the thick view of the social compact, where "human beings are ends in themselves, not means, and no one is in a position to assign value to the human life of another, for that value is a given." (Elshtain, 107)

The Communitarian Paradigm

The central issue for any political theory, however, is not the constitution of the self, because what the self does and is, is only significant in the presence of others. It is only without others that the self is truly autonomous, with no political or social constraints. But, with the addition of others, the solitary self becomes a community, perhaps only by virtue of biological relationships, or in hopes of survival, but a community, nonetheless. The community is the assortment of historical, physical, and emotional baggage that defines the self. But it is also an interactive relationship; it would be implausible to take the extreme position that one could interpret the meaning of one's roles but could not reject either them or the goals internal to them. (Kymlicka, 215)

Durkheim's persistent defense of the dignity and rights of the individual within the moral idiom of social traditions and commitment to the common good comes very close to the balance between the extremes of individualism and collectivism that can animate the nobler aspects of both social ideals. (Cladis, 1992, 1) Durkheim's attempts to connect the Kantian view of individualism with the common good, and Rousseau's intense defense of autonomy with the authority of the community, assert the possibility of the reconciliation of the tension between liberalism and communitarianism:

> This is how it is possible, without contradiction, to be an individualist, all the while saying that the individual is more a product of society than its cause. It is because individualism itself is a social product just like all moralities and religions . . . . This is what Kant and Rousseau failed to understand. They wanted to deduce their individualistic ethics not from society but from the notion of the isolated individual. This undertaking was impossible, and from it come the logical contradictions of their systems. (From Durkheim's "Individualism and the Intellectuals," translated by M. Traugott, cited in Cladis, 19)

In this interpretation, there is no conflict in principle between the moral individual and the common good of humanity. "[B]y locating autonomy within situated freedom, and by celebrating diversity within social membership . . . [Durkheim's] position satisfies the liberals' love of self-expression, as well as the communitarian's longing for socially related individuals . . . ." (Cladis, 40) This interpretation also addresses the liberal criticism that communitarianism is fatalistic and dangerously subject to the coercion of the social mass. The common good and the nature and force of moral individualism are co-joined, because the latter guides how societies establish the former. There is no philosophical reason for the community to consume either the autonomy of the individual or her secondary associations (families, unions, churches, clubs, political associations, etc.) The dispute between the liberal and the communitarian perspectives with respect to individuality is contrived. Liberals tend to ignore community, or consign it to derivative status as an aggregation of individual choices or bargains. Yet the communitarian perspective which asserts that a person is an "integral part of a community yet not consumed by it or submerged within it" (Etzioni, 1995, 18) may simply be considered the fulfillment of the social purpose of individuals. There is a tense but close bond between individuals and communities:

> The uncommunitized parts of personhood are sources of creativity and change for the community and personal expression for the person. The communitized part of the person is a source of effective psychological stability and one source of personal and social virtue. (Etzioni, 1995, 19)

Etzioni articulates an appropriate analogy to explain the tension between this "I and We" notation:

> [T]he role of bricks in an arch is instructive. There is little sense in asking which is more basic. Without the arch the bricks are a pile of rubble. And without bricks there is no arch. A proper relation among the bricks ensures that a sufficient level of tension will maintain the bond. If there is too much or too little tension, the arch will come apart and the bricks will scatter. (Etzioni, 1995, 19)

The balance of the tension between the I and the We may be weighted either toward self-interest and expressive individualism, as in contemporary American society, or in the collectivist direction, as in totalitarian societies. Communities are not necessarily or automatically places of virtue, but neither is an allegiance to individual human nature any sort of guarantee of institutional perfection. "Granting that human nature has certain attributes does not mean that we need to embrace them or approve of them." (Etzioni, 1995, 34) Nor is an homogeneous community either desirable nor possible:

> It is best to think about communities as nested, each within a more encompassing one . . . People are at one and the same time members of several communities such as those at work and at home. They can and do use these multimemberships (as well as the ability to choose one's work and residential communities) to protect themselves from excessive pressure by any one community. (Etzioni, 1995, 25)

The communitarian ethic properly fits with the idea of moral pluralism. As explained by Cladis, communitarianism does not deny one's multiple commitments and loyalties:

> Fidelity to the common good need not compromise allegiance to communities with detailed positions on "ultimate concerns" such as the nature and destiny of humans . . . It is well known that Judaism and Christianity, for example, have influenced a variety of (sometimes conflicting) moral and political positions. I see no reason why people aligned with these various religious traditions should not be encouraged to articulate public positions that have been informed by their distinctive religious commitments. And I see no reason why members of religious groups cannot remain faithful to their religious beliefs while sharing obligations and concerns for the . . . common good. (Cladis, 169-170)

Responsibilities vs. Rights

The assumption of responsibilities is fundamental to the communitarian ethic. According to Etzioni, "Claiming rights without assuming responsibilities is unethical and illogical." (Etzioni, 1993, 9) But this is not to limit responsibilities to commensurate rights; more importantly, there are also a whole host of responsibilities and duties which carry with them no immediate, obvious, or manifest right, yet they carry equal moral force. They are, by and large, the moral responsibilities and commitments that reflect one's moral compass, the ethical content of one's conscience that enables one to select between one choice that is right and another that is equally right. In an ethical sense, responsibilities are those duties and burdens one assumes, not because they bear legal force, but because they are ethically proper. In fact, the modern communitarian movement is the consequence of the observations by a small group of ethicists, social philosophers, and social scientists meeting in Washington D.C. in 1990 that while Americans were quite eager to spell out their rights, they were reluctant to accept responsibilities. According to Etzioni, "We adopted the name *Communitarian* to emphasize that the time had come to attend to our responsibilities and to the conditions and elements we all share, to the community." (Etzioni, 1993, 15)

> The language of rights is morally incomplete. To say that "I have a right to do X" is not to conclude that "X is the right thing for me to do." . . . . Rights give reasons to others not to coercively interfere with the speaker in the performance of protected acts; however, they do not in themselves give me a sufficient reason to perform these acts. There is a gap between rights and rightness that cannot be closed without a richer moral vocabulary—one that invokes principles of decency, duty, responsibility, and the common good, among others. (Etzioni, 1991, 263)

Understanding the congruity between rights and responsibilities is especially critical in the newly-formed democracies. David Hollenbach, S.J., argues that these new democracies must not elevate rights over responsibilities:

> "[S]olitary individuals, especially solitary individuals motivated solely by self-interest and the protection of their rights to privacy, will be incapable of democratic self-government. Democracy requires more than this. It requires the virtues of mutual cooperation, mutual responsibility, and what Aristotle called friendship, concord, and amity. (Hollenbach, 1995, 148-149)

Hollenbach suggests that in an interdependent world, the only way to protect both our private enclaves and our interrelatedness is by complementing subsidiarity, "with its stress on the importance of the local, the small-scale, and the particular," with solidarity that is more universal:

> Commitment to small-scale communities with particular traditions must be complemented by a sense of the national and global common good and the need for a vision shaped not only by particularist

traditions but by hostile encounters with traditions and peoples that are different. (Hollenbach, 149)

There is an indisputable philosophical link between rights and responsibilities, in that, in the long run, rights can only be assured by the cultivation of social responsibilities. According to Justice Frank Iacobucci of the Canadian Supreme Court: "Legal rights and freedoms cannot properly be understood without appreciating the existence of corresponding duties and responsibilities." (Quoted in Etzioni, 1995, 20) The assumption that for every right there is a corresponding responsibility is not too far off the mark; it is also ethically untenable to expect to benefit from entitlements without having contributed to their substantiation. This point is contested by such civil libertarian groups as the ACLU; however, it appears that it is both philosophically, socially, and ethically specious to expect that an excessive reliance on rights will not erode the social and political institutions required to protect them. According to Dallin Oaks: "[N]o society is so secure that it can withstand continued demands for increases in citizen rights and decreases in citizen obligations." (Etzioni, 1995, 20, citing Oaks, 1990/1991) Deferring to Alexis de Tocqueville, Etzioni argues that "the best protection against totalitarianism is a pluralistic society laced with communities and voluntary associations, rather than a society of highly individualized rights carriers." (Etzioni, 1995, 22)

While libertarians might argue that responsibilities are a matter of personal choice, the communitarian ethic prescribes that responsibilities are anchored in community, dependent on the diverse moral voices of citizens to define what is expected, what is valuable, and how to discipline those members of the community who depart from those values. "While the ultimate foundation of morality may be commitments of individual conscience, it is communities that help introduce and sustain these commitments." (Etzioni, 1991, 267)

> But one cannot deny that we must draw a societal line between permissible and impermissible group practices. For instance, it is hard to imagine an American court which would permit a group of African immigrants to practice clitoral circumcision in their community. We all realize that certain overarching values take priority, but which values and on what grounds remain subjects of considerable and unresolved discussion, especially at the margin. (Etzioni, 1995, 31)

Moral Conduct and Social Values

Matters of moral conduct and social values are inherent in both early and modern communitarian ethics. S. I. Benn explains the communitarian ethic through Judson Jerome's communalist ideal in the *Families of Eden*, 1975. In this context, the community is characterized as a mode of human association which combines maximum self-actualization and individuality with maximum cooperation and commitment to the welfare of others, a dynamic moral force which transmutes selfishness into self-fulfillment and dependency into love. (Benn, 1982) Jerome's "transcendent collective enterprise," arises from a common concern for some valued endeavor or worthwhile activity, and must be pursued collectively, or not at all. (Jerome, cited in Benn, 1982) Benn's observations reveal the philosophical nature of the communitarian perspective and notions of the telos of association, and are not unlike Emile Durkheim's collective consciousness theory, where morality arises out of the confluence of common languages, histories, and cultures. (Cladis, 139) True communal values are generated by the members of the community in open dialogue; they cannot be imposed by either an outside group, an internal elite, or a minority. But these values must be submitted for legitimation at some level. Communal values, according to Etzioni, are "only legitimate insofar as they are not in tension with overarching core values." (Etzioni, 1995, 17) His position is sharply differentiated from other communitarians who assert that whatever set of values the community agrees to are the ultimate criteria for moral standing.

Some communitarians, like MacIntyre and Hauerwas, argue that American society has lost its moral compass, that "our moral world is fragmented and in a grave state of disorder . . . [having] lost our comprehension, both theoretical and practical, of morality." (MacIntyre, cited by Cladis, 170) Attributing this moral rootlessness to the radical individualism of classical liberalism, this branch of the communitarian movement maintains that American society has experienced a moral catastrophe which has put in motion a whole host of drifting "should's and ought's," bereft of any moral whole. (Cladis, 170)

Etzioni argues that the moral voice of the community must be restored, but he also claims that most people are able to maintain multiple moral commitments to both their immediate community and more encompassing ones:

> Indeed, a strong case can be made that what might be called upward shifting of moral commitments, to ever more encompassing communities, is the earmark of a community which is most progressive. Such a community is likely to be more committed to widely shared values, such as peace and social justice. However, both the empirical aspects of this question (e.g., does internationalism drain local commitments?) and the moral issues involved are far from settled even among communitarians. (Etzioni, 1995, 25)

Believing that Americans have more-or-less abandoned any substantive moral and ethical claim on their lives, he argues in "The Responsive Communitarian Platform" that heeding the moral voices of her history is much like consulting what Lincoln called "the better angels of our nature." He argues that morality and right behavior are not situational, and that the disinclination to establish some sort of moral exaction frustrates the daily and routine social underwriting of morality and obstructs moral conduct in crucial situations.

> To object to the moral voice of the community, and to the moral encouragement it provides, is to oppose the social glue that helps hold the moral order together. It is unrealistic to rely on individuals' inner voices and to expect that people will invariably do what is right completely on their own. Such a radical individualistic view disregards our social moorings and the important role that communities play in sustaining moral commitments. (Etzioni, 1991, 36)

The communitarian position on morality is echoed in commentary on the breakdown of civility, a popular social and psychological topic in modern society. Robert Wright argues that modern civilization "thwarts civility." "Because social cooperation improves the chances of survival, natural selection imbued our minds with an infrastructure for friendship, including affection, gratitude and trust. (In technical terms, this is the machinery for `reciprocal altruism')" (Wright, 1995, 52) Primitive society, regardless of its hardships, possessed a primeval sense of intensive interdependence that protected and sustained both the community and its individual members. There are those who suggest that while as a society we have restrained our cruder impulses, we have also neglected our instinctive, ancestral better inclinations to our deepest moral convictions—love, pity, generosity, remorse, friendly affection, and enduring trust—all of which are equally a part of our genetic heritage: "The problem with modern life, increasingly, is less that we're 'oversocialized' than that we're undersocialized—or, that too little of our 'social' contact is social in the natural, intimate sense of the world." (Wright, 56) In *The New York Times Book Review* of Fukuyama's book, *Trust*, Fareed Zakaria, managing editor of *Foreign Affairs*, argues that what Americans really want is "not civil society, but civics—what the Romans called *civitas*; that is, public spiritedness, sacrifice for the community, citizenship, even nobility." (Zakaria, 1995, 25)

In a commentary on America's "withering civic life," Francis Fukuyama claims that the decade-long warnings of communitarian thinkers of the debasement of the moral community and the demise of trust in American society are valid. Joining the communitarian admonitions, Fukuyama denounces what he calls the "associational crisis" in American society, which leads it to squander its rich endowment of social capital. (Herbert, 1995, 52) In a speech on July 6, 1995, American President William Clinton implored community leaders to become role models of moral character and civility, to spread the gospel of citizenship and individual responsibility. Unless the issue of civility and moral virtue had been perceived as a matter of national interest, it is unlikely that an American president, troubled as this one is by his own problems of personal virtue and morality, would broach the issue. (Malone, 1995, A7)

Richard Armstrong claims that most recent polls indicate that Americans themselves believe their society to be rude and uncivil, its values eroded by violence and vulgarity in the public media. But much of the nature of modern society is also a reflection of its denial of its traditions; quite simply, as Armstrong quotes Peggy Post, great-granddaughter-in-law of Emily Post, "I don't think people are any meaner or more awful than before. We've just become lazy about thinking about the other person." (Armstrong, 1996, B1) Post is invoking the communitarian ideal when she concludes that "people grasp for a deep down need to know how to get along." (Armstrong, B1)

But Richard Morin, commenting on the "Bowling Alone" thesis of Harvard's Robert Putnam, and the decline of civic trust and community participation, argues that "Individualist America in its post-industrial era is vigorously civic America." (Morin, 1996, 37) Encouraged by figures from the Roper Center which reflect increasing numbers of

Americans participating in the social lives of their communities, Morin argues that this is "good news for America . . . encouraging for all of us who see vigorous civic participation essential to the nation's health." (Morin, 1996, 37)

Civil Society and Civic Virtue

Communitarians insist that the breakdown in civil society and its moral infrastructure are a threat to democracy and political freedoms. To draw a line from the individualism of classical liberalism to the demise of the democratic state is perhaps a philosophical reach, but, nevertheless, Jean Bethke Elshtain makes a strong argument for the concept that when the bonds of social trust and competence collapse and faith in our neighbors dwindles, democratic society is in peril. Not unlike the counsel of Alexis deTocqueville, modern communitarians like Elshtain are unrelenting in their call for a return to a sturdy civil society in which individual citizens assume their vital stations.

> Communitarians, inspired by the republican insistence upon the necessity for "civic virtue," reject the normative focus of liberalism upon rights claims and instead insist upon the necessity of correlative or supervening responsibilities that a democratic citizen owes to society. Empirically, communitarians depart from liberalism's nominalist resolution of society into an aggregation of individuals, insisting instead upon the irreducible corporate features of society. (Spragens, 38)

Tocqueville warned Americans about the possibility of the corruption of their way of life, a corruption they themselves would facilitate if they succumbed to the relative ease of allowing a centralized, top-heavy state to usurp the social responsibility of the citizens. "In Tocqueville's worst-case scenario, narrowly self-involved individualists, disarticulated from the saving constraints and nurture of overlapping associations of social life, would come to require more and more restraints from above in order to muffle the disintegrative effects of `bad egoism.'" (Elshtain, 1996, C4)

According to Elshtain, "If we have lost the sturdiness and the patience necessary to sustain civil society over the long haul, democracy itself—as a political system, and social world, and a culture—is in trouble." With other communitarians, Elshtain cautions that one must accept the discipline of the community in order to sustain it:

> This discipline consists, in part, in a recognition that the world doesn't begin and end at the perimeter of me, as in "me, myself, and I"... It consists in recognition of the fact that, even as I restrain myself and expect others to restrain themselves in the interest of sustaining a way of life in common, we are all of us beholden to something bigger and beyond—to purposes not reducible to the sum of our private passions and interests. (Elshtain, C4)

Her comments are supported by the comments of Common Cause founder John Gardner:

> Families and communities are the ground-level generators and preservers of values and ethical systems. No society can remain vital or even survive without a reasonable base of shared values... They are generated chiefly in the family, schools, church, and other intimate settings in which people deal with one another face to face. (Quoted in Etzioni, 1993, 31)

Philip Selznick reminds us that the fundamental source of moral obligation is our own sense of identity and relatedness; it is difficult to conceive of moral duty and civic responsibility outside the bounds of an overarching social interrelatedness. That liberal capitalism attempts to do so—identifying individuals under the rule of law, political democracy, or free enterprise—has the effect of negating the concreteness of selfhood, connection, and context. The "abstract individual" becomes the barren, dehumanized legacy of rationalism. But the concept of *person* retrieves the texture of the moral order, with all the Latin and Greek baggage of moral and civic duty:

> [P]ersons are at once socially constituted and self-determining. To be socially constituted is not, in itself, to be imprisoned or oppressed; it does not require that people be puppets or act out prescribed roles in excruciating detail. Nor is self-determination properly understood as gratification of impulse, compulsive dependency, or opportunistic decision. Insofar as it has moral import, the theory of the social self makes plain that a morally competent self must be a product of

affirmative social participation and of responsible emotion, belief, and conduct. (Selznick, 1995, 125)

The communitarian ethic mandates the participation of non-state actors in society. Not unlike the philosophy of the ancient Greeks which championed the affinity between one's public and private responsibilities and virtues, the communitarian ethic declares that the health of the institutions of civil society is fundamental as the critical and natural expression of social men and women to each other and their mutual responsibilities. In principles shared by modern political advocates of smaller government, communitarians believe that "Some measure of caring, sharing, and *being our brother's and sister's keeper*, is essential if we are not all to fall back on an ever more expansive government, bureaucratized welfare agencies, and swollen regulations, police, courts, and jails." (Etzioni, 1993, 260)

The communitarian notion of civic virtue and responsibility affirms that no task should be assumed by any institution that is larger than is minimally required to do the job. This means, in essence, that the jobs and responsibilities of families should not be passed on to larger institutions, and that what can be done locally should not be bumped up to a higher level. "[T]o remove tasks to higher levels than is necessary weakens the constituent communities." (Etzioni, 1993, 260) This suggests a national government limited to only those functions of national and international import, a concept which echoes Tocqueville's comments about the definitive nature of despotic democracy in Book IV of *Democracy In America*. Tocqueville, concerned that an obsession with equality would predispose men to servitude of "an immense and tutelary power," is anticipating the communitarian ethic in these famous words:

> After having thus successively taken each member of the community in its powerful grasp and fashioned him at will, the supreme power then extends its arm over the whole community. It covers the surface of society with a network of small complicated rules, minute and uniform, through which the most original minds and the most energetic characters cannot penetrate, to rise above the crowd . . . . Such a power does not destroy, but it prevents existence; it does not tyrannize, but it compresses, enervates, extinguishes, and stupefies a people, till each nation is reduced to nothing better than a flock of

timid and industrious animals, of which the government is the shepherd. (Tocqueville, 1990 Ed., 319)

Communitarians believe that the intimate relationships between human beings and all their institutions generate social capital; to bypass these critical connections has the effect of obliging citizens, and their diverse and voluntary associations, to abandon their moral and virtuous purposes. Taking responsibilities away from civil society—the buffer between the individual and the state—is to impoverish all three:

> What we must try to avoid is relying on the state to maintain social order, which can be achieved more humanely and at less cost by the voluntary observance of those values we all hold dear . . . . In short, the more people generally agree with one another about what is to be done and encourage one another to live up to these agreements, the smaller the role that coercive authority will play and the more civil the community. (Etzioni, 1993, 44)

A COMMUNITARIAN EPISTEMOLOGY

The communitarian ethic directs individuals, organizations, and societies to aspire to noble ideals with respect to shouldered responsibilities, ethical conduct, and civic virtue. The communitarian ethic rests on the social thesis of civil society, not unlike Rawls' liberal neutrality, which rests on a faith in non-state forums to support individual judgments and cultural development.

There are numerous definitions of community. Scott M. Peck defines community as "a way of being together with both individual authenticity and interpersonal harmony so that people become able to function with a collective energy even greater than the sum of their individual energies." (Zemke, 27, quoting Peck, 1993) According to Corlett, community is the foundation that exists before interaction: "Mutual service, reciprocity, and communion form three different ways of being communitarian." (Corlett, 1989, 19)

Schaffer and Anundsen describe community as a dynamic whole that emerges when a group of people: (1) Participate in common practices; (2) Depend upon one another; (3) Make decisions together; (4) Identify themselves as part of something larger than the sum of their individual relationships; and, (5) Commit themselves for the long term to their own, one another's and the group's well-being. (Zemke, 27, quoting Schaffer and Anundsen, 1993)

An epistemological examination of the communitarian ethic reveals it to be, much like democracy, both prescriptive and descriptive, both intimate and public. At the personal level, the communitarian ethic directs one to be honest in one's relationships, to be mindful and protective of one's personal integrity, and to be decent and honorable in one's dealings with others. The communitarian person is motivated in all her behavior out of concern and care for others, relying for moral guidance on the constant of "love thy neighbor." The communitarian embraces personal responsibility for all her actions, ever mindful of her own selfhood and the selfhood of others. There is a strong sense of obligation to others in the communitarian spirit, an "other-regarding" compulsion that recognizes the interdependence of all human beings in pursuit of the common good. The communitarian ethic obliges one to exercise self-constraint, self-discipline, and service to others in a general spirit of ordered liberty and ethical behavior which reflects a concern for rightness over rights and benevolence and charity over hostility and selfishness.

Civil society is the heart of the communitarian ethic, which envisions a host of associations, beginning with the family, whose members are bound together by their traditions, their histories, and their mutual needs and responsibilities. Communitarians insist that bringing children into the world is not a matter of biological regeneration; it is a moral act which brings with it a moral commitment to provide one's children with a conscience, a lifetime commitment to the most basic of the communities of man, the responsibility for which is not justifiably relieved by frivolous desires to put the preferences of the parent above the good of the child. "Fathers and mothers consumed by `making it' and consumerism, or preoccupied with personal advancement, who come home too late and too tired to attend to the needs of their children, cannot discharge their most elementary duty to their children and their fellow citizens." (Etzioni, 1993, 257) As the immediate community, the family—meaning two parents and all the children—are society's basic unit. When it fails, the society fails. The communitarian ethic is unequivocal in its advocacy of marriage and childbearing as more than a personal, private matter: "It is an act that has significant consequences for the community. Hence those who bring children into the world have a social obligation to attend to their moral education. Children have no inborn moral values, and unless these values are introduced, they will not become civil members of the community." (Etzioni, 1993, 88)

The communitarian ethic is an ecumenical notion of multiple affiliations. The family may be the basic unit of civil society, but its other institutions—schools, churches, clubs, economic enterprise—all the rich fabric of voluntary associations in everyday life—are the repositories of shared experiences that define a participatory community. The communitarian ethic visualizes a civil commitment to activities which bring together people from different backgrounds, but which are not coercive. In fact, the communitarian ethic proposes that the best way to minimize coercion is to enhance the moral voice of the community. The institutions of a community are its common cores, its mainstay of stability and spirit, the enhancement of its moral purpose. A community is not an homogeneous monolith; its nested nature guarantees that everyone has *a* place in the community, but there is neither a requirement nor guarantee of *specific* place. (Etzioni, 1993)

The intermediate associations of life, or civil society, represent the significant connectedness of human beings which relieves the alienation people feel when they suspect that they have lost control over their own lives. The philosophical paradox of the communitarian ethic is that to collaborate in the human endeavor is not to lose one's personal identity, but rather to strengthen it. Focusing an inordinate amount of attention and effort on singularity results not in self-satisfaction, but in alienation; focusing on one's mutualities and the common good, to the contrary, results in the self-fulfillment that remains elusive to the egoist.

Walzer has a name for the dissociation and separateness of modern American society: The Four Mobilities, an imitation of the Brownian movement in physics which draws people apart. He argues that in a society so unsettled, it is not surprising that citizens experience a very real sense of loss of place and purpose. Walzer insists that geographic, social, marital, and political mobility have followed on the coattails of increased knowledge and technological progress, but instead of bringing contentment and fulfillment, the consequences have often been psychologically and spiritually, perhaps even physically, disagreeable. The joy of personal liberation may be lost in the detritus of social disintegration.

> Moving may be a personal adventure in our standard cultural mythologies, but it is as often a family trauma in real life. The same

thing is true of social mobility, which carries people down as well as up and requires adjustments that are never easy to manage. Marital breaks may sometimes give rise to new and stronger unions, but they also pile up what we might think of as family fragments . . . . And independence in politics is often a not-so-splendid isolation: individuals with opinions are cut loose from groups with programs. The result is a decline in "the sense of efficacy," with accompanying effects on commitment and morale. (Walzer, 60)

Schaffer and Anundsen, with Wendell Berry, represent the viewpoint of one wing of the communitarian movement that points to a "plethora of provocative medical, psychological, and sociological studies" that "attribute illness, despair, and sundry other maladies to a literal rootlessness and lack of community in the physical, as well as emotional sense." (Zemke, 27)

To limit the communitarian ethic to matters of geography, is to ignore its broader philosophical relevance of the multitude of communities of mankind. In spiritual matters, one may be a member of a community of believers, or non-believers. The information highway has created a community in cyber space, whose members may develop quite intimate and personal relationships with each other, though physically unseen and geographically diverse. Members of the military, as well as retired and those otherwise separated from active duty, enjoy a communal bond that spans the globe, as well as crossing nationalities and political inclinations. Professions have a non-geographic, as well as a geographically-situated nature, as do avocations and other commitments to particular and sundry causes. Kazimierz Gozdz of Stanford University speaks to the philosophical stretch of the ethic when he advises that "We need to talk about community as a state of being, a spiritual and psychological experience—psychospiritual—a geographic location, an affinity group. All those and more." (Zemke, 27, quoting Gozdz) And not unlike Wolfe's comments as to the limitations of looking on community as a biological phenomenon, Gozdz separates the *experience* of community from the concept of a *sustainable* community. The former, according to Gozdz, is simply a momentary, short-lived interconnectedness that arises out of the dynamics of human nature; but the latter, the sustainable community, is defined by its ongoing sets of relationships, which transcend "touchy-feely" sensations and ephemeral feelings of wholeness and interconnectedness. (Zemke, 28, quoting Gozdz)

At the public level, the communitarian ethic brings with it an expectation of cooperation, justification, and a substantive moral discourse. Communitarian persons create participatory communities, whose general republicanism arises out of a thick view of embedded selves, bounded by citizenship and the moral certitudes of justice and mercy over rationality and legalism. What William F. Buckley calls "civic sacrament," political participation is an expression of the communitarian convictions of personal responsibility and public-spiritedness. (Etzioni, 1993)

The communitarian belief in civil society is attendant to the communitarian conviction that the state has its own rightful purpose. In fact, the communitarian position is that a free public state is dependent on a free civil society:

> The notion of civil society comprises the host of free associations, existing outside of any official sponsorship, and often dedicated to ends which we generally consider nonpolitical. No society can be called free in which these are not able to function, and the pulse of freedom will beat very slowly where they are not being spontaneously formed. (Taylor, 1995, 185)

Contrary to the usual interpretation of a liberal society, the communitarian conceptualization of American citizenship emphasizes participation in democratic self-governance and public service rather than individual rights. Rogers Smith muses that "American citizenship is said to rest on consent to the political principles valorizing personal liberties and democratic self-governance that are enshrined in America's Constitution and laws." (R. Smith, 1995, 234) But, he continues, this standard perception of citizenship contains two distinguishable conceptions of citizenship. One, the liberal notion of citizenship, focuses on the American citizen as the bearer of individual rights first—economic, spiritual, intellectual, and procedural. The second component, in his view submerged beneath the first by the liberal tradition, is the concept of political liberties. According to this view,

> She or he [the American citizen] is likely to be most absorbed in pursuing happiness in forms of 'private' life, work, church, and family and to act in national affairs, even to the modest extent of voting, only sporadically. Those brief interventions are likely to be

The Communitarian Paradigm

aimed at protecting personal interests and making sure the government does not trample rights. (R. Smith, 234)

While Smith is not denying the aspects of The American Creed which validate personal relationships, in his view, citizenship must also rely on a more "civic republican" reading which emphasizes not individual rights but rather active participation in forms of democratic self-governance and public service:

> It is our prime civic duty, part of a shared commitment to help shape our lives in common and serve our common interests. It is also a vital fulfillment of our potential for both freedom and moral dignity, as we bring the social constituencies of our lives under more conscious collective control." (R. Smith, 234)

Smith admits that most Americans probably want the best of both worlds—the institutions, programs, and policies that nurture the sense of civic obligation and bond all in pursuit of the common good; but they also want to be free to pursue their self-chosen courses as much as possible. (R. Smith, 236)

Durkheim made a similar distinction, but added that the legitimate purpose of the state is to sustain the highest ideals of society. In this manner, Durkheim answers the critics of communitarianism who are persuaded that the communitarian ethic may release bigotry, coercion, and intolerance.

> The state, as a servant of the common good, blocks secondary groups from dominating the individual, an important feature of the common good. Secondary groups reciprocally prevent the state from becoming a Leviathan, and hence they, too contribute to the common good. (Cladis, 156)

As Etzioni would explicate many years later, the government is not empowered to replace local communities, although it is expected to support them in the event of need, in public-private cooperative efforts: "The government should step in only to the extent that other social subsystems fail, rather than seek to replace them." (Etzioni, 1993, 260)

THE COMMUNITARIAN PARADIGM FOR CORPORATE ORGANIZATIONS

The communitarian ethic prescribes that membership in society is accompanied by both the rights-of and the responsibilities-to that society. There is no escaping the certainty that economic organizations belong in the intermediate realm of civil society, where, according to the communitarian ethic, individuals are fulfilled, mutualities are fused, the common good is realized, and cultures are sustained.

The presumption of economic organizations as constituted selves in civil society vests them with civil purpose, controlled by both subsidiarity and solidarity as economic and social agents. Organization policies devised to recognize the institutional role in civil society and the responsibilities attendant to the rights of enterprise expand the corporate purpose beyond profit. Quite simply, the organization would discover its role in the community, much as the individual discovers her role in the community. As an embedded self, the organization would then act in concert with the community, not contrary to it. Much like a marriage, there is a presumption of purpose in common, pursued in an attitude of give-and-take which seeks to confirm the values of all parties to the union. This approach does not presuppose that the community would remain unchanged by the organization, nor that the organization would remain unchanged by the community. But it does presuppose that it is the community discovered in this union that will remain the repository of values. Note that as a marriage creates a new family unit, the fusion of corporation and community creates a new community, where the predominate values and norms are both greater than and less than those of either of the two parties.

The implications of this perception for American organization theory are complex. Much like Etzioni's notion of "nested" communities, we are looking at two communal relationships. On the one hand, the organization itself is a community, albeit an economic community. The appropriation of the communitarian ethic to the organization as a community would encourage organizations to allow autonomy and sustain mutuality among its members, rather than to pre-ordain a struggle between the individuals who work and the organization as employer. Beyond the paternalism of Japanese management, and contrary to the over-organized and rationalized competitiveness of typical American organizations, understanding the organization as a community exponentially elaborates the unity of

The Communitarian Paradigm

purpose critical to successful enterprise. Surely economic organizations can be characterized as consisting of webs of relationships with shared meanings and shared values. They are part of the pluralistic tangle of communities, whose members are also members of other communities. And it would be too simplistic to try to define the scope of economic organizations as bounded communities; modern corporations, like their workers and managers, also belong to other sets of communities, subjected to an assortment of mutual expectations and obligations.

Secondly, economic enterprise organizations are also contextualized by the national societies in which they are located. American organizations, multinationals, giant corporations, and energetic entrepreneurs responding to the opportunities of expanded resources and markets, are nevertheless limited by traditional Western techniques and philosophies which may confront, or affront, national cultures with unfamiliar social, historical, and personal patterns. Bound together by technology and economics, the challenges to organizations are likely to be of a cultural nature, exhibited by unfamiliar social customs and norms, dissonant work habits and goals, and complex and dynamic political environments. The communitarian ethic would encourage the development of cross-cultural organization philosophies and plans of action and the development of cooperative and nurturing mutual relationships which respect rather than pervert the native culture. Bruce Kogut of the Wharton School, citing the work of Stephen Hymer of MIT, argues that companies expand their operations in foreign and alien societies for reasons other than return on investment:

> If a firm wants to invest and own physical capital in a foreign country, it must believe that there is some additional advantage that outweighs the added costs of operating at a distance in an unknown business environment. Moreover, it must also believe that this advantage can only be exploited through the ownership and control of foreign operations. (Kogut, 1998, 154)

The communitarian ethic is clearly implied in these FDIs, since there is also a presumption that ownership brings into play a panoply of other resources that might otherwise remain un- or under-utilized. In other words, ownership through foreign direct investment creates a new community with an array of new resources at its command.

Etzioni's work leaves no doubt as to the efficacy of the communitarian ethic as a moral compass for organizations:

> Too many businesspeople no longer accept the responsibility of *stewardship*, at the very least to leave their communities no worse off than they found them. They no longer see it as their duty to reach beyond furthering self or corporate advancement or to serve as trustees of a social undertaking. (Etzioni, 1993, 28)

The Japanese model exhibits a communitarian orientation in organization theory in large corporations, but its particular Japanese articulation tends to encourage a paternalistic, lumbering corporate monolith rather than the energized and innovative environment possible when cooperation displaces manipulation.

The Theory Z organization is revealed to be little different from the Japanese model; it is a more humane American model, but fundamentally unchanged from the Japanese paradigm. Much of the usefulness of the Japanese and Theory Z models is diminished as an intercultural model by their paternalistic and discriminatory tendencies. Much of the strength of the Japanese model, and to a lesser extent the Theory Z model, is predicated on the presence of an homogeneous workforce; intercultural workforces are not homogeneous. With the loss of homogeneity, there is a loss of much of the basis of the trust that is so intrinsic in these models. Further, the environment is much more dynamic than these models; there is little match between the environment and the ability to respond. Theory Z has not reconciled its lifetime employment variable, but even the expectation of long term employment may be unreasonable in emerging nations or other nations whose traditional work habits and customs are of a contrary inclination. While the Theory Z model is somewhere in between the two extreme individualistic/ collectivist styles of organizations, nevertheless, it would appear to be too inflexible and parochial to serve our purpose. Indeed, there is a need for a new paradigm which minimizes the weaknesses and maximizes the strengths of the models considered.

The exercise of the communitarian ethic would encourage groups of human beings to allow autonomy and still sustain mutuality, in fresh, new, and innovative types of organizations, rather than to pre-ordain a struggle between the individual and the collective. It is an expression of the innate sociality of human beings in all their associations, and it allows for the situation of the "I and We" within an institutional

The Communitarian Paradigm

framework which respects both orientations. The I and We paradigm represents the sympathetic relationships of society. Communitarianism is empowering, because it taps the resources of all members of the enterprise, a force which acknowledges that individuals working together can change the collectivities of which they are a part and compel them to be more responsive to human needs and aspirations. (Etzioni, 1988) The organizations of a community are parts of its collectivities; whether compelled by its members or self-determined, organizations that adopt the communitarian ethic are expressing an allegiance to values and ethics beyond, but not antithetical to, economic gain.

Some social awareness of the moral rightness of loving one's neighbor exists as a religious principle and as both a modern and ancient tradition of natural law in most societies, but it has generally been ignored as a conscious consideration in modern decisionmaking. However, the possibilities of this principle as a means of injecting an ethic of care into organization theory are profound, as evidenced by the impact of the Confucian adaptation on the Asian familial orientation of doing business.

Communitarian organization theory appears to be particularly appropriate for the conditions of an interdependent world. Organization theory post-1990 is necessarily social theory; issues of sovereignty, mutuality, interdependence, fairness, values, and unity have become as germane to organizations as to sovereign states. Indeed, the declining power of the nation-states as protectors and defenders of conflicting political ideologies encourages a reconsideration of moral responsibility, since the communitarian ethic is predicated on the idea that "If communities are to function well, most members most of the time must discharge their responsibilities because they are committed to do so, not because they fear lawsuits, penalties, or jails." (Etzioni, 1993, 266)

Kymlicka tells us that this sort of mutual interdependence is the foundation of a broad conceptualization of citizenship which does not depend on the nation-state, but rather upon the free association of individuals. (Kymlicka, 220-221) He strengthens this link between the communitarian ethic, Rawls' liberalism, and the non-essentiality of nation-states in associations, citing Rawls' claim that "good ways of life will in fact sustain themselves in the cultural marketplace without state assistance, because in conditions of freedom, people are able to recognize the worth of good ways of life, and will support them." (Kymlicka, 217, citing Rawls 1971)

Global economic enterprise demands stability as much as Augustine's earthly city demanded peace. But, unlike the Augustinian and Hobbesian solution of a powerful, unitary state to provide the peace necessary for self-interest to flourish, stability in the post-1990 global society is an illusion. The elite economic institutions who are reaping the profits of a generally politically-compatible international order may also find that they are vested with the duty and responsibility to sustain it.

But Plato's admonitions are pertinent. Plato maintained that the relationship between community and the *polis* reflect a clear expectation that personal and civic virtue may not be detached from one another. At the end of Book 9 of the *Republic*, in the dialogue with Glaucon, Plato articulates the view that justice in the *polis* demands that man conquer the inner monsters of his greed:

> Then how would a man profit if he received gold and silver on the condition that he was to enslave the noblest part of him to the worst? Who can imagine that a man who sold his son or daughter into slavery for money, especially if he sold them into the hands of fierce and evil men, would be the gainer, however large might be the sum which he received. (Plato, 1952 ed., 427)

A recognition of community and the social space in which traditional values are defended, not diminished, relieves the pressure to conform in order to cooperate in the joint global venture. (Novick, 1995) In so doing, it also removes much of the neo-nationalist hunger for recognition and acceptance. Survival of diverse societies is predicated on an understanding of the historical ties and traditions, the loyalties, mutualities and character of communities, not states, which cannot be defined exclusively in individualist or contractual terms. (Elshtain, 1995, 107-109) Without a just consideration of the importance of these characteristics of community, neonationalism will rend asunder global security and strip the international order of its opportunity for creating mutual justice and reciprocal support.

There is somewhat of an analogy between the individualistic fervor which divides one person from another, and the neonationalistic zeal which separates families of society from their neighbors. An assumption of the communitarian ethic relieves both these pernicious

The Communitarian Paradigm

predicaments. An infatuation with a misconstrued neonationalist/individualist ethic should not be allowed to subvert the chances for progress and stability inherent in adopting a communitarian ethic within and among the interdependent communities into which the populations of the world have sundered.

The communitarian ethic allows organizations the freedom to explore possibilities and consider options as a full-fledged member of a community, rather than as an outsider. This distinction is the wellspring of communitarian theory; its implications for organization theory lie in its acceptability as appropriate ethical input to a nascent consensus that productivity and earnings in an interdependent global marketplace are subjected to the imperatives of a complex set of social considerations.

The Internal and External Communities

There is a good deal of evidence that numbers of American and transnational corporations are embracing organizational styles and philosophies that strengthen, rather than dilute the personal and collective conscience, opting to introduce organizational notions of reciprocity and mutuality among individuals and communities. Numbers of organizations are finding that creating a corporate culture based on collaboration, cooperation, and consensus is far preferable to models which deny the integrity of the parts of the whole. Neither Japanese, American, or Theory Z organizational clones, many of these organizations illustrate features of a communitarian enterprise theory, a theory for organizations which leads a corporate culture to discover its broader social and moral responsibilities. As the organization thus discovers and acquiesces to its greater social role, it attempts to fulfill its economic role with a minimum of rancor, hostility, and enmity.

There is much similarity between the communitarian framework presented herein and the internal management styles of corporations who have abandoned the traditional American mass production model for participatory and empowering management strategies in which the worker defines the task, rather than vice versa. There is a real affinity to the communitarian ethic in the team-based approach to organizing where quality is the ultimate product and credit and recognition is shared, rather than stipulated to one individual. Communitarian enterprise organizations enhance personal responsibility, accountability, and pride of accomplishment, which is supported by management theory which promotes employee "ownership" of their tasks. By so doing, there is a validation of the self-worth of the employee, which builds both personal character and enlarges individualism, much in the manner of the arguments of Durkheim, Spragens, and Etzioni. Nonhierarchical management schemes may also diminish hierarchy in the larger society, fulfilling the communitarian ideal of nested and reciprocal communities. Innovative organization plans which match employees with their work, allowing at-home networking, flex-time, and substitutability are essentially a communitarian expression of the cooperative spirit which values the contributions of all the members of a community.

Robert Waterman reminds us that corporate success is related to organizational arrangements: "What makes the best firms the best cannot be attributed to such things as technology, a bright idea, a masterly strategy, the use of a tool, or the slavish following of guidelines . . . what makes top performing companies different . . . is their organizational arrangements." (Waterman, 17) His survey of a number of large, well-known firms, which are enjoying continued conspicuous success from the standpoint of productivity and earnings, reveals the organizational tools which appear to be most successful from both the economic and social standpoints. These are firms with strong cultures, well-defined perceptions of themselves, and acute sensitivities to the ethical and social contexts of economic organizations. (Waterman, 15-25)

Proctor & Gamble began tinkering with organizational forms in the 1960s, largely as a result of a leadership belief in employee self-direction. Troubled by a lack of communication between managers and workers, and motivated by the conviction that individuals have a desire to shape their own world, David Swanson, (who was to spend thirty-seven years at P&G) designed his own version of a Theory Y Plant, after the model of Douglas McGregor's treatise *The Human Side of Enterprise*, published in 1960. Convinced that the assumption of the mediocrity of the masses was erroneous and unsuitable as a basis for plant management, Swanson designed an open system plant where communications would flow freely in all directions. His theory required a different view of human beings, and required changes in the attitudes of both managers and workers. But most of all, it demanded a faith in the ability of workers to rise to responsibility and commitment. (Waterman, 29-39)

The first P&G Theory Y plant was located in Augusta, Georgia, in 1961. It was an egalitarian experiment in organization arrangements, with few tangible barriers and no symbols of rank. Designed around self-disciplining and self-sustaining flexible teams, the P&G experiment proved immensely successful. By the mid-1960s the productivity at the Augusta plant was about 30 per cent better than at any other P&G plant. Attempts to transplant their success met with difficulties, however, in older plants with older attitudes and entrenched hierarchical habits. But over time, the removal of traditional management structures, the empowerment of workers, and the commitment to systemic change seem to have worked for Proctor & Gamble. The organization created an atmosphere of trust, backed it up with a vision statement, and practiced what they preached. According to Waterman, the P&G system version of a self-managing system has been successful in increasing productivity and earnings while allowing workers the control they need to feel and be their personal best. (Waterman, 39-46)

At Federal Express the systems infrastructure has the effect of putting its own people in charge of the company. The corporate philosophy is simple: People—Service—Profits. And the workforce understands the concept well. With a strong commitment to quality, and constant effort to provide employees with flexibility and the information they need to do their work, Federal Express serves as an example of a goal-oriented corporate culture which encourages employees to feel good about themselves, their job, and the place where they work. According to Waterman, the pressure of strict delivery standards and strong competition is relieved by the freedom and trust inherent in the feedback systems available to all employees. Waterman believes that by continuing to put people first and allowing their employees the autonomy to decide how to get their jobs done, Federal Express has found a certain simplicity beyond the complexity of automated equipment and control systems, high-volume service requirements, and systems technology that regulate and dominate the highly competitive delivery industry. (Waterman, 87-110)

At AES the presumption since inception has been that values are more important than strategy; when confronted with trade-offs between values and profits, AES management has consistently contended that their company will always favor values. In a clearly communitarian posture, AES leadership has sought to create a "noble" culture with written value statements on fairness, integrity, and social responsibility.

This conspicuously-committed organization has not suffered financially; in fact, caring more about the kind of company they have rather than the bottom line has enhanced both; in 1994 the AES stockmarket value of $1.5 billion provided a return to shareholders that rivaled even the best high-tech venture-capital arrangements. (Waterman, 111) AES is a prototype of the socially-responsible corporate model; as a model of the communitarian enterprise, they promote corporate values which have both intellectual and emotional appeal. Organized into family-type work groups, with one-half of the yearly salary increase and bonus dependent on how well the employee upholds AES values, the corporation seems to thrive on its value-based infrastructure. "There is no understanding AES without understanding its culture—in other words, the shared values that give its people a sense of purpose." (Waterman, 112) In an industry not known for its sense of social responsibility, AES has a standard policy of attempting to offset the damage from its coal-fired plants by planting enough trees to soak up the carbon dioxide produced. Roger Naill, one of its founders, considers the 52 million trees planted by AES as simply an expression of the company's sense of responsibility. ("Companies find . . . , 1996, 4B; Waterman, 111-136)

Levi Strauss & Company serves as an example of a corporate tiger that changed its stripes. In a sort of "industrial epiphany," Levi turned its back on the mass production model to embrace a communitarian-type enterprise organizational culture based on ethics, diversity, trust, recognition, responsibility, belief, and commitment.This company answered in the affirmative the question of whether or not a company can "make life more meaningful and exciting for down-the-line people who have spent their whole lives stitching, sewing, packing, and selling jeans?" (Waterman, 137)

The Levi Aspiration Statement reveals the communitarian paradigm:

> We all want a Company that our people are proud of and committed to, where all employees have an opportunity to contribute, learn, grow, and advance based on merit, not politics or background. We want our people to feel respected, treated fairly, listened to, and involved. Above all, we want satisfaction from accomplishments and friendships, balanced personal and professional lives, and to have fun in our endeavors. (Waterman, 141)

With an average growth rate from 1982 to 1992 of fifty percent, there is little doubt that Levi's culture has been successful on both the economic and social fronts. With a credo that reminds the employee that "You don't work *for* Levi's, you work for yourselves; you just happen to work *at* Levi's," (Waterman, 142) the company dismantles the individualist/collectivist dualism. In extending its statement of corporate values to its overseas operations, Levi accepts the communitarian responsibility to cultural diversity. But its most direct affiliation with the paradigm is its statement of "Ethical Principles," a document based on the straightforward idea that its employees should "strive to live up to six principles: honesty, fairness, respect for others, compassion, promise keeping, and integrity." (Waterman, 162) Asserting that ethical principles trump business and profit considerations, Levi joins AES in an institutional expression of a communitarian ethic.

Perhaps one of the best examples of the communitarian enterprise is the oft-reported case of Ben and Jerry's Ice Cream, whose chairman Jerry Greenfield and Ben Cohen have been leaders in the corporate responsibility movement. But they do not see their policy of giving away 7.5 percent of the company's pretax profits as the full measure of the concern. "The major benefit that Ben and Jerry's provides for the community is not based on contributions and donations. It's based on factoring in the concern for the community on the basis of our day-to-day activities." ("Companies find . . . . , 4D, quoting Ben Cohen) Cohen and Greenfield are very vocal supporters of the notion that social concerns are a rightful responsibility of businesses. They clearly acknowledge the point we have made about the power of corporations in the lives of workers, as well as in the larger society; but their position is all the more significant because their financial success has not been diminished by their communitarian philosophy. Granted, they operate out of the state of Vermont, a very community-oriented region of the country famous for its sense of solidarity, honesty, and social uprightness. (Novick, 1995) But their philosophy is woven into the worldwide operations of Ben and Jerry's Homemade Inc. Of over 130 ice cream scoop shops, ten are run and owned by nonprofit groups that use their revenues as a means of raising funds; when the company expanded into Belgium and Luxembourg, Human Rights Watch became a fifteen percent owner of the franchises. ("Companies find . . . , 4D) According to Cohen, "I think businesses are more receptive to the message of responsibility . . . They are realizing now that their customers are demanding that businesses use their power to help the community as opposed to exploiting the community." (Frandsen, 1996, 5B)

BUSINESS ETHICS

The communitarian enterprise is an idealized model of ethical business practices. As the significance of a code of ethics for business has grown over the last eighty years, so has the recognition of its worth. "Such codes encourage managers to do more than just follow the letter of the law; they demand that entire companies should be open, trustworthy and green. Altruism, say the ethicists, is good business." ("The uncommon good," 1995, 55)

But syndicated columnist Edwin Yoder, assuming the role of cynical curmudgeon, claims that American firms have gone too far along the profit-maximization path to change their corporate spots:

> There was a time when corporations were identified with the personal ethics of those who owned and ran them—Ford, Vanderbilt, Carnegie, et al. It might have made sense then to personalize such issues as who could be laid off in good conscience, and why. But by the time I studied the dismal science, the "managerial revolution," as James Burnham called it, had occurred and the all powerful old pirates of the boardroom had vanished. Hired professional managers had replaced them; and their managerial strategies were—and were meant to be—as unsentimental as those of an engineer building a bridge or a dam. (Yoder, 1996, 18A)

But Yoder may well be mistaken. Research reveals numerous examples which dispel the image of the cold-hearted capitalist. Deal and Kennedy discovered that corporations with strong ethical values are generally highly successful; they link this strength frequently to the presence of those they label visionary heroes who knew without being told that ethical and caring behavior was a given. Of course, there are successful tyrants who follow no corporate or personal conscience. But to be remembered for one's decency and fairness is to become a part of the roll call of the giants of American industry, whose reputations are enviable, such as Tom Watson and IBM; Will Durant and General Motors; Helena Rubenstein; Mary Kay Ash; Dave Packard and Hewlett-Packard; and Jim Treybig and Tandem. (Deal and Kennedy,

38) Deal and Kennedy tell the story of Charles Steinmetz, who was responsible for dozens of inventions used by General Electric and other companies, but whose humanity exceeded his professional talents:

> Whenever young engineers joined GE, Steinmetz would invite them home for the weekend in order to learn, sincerely and without political intent, what kind of people they were. Once he adopted one of GE's leading engineers as his own son—and the man's whole family. They all moved into Steinmetz's house and lived with him for twenty years. (Deal and Kennedy, 45)

The public perception of issues of corporate responsibility and business ethics has generally been in terms of either-or: "At times, Americans have celebrated corporations as benevolent agents of growth and prosperity; at other moments, they've viewed corporate managers as ruthless profit-maximizers, greedily sacking workers to appease the gods of Wall Street." (Chandler, 1996, 16) But this duality may be fallacious: Caring about the interests of the larger society does not necessarily lower profits. According to Laura D'Andrea Tyson, "There tends to be this oversimplified notion that offering workers a good health plan or skills training always hurts the bottom line . . . But a lot of companies don't see it that way. They think these things are in their interest." (Chandler, 16 citing Tyson) The interests between the larger needs of the society and the interests of business are mutual; in fact, communitarians would propose that the interests between the business and the larger society must be matched if either one is to be sustainable.

Corporate Citizenship.

As the citizen is expected to fulfill her responsibilities to her society, so the corporate citizen is expected to render service as a corporate citizen. This is a concept almost as old as American economic enterprise itself. While the paternalistic "company towns" are a thing of the past, they were the outgrowth of an age where the life of a community was largely determined by the health, and wealth, of its industry. Of course, with modernity, the expression of corporate citizenship has changed, but it is still based on the notion that the enterprise will give something back to the larger community, or will simply be a good neighbor. And evidence that this quality still exists is abundant. Rhino Records offers its employees the opportunity to earn time off in exchange for community service; the particular type of service is up to the employee, but it must be non-profit, non-political, and non-partisan. Reebok sponsors an annual volunteer fair, which is designed to inform its employees of volunteer opportunities in their locations. Franchisees of The Body Shop are also encouraged to set up employee volunteer programs in the local community, and Honeywell offers grants of between one and five hundred dollars to support community volunteer involvement by its employees, retirees, and their families. (Makower, 234-236)

There is as great a variety of corporate community effort as there is variety of organizations. Loews Hotels' Good Neighbor program lends all sorts of support to the communities where Loews owns and manages hotels, everything from donating excess food to local food banks, to providing space and instructors for literacy classes. The Longfellow Clubs, a $4.5 million health and recreation company in Massachusetts, donates the use of facilities to special needs children; Just Desserts, the San Francisco-based bakery, persuaded thirty-five other businesses to join it in adopting an elementary school in a low-income area. In a particularly innovative plan, Gardeners' Supply, a $20 million mail order company out of Burlington, Vermont, collects and composts grass clippings and leaves for residents of the Burlington area at no charge. The project has become so successful over the years that the company now collects up to 4,000 tons a year, then making the compost available to gardeners. Hanna Andersson, a children's clothing mail order service based in Portland, Oregon, asks its customers to recycle its products by donating them back to the company when they are outgrown. The company then donates the goods, called "Hannadowns," to local shelters and children's organizations. Since 1984, the company has donated more than 100,000 garments for needy children. (Makower, 236-238)

Most business members of a community are anxious to make a contribution, and for the most part, contributions reflect the corporate culture and leadership. Local symphonies and art museums often benefit from corporate leadership that has a specific interest in the arts. Good corporate citizens would rather donate out-dated equipment than trash it, which works to the benefit of, perhaps, municipal offices whose tight budgets prohibit the acquisition of the furniture and equipment they need. Donations and participation in local events, sponsorship of athletic teams, entering into community blood drives, and funding activities for an endless variety of charities, diseases, and disasters take large chunks out of corporate budgets. But they are not without tangible results.

Not unlike communitarians, Michael Novak connects the argument for corporate citizenship to the success of self-government:

> And this project of self-government requires an active private sector as an alternative to the state. The business firm therefore has a responsibility to become a leader in civil society. To this end, it should contribute to the good fortune of other mediating structures in the private sector, whether in areas such as education and the arts, healthful activities for youth, the environment, care for the elderly, new initiatives to meet the needs of the homeless and the poor, and other such activities . . . it does well to nurture the networks of civil society and to strengthen those of its allies who provide an alternative to government. (Novak, 150)

Attention to corporate responsibility, or that "ill-defined but good intention embraced by corporations that believe their responsibility extends beyond the bottom line to employees and the community," appears to be changing the way many corporations do business. The association of Businesses for Social Responsibility boasts more than eight hundred member companies, and two of America's Big Six accounting firms have created offices to help corporations create effective business ethics programs and socially responsible practices. (Frandsen, 5B)

Whether the behavior of firms who choose to exercise a social conscience in their corporate behavior are acting out the declaration of a philosophical communitarianism or an expression of some variant of corporate altruism or enlightened leadership is moot; the benefits which accrue to the communitarian enterprise do not appear to diminish corporate profits. While it is admittedly analytically difficult to discover a causal relationship between acts reflecting corporate social responsibility and profitability, nevertheless, some researchers have attempted to do so. Joel Makower cites a variety of research studies intended to test the hypothesis that "strong social performance is associated with strong financial performance.

The Erfle-Fratantuono study of 1992 compared companies' ratings in *Shopping for a Better World*, a publication of the Council on Economic Priorities, a New York-based research group which has compiled ratings of companies revealed through a set of criteria to be socially responsible. These companies are rated for social responsibility by CEP based on thousands of consumer products reports, manufacturers' records, media reports, questionnaires, and other sources such as the Center for Science in the Public Interest, labor unions, and outside advisers. While the rating system may be imperfect, it includes a considerable variety of social issues including environmental performance, advance of women, promotion of minorities, charitable contributions, community outreach programs, research conducted on animals, military sector involvement, nuclear power involvement, and disclosure of information. Economists Erfle and Fratantuono compared the companies' ratings with their bottom line results, assuming that their findings would demonstrate, and perhaps measure, the financial costs to companies highly rated for social performance.

But the study revealed, instead of significant costs, that at worst, socially responsible behavior had no financial impact, and in some cases had a strong financial payoff. Compared to the bottom-ranked companies, this 1992 study found that the top-rated companies had:

16.7 percent higher operating income growth
13.3 percent higher sales-to-assets ratio
9.3 percent higher sales growth
4.5 percent higher return on equity
4.4 percent higher earnings-to-assets ratio
3.9 percent higher return on investment
2.2 percent higher return on assets
1.9 percent higher asset growth

The Erfle and Fratantuono study revealed a particularly positive relationship among five dimensions of social performance: environmental performance; promotion of women; promotion of minorities; charitable contributions; and community outreach programs. (Makower, 70-71, citing Erfle-Fratantuono, 1992)

Makower also cites a number of other research efforts by academics in recent years to discover whether or not there is a link between social performance and corporate performance. "And although the evidence to date is mixed, there is some compelling evidence that an empirical relationship exists." (Makower, 72) Citing a compilation of reports from Levi Strauss & Company (who we have already

The Communitarian Paradigm

identified as committed to socially responsible behavior and the development of a strong corporate culture), Makower includes:

> A 1988 study at the University of Massachusetts which linked financial performance to *Fortune* magazine's ratings of corporate reputations, a compilation of corporations gathered from surveys of 8,000 executives. The Massachusetts study found that firms low in social responsibility had lower returns on assets and stock market return than those rated highly in social responsibility.
>
> A 1993 Wright State University study based on questionnaires submitted to corporate managers asking them to rate the perceived effect of nine socially responsible issues on their organization's market share. Of the nine, actions related to environmental pollution, corporate philanthropy, and disclosure of social information were perceived to have the greatest effect.
>
> A 1993 Rutgers study which examined the relationships between workplace practices, such as promotion and incentive systems, grievance procedures, and labor-management participation, with financial performance of 700 publicly held firms. Using an index of "best practice" prevalence, the study concluded that 25 percent of the firms scoring highest on the index also performed substantially higher on key financial performance measure than lower-rated companies—firms in the top 25 percent had an 11 percent gross rate of return on capital, which was more than twice as high as the remaining firms.
>
> A 1994 Florida International University study found a significant positive relationship between social responsibility, growth in sales, return on assets, asset age, and was significantly related to free cash flow and debt to equity over the long term.
>
> A 1994 study by the Gordon Group of Waban, Massachusetts found that companies with a broad reputation for good workplace practices overwhelmingly had higher price-to-book valuation ratios than their industry peers; these researchers also concluded that "a large portion of companies with the worst reputations on workplace issues are either taken over or experience bankruptcy.(Makower, 72-73)

Considering the issue of social responsibility from another angle, Walker Research, a business unit of Indianapolis-based Walker Group, a research firm that specializes in measuring the impact of social responsibility, conducted interviews with 1,037 households to determine if socially-responsible behavior is a factor to consumers and investors. This study found:

> 26 percent of potential investors say social responsibility and good corporate citizenship are extremely important to their investment decisions.
>
> 39 percent of current or previous investors say they always or frequently check on business practices and values before investing. 21 percent say they always do.
>
> 92 percent of consumers are much less or somewhat less likely to buy from a company that is not socially responsible and not a good corporate citizen; 70 percent say they will not buy from this type of company even if the product or service price is substantially discounted.
>
> 88 percent of the public is much or somewhat more likely to buy from a company that is socially responsible and a good corporate citizen, all other things being equal.
>
> 13 percent say they always or frequently seek information about a company's practices or ethics before purchasing.
>
> 35 percent say they always or frequently avoid a product or service from a company perceived to be unethical.

Walker Research concluded: "The study shows that not only does being socially responsible pay off today, but also that the public's interest in corporate reputation and social responsibility is growing and will be even more important in the future." (Cited in Makower, 74-75)

Philosopher Tom Morris makes a powerful argument for business ethics in his 1997 book *If Aristotle Ran General Motors*:

> Too often in business today people tend to take a negative and legalistic approach to ethics as fundamentally no more than a matter

The Communitarian Paradigm

of mere compliance, as if the main point of ethics or morality were just staying out of trouble, legally and otherwise. This gets the focus all wrong. Ethics is not first and foremost about staying out of trouble. It's not primarily about avoiding problems at all. Ethics is mainly about creating strength, in an individual person, a family, a community, business relationships, and life. (Morris, 1997, 120)

Is there a subjectivity to economic choices that supplants the market rational theory of choice? Is an insistence on ethical behavior a valid criterion to impose on corporations at all? I believe there is little doubt that some members of the buying/investing public are concerned about corporate ethics; they express their preferences when they refuse to buy sneakers produced by child labor; they try to find compensatory means of preserving the rainforest; they boycott companies that violate their religious principles; they pay more for products whose use and production are environmentally sound; they follow their convictions in many economic decisions. Are there investors who shy away from Walmart stock because the stores tend to displace local retailers and ravage downtown shopping districts?

Tom Morris' commentary on social harmony is expressive of the ethic of working in communities:

Social harmony is not only a state of the absence of conflict but one of positive, vibrant consonance and interpersonal strength, a relationship within which individuals can attain the development of their highest gifts and enjoy the fullness of life together. This is the concern of ethics. (Morris, 119)

Toward More Collaborative Corporate Strategies

Moran, Harris, and Stripp argue that corporate leaders are leaders of cultural renewal:

We are in passage from a work culture that conditioned most of us when the Industrial Revolution recast our physical world and reality through mechanization, quantification, and consolidation. We are in transit to a Knowledge Society, dominated by high technology and information processing, a culture marked by mediation ... by simulation and virtual reality ... and by circularity. In these circumstances, between epochs, everything we do is cross-cultural and dynamic. (Moran, Harris, and Stripp, 10-11)

These authors suggest a seven-point syndrome based on communication, autonomy and participation, innovation, enhancement of the quality of life, high standards of excellence, cross-functional organizational style, and advanced technology to transform the industrial mind-set and environment into a "high performing, superindustrial work environment." (Moran, Harris, and Stripp, 12)

Peter Lorange claims that the increase of cooperative ventures demand new strategic thinking in human resource management techniques based on a value-added chain of synergistic factors "for a combined output greater than the sum of the outputs of each participating partner." (Lorange, 1993, 227-228) There is no more communitarian notion than that which assumes that the sum of the parts is greater than any of the parts alone. But Bennett Harrison is not so sure that the new "networked" alliances in the global market will fulfill that spirit. Critical of the emerging paradigm of flexible specialization and networked production characterized by concentration without centralization, and dominated by big corporations and their partners, but nevertheless convinced that the thesis of alliance capitalism is the economic vanguard of the future, Harrison questions both the viability and prudence of the consequences of the social arrangements that will arise from such economic partnering. (B. Harrison, 1994) Perhaps Harrison has neglected to notice the potential for mutuality and cooperation imposed by these new organizational forms, as well as the expectations for the assumption of responsibilities and accountability. As companies must be more competitive, so must the worker. The work force, which Harrison depicts as rather passive, reactive, and victimized can become their own masters in the collaborative workplace. Enlightened leadership cannot achieve a communitarian enterprise on its own; it must be assured its work force is both willing and capable of becoming vigorous teammates. Flexible specialization has opportunities for those members of the work force who are willing to upgrade their skills, accept transfers, and become a part of a dedicated, committed team. Uneducated, lazy, self-centered, and uncooperative workers will never equal the personal or social accomplishments of trained, energetic, interested, caring, self-starters who perceive of themselves as worthy members of a team with both rights and responsibilities.

The Communitarian Paradigm

There is an analogy to be drawn between fruitful relationships between workers and their employers and between firms and their partners. Both relationships demand collaboration rather than domination; dependability as well as responsibility; honesty rather than duplicity; patience in the face of confounding change and uncertainty; and an optimistic view of the future rather than nostalgia for a past that had its own flaws and inequities.

Affiliation can also be a strong source of community strength in localized arrangements. Piore and Sabel argue that the collaborative effort of small firms is fundamental to the reclamation of economic and social vitality in modern capitalist countries. Their conceptualization of flexible specialization is clearly a communitarian approach to cooperative industrial organization. It is an industrial replica of nested communities, which rests on cohesion among industrial districts, federated enterprises, and the solar-system model of orbiting suppliers and the workshop factory. The authors validate a number of communitarian principles: the need for community ties to nurture solidarity and temper competition; the recognition of alienation which occurs when one is excluded from one's community; the need for a sense of common, quasi-familial identity; the sense of collaboration, rather than subordination in relationships; the importance of neighborliness and social sensitivity; the establishment of community norms as a standard of behavior. (Piore and Sabel, 1984)

Piore and Sabel are advocates of the philosophy of small-firm-led economic growth. Contrary to the gargantuan image of Harrison's networked affiliations, the Piore and Sabel position is that real economic growth and social progress has always been situated in the vitality of craft economies, and can remain so, under what I would describe as communitarian conditions. (Piore and Sabel, 4-35) Arguing that the American corporate model and American-style mass production have generated economic crisis in advanced capitalist countries, Piore and Sabel examine the histories of mass and craft production and the vagaries of political and social struggles that have expedited the mass production paradigm. They conclude that if change is to come, revitalizing and re-energizing economic growth and complementary fairness to labor, there must be comprehensive restructuring of production and organization styles away from mass production technologies toward a craft method of production reminiscent of nineteenth century British and American systems. (Piore and Sabel, 1984)

There is evidence to support the notion of small-firm led economic growth, but whether these are in reality the distinct firms cited by Piore and Sabel or the satellites in Harrison's treatise, the same communitarian ethic applies. The American tradition of mom-and-pop stores and individual entrepreneurship may well still obtain—certainly the mayor of Tucson believes so, making the point in an address in Tucson, Arizona, in March 1996 that more than eighty percent of Tucson's economic growth was in firms of less than one hundred employees. But the larger point is that affiliations of small firms are an exercise of the communitarian spirit and increase the viability and vitality of the member firms.

In a business report in June, 1996, *The Macon Telegraph* (Georgia) featured a report on Forsyth Landing, a "female-dominated shopping center [which] enjoys a spirit of community, merchants say." (Johnson, 1996, 1) At the time of its development in 1985, the center's main concern was to simply fill rental space, but nine years later, Forsyth Landing is indeed a distinct image of a modern retail district with a strong communitarian orientation with a gendered variation—more than half of the stores, ten out of seventeen, are owned by women.

> The women not only share the distinction of being successful business owners, but also share their expertise and experiences with each other. A spirit of community exists within the shopping center. They look out for each, [sic] share information with each other and pass along customers to the other stores. (Johnson, 1)

According to the report, the owner-tenants "want . . . everyone to be successful . . . ." This center makes several communitarian statements: It functions like a family, where owners and employees look out for each other; the tenants buy from each other, and encourage their customers and clients to do likewise; there is a friendly atmosphere which is both supportive and protective; two of the stores actually open to each other, where customers can walk directly from one store into another; and they are kindly and sympathetic counselors and advisors to one another. The stores also try to schedule special events together, which often leads to friendships between one store's customers and those of another that would not otherwise exist. (Johnson, 1, 8)

Doubtless Forsyth Landing has its equals in the hundreds of thousands; but it is as clear an example of the force of the communitarian ethic as Piore and Sabel's industrial districts, Mexico's *maquilladores*, Italy's innovative textile cottage industry, the Silicon Valley, Austin, Texas, and Durham, North Carolina, models of concentrated high-technology firms. (Piore and Sabel, 1984) B. Harrison praises the emerging affiliations in Europe and the protective covenants of the Japanese *keiretsu* as examples of mitigating forces to dispel the dark shadows of networked production. Enabled by laws and customs in Europe and Japan which discourage hostile takeovers, and government policies which facilitate rather than frustrate joint ventures, the development of closer relations among firms, and beneficial financial arrangements which encourage vestment and research and development, European and Japanese networks bear little of the taint of collusion and monopoly as such practices would suffer in the United States. Such an environment has sanctioned numbers of innovative arrangements, particularly cross-border alliances among countries of the European Union which allow them to bypass the serial, atomistic calculus so embedded in American management practices. (B. Harrison, 187) Purposeful alliances which benefit all the members of the alliance, rather than domineering core-ring arrangements where the secondary firm is placed in competition with like firms, and entirely at the mercy of the profit expectations of the core firm create diametrically opposed corporate environments. Under the former, there is a communitarian, cooperative spirit that predicates success of the whole on the success of each; under the latter, the secondary firm has "no room to wiggle." But legal and political restrictions largely prevent American companies from enjoying the full fruits of strategic alliances, public-private cooperatives, collaborative manufacturing with suppliers, and other forms of inter-organizational networking. These restrictions may limit the ability of American firms to respond creatively to the expectations of high returns on investment and increasing market competition. (B. Harrison, 190)

HUMAN CAPITALISM: A NEW LOOK

Ozaki's thoughts on the development of human capital have a communitarian implication. Also incorporated into the Clinton administration's "New Enterprise Economics," the development of persons as both workers and citizens is akin to the communitarian ideal of strengthening moral and civic virtue. Many American corporations, as Bennett Harrison notes, have been derelict in their duty to develop, rather than exploit their workers. One of Harrison's most serious charges against the response of American companies to the changing economic landscape has been that they have taken the "low road to profitability," built on a foundation of cheap labor, emphasizing cost reduction strategies to maximize profits in the short term. Harrison argues that American companies would rather compete by cutting wages than by increasing productivity through the positive development of its work force and its partner organizations by means of technology, training, and technical assistance. (B. Harrison, 213)

While much of what Harrison has to say is cogent, it is apparent that ways can be devised to manage both large and small companies where profits are enhanced with less negative repercussions to the work force. There is also strong evidence of numbers of highly successful American companies that are pursuing what Harrison would call "the high road" to profitability. What Harrison is describing is clearly a breakdown in the cooperation and mutuality expected in the organizational community.

We are given certain circumstances—dealt certain cards, if you will—of global competition, thriving technological development, and eased political tensions that obviously bode both well and ill for the human side of economic progress. While it is likely, as Harrison argues, that big firms are quite likely to gobble up small firms, or to co-opt them. But this process is neither unique nor new; many small business owners have made their millions by selling out what they have achieved over a lifetime of the risk-taking and hard work of entrepreneurship. Others, perhaps not as financially stable, have opted for the security of arrangements with large firms that can guarantee them markets and resources; these are common occurrences. "Playing in the big leagues" has a price, but it also has a profit; these dualities drive the inquiry into corporate communities. It is more ethically sound to take the high road to productivity; the communitarian ethic mandates it. But the reality is that the partner firms of the world's biggest companies are oftentimes caught in a squeeze between their sense of ethics and the demands of their larger partners, and their own stockholders, who expect a hefty return on their investment. Often unfamiliar with either the product or service provided by the firms in which they have invested, many stockholders are not always concerned as to how profit is achieved—hence the "low road" syndrome; but they are unequivocally concerned when a contract is lost. Many board members are also uninformed and aloof, yet powerful, directors of their vested industry. This is a good example of what Harrison refers to as the "low level equilibrium trap," which he indicates is unlikely to change unless ". . . a sufficiently large number of companies make the shift to a high-road strategy together . . . ." (B. Harrison, 181)

While other firms are taking different routes to true profits, or what Harrison calls the "high road to productivity," the larger communitarian question would be how to bring more workers into full partnership in the businesses of which they are a part. Many companies, both large and small, are bringing employees into full partnership through shared ownership. The National Center for Employee Ownership keeps watch over numbers of plans to involve employees in ownership, not just management, as is accomplished through some of the other strategies discovered at P&G, Levi Strauss, and Federal Express.

Ownership plans, information sharing, and schemes to involve workers in the state of the overall financial well being are specific ways in which companies can build a strong communitarian culture. At Foldcraft Company, a manufacturer of restaurant and cafeteria seating, all 230 employees—who are referred to as members—take part in the monthly business meeting in an effort to help workers know and understand the dollars and cents involved in their own enterprise. Management designs the meetings as games, complete with vice presidents in referee stripes and carrying whistles. Employees compete with one another in a game called "Pass or Play," with victory, and monetary reward, going to the player who can answer questions on obscure, yet significant issues such as the company's workers' compensation modification ratio. Strategies such as these build human capital, as they build trust and reinforce mutuality. According to Doug Kruse, a Rutgers University economist who studies employee participation, "With businesses worried about a shortage of highly skilled workers in the next 10 years, they'll be trying to pay more attention to current employees. Sharing business information is one of the strategies they'll use." (Mitchell, 1996, 6A)

The Economist makes the point that sharing profits with workers is a significant means of motivating and integrating employees into the necessity of increasing productivity and earnings. Plans which allow workers to share in the financial success of the American firms have grown rapidly in the last ten years. According to the OECD Employment Outlook of July, 1995, there are substantial benefits to this practice:

Profit sharing may give workers an incentive to work harder. It may encourage co-operation, because it helps employees to identify more closely with the fortunes of the firm. It may also produce a more skilled workforce by increasing loyalty, and so reducing labour turnover . . . there is also evidence that firms which share profits tend to get rid of fewer jobs in economic downturns." ("True profits, 1995, 68)

Naisbitt and Aburdene claim that employee ownership is the "ultimate in employee capitalism." (Naisbitt and Aburdene, 58) They cite a number of examples of this trend which reach back into the 1980s:

Weirton Steel of Weirton, West Virginia became the nation's largest employee-owned company in early 1984. It turned profitable almost immediately, earning $9.7 million the first quarter and $60 million in 1984, which was the first profit since 1981.

Linnton Plywood Association, Portland, Oregon, a $20 million a year plywood manufacturer is a worker owned cooperative. Workers earn more than $50,000 per year—much more than people at larger mills such as Weyerhaeuser. But they must invest a substantial amount to buy and share and join the collective, a figure of $75,000 in 1985.

Publix Super Markets, Florida's largest retail food chain, is wholly owned by its employees. Its profit per dollar of sales is twice that of Safeway, which has the country's biggest sales figures.

Colorado's Fred Schmid Appliance & TV Company, with fifteen stores and $62 million in annual sales, transferred 100 percent of stock ownership to employees in 1984 rather than sell the company to outsiders for nearly $10 million.

(Naisbitt and Aburdene, 58-59)

Linnton Plywood is patterned after a worker-owned cooperative model developed in Spain; according to Naisbitt and Aburdene, this model is the more radical type of the employee-owned firm in the United States. In the mid-1980s they found some two hundred worker-owned American cooperatives, most with fewer than fifty employee-owners. (Naisbitt and Aburdene, 58)

Louis and Patricia Kelso's investigation of employee stock ownership plans (ESOP) makes some important conclusions about the business and social logic of employee shareholding. In their opinion, "The ESOP utilizes the same business logic that capital-owning families have always used to acquire capital ownership for themselves; the same logic that corporate managements use in deciding to expand production." (Kelso and Kelso, 1987, 201) ESOP provides individuals two ways to participate in production and earn income in a private-property, free-market, capitalist economy, as both labor workers and capital workers. They believe that the ESOP system of providing industrial productive power to all families, rather than allowing capital ownership to remain concentrated in the approximately five percent of American families who own capital wealth, is intrinsic to the sustainability of a private property, free market, capitalist democracy, and is an important means by which to eventually relieve government of the need to offset the effects of poverty. They point out that ESOP's do not redistribute income from present shareholders to employees; to the contrary, they are a "credit mechanism that enables employees to buy stock and pay for it out of the earnings of the assets it represents, not out of their wages, salaries, or savings." (Kelso and Kelso, 201) They claim that there are important positive consequences to policies that legitimate labor work and capital work as equally legitimate ways to engage in production and earn income: (1) As a means to restore the integrity of the capitalist system; (2) To eliminate most adversarial relations between management and labor; (3) To protect private capital; (4) To eliminate the worst excesses of business cycles. Ultimately, they argue, such policies are simply within the rights of individuals to earn a good living. (Kelso and Kelso, 206-207)

There are a variety of research designs which focus on employee ownership. A 1987 survey by R. H. Bruskin Associates sought to determine the attitudes of workers at employee-owned firms and those at non-employee owned firms. Based on 1,001 completed telephone interviews, this survey found:

> 93 percent believed that workers at employee owned firms paid more attention to quality;
>
> 81 percent believed that employee-owned company workers paid more attention the financial performance of their firm;

69 percent thought workers at employee-owned firms worked harder than workers at non-employee owned firms;

57 percent of workers said they would be willing to trade their next wage increase for a share of company ownership. (*Employee Ownership Plans* . . . , 1987, 16-17.

A 1987 Report of the Bureau of National Affairs reported that according to the National Center for Employee Ownership the actual percentage of American workers in employee-owned firms was under 10 percent. (*Employee Ownership Plans* . . . , 18) But more recent publications make some important points about the growing trend of employee ownership in the United States. In a report of their two-year study published in 1991, Blasi and Kruse examined employee ownership in public companies. They claim that in 1991 there were over one thousand publicly-traded American corporations in which employees own substantial stock in the company, about 14 percent of the publicly traded corporations in the U.S. economy. But they contend that this is but the "toddler stage" of a transformation in the structure of ownership. Citing research of the Columbia Institutional Investor Project, Blasi and Kruse claim that institutional investors controlled 45-to-50 percent of the stock market in the United States, and 48 percent of the top one thousand corporations. In 1991 they predicted:

> By the year 2000, more than a quarter of the companies traded on the New York Stock Exchange, the American Stock Exchange and Over-the-Counter Market will be more than 15 percent owned by *their* employees. Most corporations will also be more than 25 percent owned by pension funds, representing large segments of the population, and larger corporations will continue to be 50 to 70 percent owned by institutional investors as a whole. (Blasi and Kruse, 1991, 3)

And they point out that employee ownership is accompanied by enormous risks in investments, longevity, contributions, and inflation. Employees can lose money if stock does poorly; or one may live longer than one's assets last; contributions are high; and inflation can reduce stock value. They also advise that the "trusteeship" notion of employee ownership is as much a part of the trend as the "rights" notion, not dramatically different from the comments of Kelso and Kelso, above:

Trusteeship ... is really ownership held in trust for employees ....
but it is an attempt to broaden the wealth-holding .... Employees
really do own the stock "in a beneficial way," and they do get money
for it in return. But anything beyond that is viewed as unrealistic.
(Blasi and Kruse, 4)

On the other hand, "rights" represents substantial change, because it is a recognition of money and influence: "Rights says that, perhaps, employees can strike a deal to be viewed as capitalists." (Blasi and Kruse, 5) They do point out, however, that trusteeship can degenerate into paternalism, and the extreme explication of rights involves the pursuit of control and the replacement of the managerial hierarchy with a worker hierarchy unless "groups in a company or organization ... find ways to cooperate rather than solve problems of dominance." (Blasi and Kruse, 5-6)

Their research revealed that the total value of employee ownership estates in public corporations in 1991 was over $99 billion, monies held by 12.5 percent of the private-sector workforce, representing 10.8 million American workers who own stock in companies where employee ownership exceeds 4 percent of total company market value. They point out that in 1991 there were more employee-owners in these firms than in the entire trade-union movement in the United States. (Blasi and Kruse, 12-13) Citing Ken Lindberg of Hewitt Associates, a compensation consulting firm:

Employee ownership has become socially acceptable. When some of the big companies started putting in ESOP's, it was oh no, they are afraid they are going to be taken over. Now we have a lot of companies putting in ESOP's who are not even close enough to the amount of employee ownership that would give them any protection. But now it has become more of an acceptable business practice to do it. It used to be you could not open a newspaper and see that a company is implementing employee ownership. Now, there are more plans than before but you do not see anything in the paper. It is not sensational but it is still happening. (Blasi and Kruse, citing Lindberg, 20)

As editor of a collection of articles regarding productivity and worker participation, Alan Blinder argues that the sum of the collective investigations, along with the results of related studies of European cooperatives, found the evidence too mixed to support any strong conclusion that having an ESOP raises productivity. While none of the collected studies found that ESOP's harm either productivity or any other standard measure of company performance, several suggested that they did help. The point of their agreement, however, was that when ESOP's were combined with worker participation, there is much stronger evidence of a correlation with productivity:

> Solid empirical evidence on this question is hard to come by, however, because *participation* is a vague term encompassing a wide variety of labor-relations practices, including quality circles, work teams, labor-management consultation, and employee representation on corporate boards. (Blinder, 1990, 9)

Blinder cites the research of Levine and Tyson, who argue that there are four mutually supporting conditions under which participatory arrangements work best: (1) Profit sharing, which makes workers feel that cooperative behavior is rewards; (2) Guaranteed long-term employment, which makes workers feel less threatened; (3) Relatively narrow wage differentials which promote group cohesiveness and solidarity; and (4) Guarantees of worker rights, such as dismissal only for just cause. (Blinder, 9)

Education, training, and re-training strategies are common means of building the human capital Ozaki and others insist is so important to productivity. Much of the debate between the East Asian and American organization paradigms is predicated on the skill and academic level of the worker. In reality, education and skills are among the most basic components of any society, and any of its organizations, but they are especially critical elements in those organizations who are seeking to develop a more trusting, responsible work environment which moves away from the mass production model. And it is even more critical as technological advancements of the Information Age exert new pressures for high levels of worker skills and analytical thinking.

Ozaki insists that it is the human capacity to learn that enables them to increase their productivity over time. "Formally or informally, workers can learn skills, knowledge, and know-how from others, and can become capable of producing more as well as performing progressively more difficult and differentiated skills." (Ozaki, 27) The community of workers is the organization's most important asset, but the skill each worker possesses may also be her most important asset.

The Communitarian Paradigm

And according to Bob Dunn of Levi Strauss, educated workers are intrinsic to the good of both society and enterprise. He believes, reflecting his communitarian philosophy, that "if you neglect educating people, you don't have a competitive work force." (Makower, 226)

Naisbitt and Aburdene maintain that American business must make a forceful effort to strengthen and enhance the quality of education in America, reminding us that "Today's ill-prepared graduates become tomorrow's corporate burden." (Naisbitt and Aburdene, 145) In a very large sense, corporations have been compelled by the failures of public education to provide education and skills to the workforce. Naisbitt and Aburdene cite figures that reflect that three-fourths of large American corporations teach remedial education and basic skills, with the yearly cost for remedial reading programs alone near $300 million. Frustrated by workers who are both illiterate and innumerate, and who lack even basic lifeskills, corporations have assumed new roles as educator-activists. But while such action may be self-serving behavior to protect themselves from mistakes and lost revenues because workers cannot read and count, nevertheless, broad, non-company-specific aid to education serves the educational needs of the broader community as well. (Naisbitt and Aburdene, 145-146)

There are any number of horror stories about the education level of the American worker, from the New York insurance company which reports that 70 percent of all its dictated correspondence must be redone at least once because of errors; to the clerk who reimbursed a $22 dental claim with a check for $22,000 because she did not understand decimals; to the $250,000 yearly figure a medium-sized manufacturing company estimates it loses because of mistakes due to poor education and illiteracy. (Naisbitt and Aburdene, 152-153)

Democracy requires an educated populace; none of its institutions function well when the literacy level of the citizens tumble. Communitarians, particularly Etzioni, are strong supporters of movements to educate the American voter to enable her to exercise her civic duties. And corporations, tinkering with all manner of plans from contributing computers to classrooms, guaranteeing jobs for every high school graduate or promises of college funding, providing volunteer teachers and mentors, not to mention dumping millions of dollars into public school systems and matching employee contributions, are perhaps education's most crucial source of funding and moral support in the absence of a strong national education policy. (Naisbitt and Aburdene, 146-147)

Corporations are obliged to take up the education slack, not only because there is no strong government support of education, but also because they are largely forbidden to require explicit pre-employment tests under the authority of the Equal Employment Opportunity Commission. Employment tests are subject to scrutiny under the rules against discrimination; this largely prevents any substantial pre-employment screening as to skills. Whether self-serving or altruistic, most companies are quite proud of their educational activism. Honeywell's most prized educational effort is its New Vistas High School, a high school for pregnant teenagers and teenage mothers located in its headquarters in Minneapolis, Minnesota. A collaborative effort among Honeywell, the Minneapolis public schools, and several community and social service organizations, the New Vistas program has been quite successful in its efforts to turn out employable citizens. But Honeywell's involvement has enabled the company to enter the educational market with its climate-control systems. Honeywell was a good corporate citizen; but the benefits also accrued to the bottom line. Honeywell's communitarian attitude is reflected in the comments of M. Patricia Hoven, Honeywell's vice president of community and local government affairs:

> I think we do a lot of the things we're doing because we believe that communities have to be viable or companies can't function . . . And so we work to keep the community functioning as well as it can. We do these things to help the community, but also the company benefits. If we don't have an educated citizenry, they're not going to buy our products, nor are they going to be good employees. And I think one of the reasons that companies have gotten so involved in the public education system over the last ten years is that to stay competitive worldwide, we've got to have better public schools. (Makower, 233)

Management Praxis in the Communitarian Enterprise

As the traditions and history of a society are buried in its culture, so it is with organizations. There are numbers of organizations which have changed their cultures, and organizations which were structured from inception to fulfill a communitarian agenda. There are analogous relationships between the organization and worker, solar firms and satellites. There is abundant evidence of the expression of communitarian principles in numbers of American firms whose social conscience and sense of corporate responsibility and ethics are vigorous; and the nature and quality of the corporate culture enables the enterprise to either embrace or repudiate its communitarian character. The path to achieving a participatory, honest, and ethical corporate culture, however, while oftentimes experiential, is not a haphazard journey. In fact, the communitarian enterprise must rely on guidance and leadership, particularly when there is diversity between the corporate culture and the larger society. While a great deal of research has focused on American firms doing business in America, analysis suggests that such commitment to the communitarian ethic can be especially serviceable in cases of intercultural interactions, where host and visitor are separated from each other not only by diverse cultural accoutrement but in the most basic philosophical marker of all—whether man is by nature social or solitary.

As American companies have responded to the challenges of concentration without centralization and flexible specialization, to borrow the phraseology of Bennett Harrison, so have they also risen to the challenges of the global marketplace in issues of managing across borders. Again, while there is little evidence of abstract philosophical motivation, there is clear evidence that companies are arranging and managing themselves to meet the needs of idiosyncratic cultures and unfamiliar behavior patterns.

Cross-cultural Learning

In an examination of Toshiba's management strategies in its United Kingdom operation, Hoecklin discovered a distinct effort to effect a team spirit/equal status industrial culture between two very different national cultures. She describes a learning experience on the part of both host country and alien firm that focused on the ways each culture worked, their expectations, and the desired goal:

> Every aspect of the business was discussed, the desired outcomes were agreed and the ways to make them happen. There were not only financial objectives, but also objectives aimed at developing a particular company culture. For each aim, a team of Japanese and English managers discussed every detail and worked through them together. They discussed their different approaches and negotiated the most effective way of ensuring the desired outcome. (Hoecklin, 82)

In Toshiba's American operations in Lebanon, Tennessee, there was an equal focus on blending the best of Japanese culture and American culture to create sources of competitive advantage. This involved a joint American/Japanese management team, as well as the development of complementary skills among the American and Japanese engineers to get the best performance from each. (Hoecklin, 84)

Corporations are developing strategies to identify and maximize individuals with particularly robust intercultural skills. Citing Hawes and Kealy, Brislin lists seven specific indicators of good intercultural interaction, including the ability to interact socially with nationals, as well as on the job; an interest in and some knowledge of the local language, particularly greetings and salutations; knowledge of local nonverbal modes of communication; factual knowledge about the local culture; concern for training; tolerance and openness toward local cultures, conditions, mentalities, and customs; and attitudes of collaboration and cooperation. (Brislin, 23-25)

Neal Goodman claims that it is vitally important for businesspeople to develop skills in communicating with culturally-different others in order to increase awareness of hidden cultural assumptions, how they impact on job performance, and how they can be overcome. With Brislin, Goodman proposes that there must be a wholistic approach to cross-cultural learning, incorporating how the history and geography of a country impact on business practices; social, demographic, and business trends; the linkage between politics, government, and economics; different communication styles; habits of entertainment and gift giving; and decisionmaking and negotiation styles. (Goodman, 35-51)

Mole contributes to the compendium of cultural interaction points, adding geographical factors such as regionalism, which reflects how countries are aligned with other countries, and how that affects their organizations; traditional authority systems and the generation gap as reflected by changing habits and social norms; and gendered attitudes. He also points out that the work ethic varies from culture to culture, with the tongue-in-cheek remark that "Southern Europeans work to live and Northern Europeans live to work." (Mole, 1990, 6) He emphasizes that the national stereotypes one should be most wary of are those propagated by nations about themselves, in that they express more myth than reality. (Mole, 3-10)

The Communitarian Paradigm

Goman's description of the "boundaryless organization," is quite appropriate. What other authors have called the "diversified multinational corporation," (Doz and Prahalad, 1993, 24); the "interorganizational network," (Ghoshal and Bartlett, 1993, 77); and the networks, strategic alliances, and solar firms cited by Bennett Harrison (1994) represent demands for intercultural training, if there is to be any consideration of the communitarian ethic as a theory for organizing. Goman also refers to another variant of transnational organization as "virtual corporations," groups of collaborators that are more-or-less ad hoc bodies who come together because each has something to offer, creating a somewhat "best-of-everything" organization," sharing costs, skills, and global market access, linked by information networks, and united by a mutual dependency. According to Goman, Corning, Inc., is highly successful at partnering, with nineteen partnerships, accounting for nearly thirteen percent of its 1993 earnings. (Goman, 23)

Terry contends that the Japanese corporate culture, unpopular with its Asian subsidiaries, is being co-opted by local business cultures. While in the early economic development of the Pacific Rim the Japanese model dominated, leading to predictions that it would become the standard for transforming business practices, Terry's research leads her to conclude that even the heart of Japan, Inc., the *keiretsu* system of subcontracting, is not being sustained in the other East Asian economic cultures. According to reports from Thailand, "The results you get in Japan don't guarantee the same results in business in Asia." (Terry, 1995, 9) And other aspects of the Japanese business culture—lifetime employment, and paternalistic and prolonged promotion and management policies—are being eroded, albeit slowly.

The Chinese, particularly, are disinclined to accept either Japanese management teams or practices: "The ways Japanese and Chinese think about business clash head on." (Terry, 9) And slowly, but surely, Japanese firms are being forced to respond to pressures to promote local managers in their operations and recognize that just because they are Asian does not automatically mean that these diverse cultures are willing to accept the Japanese management style as whole cloth. (Terry, 9)

Hampden-Turner and Trompenaars argue that much of the success of intercultural interactions depends on how well companies are able to react and respond to exceptions to their conventional wisdom, claiming that "the integrity of the enterprise, its value to stakeholders, must depend in part on how well *universalism* (rules of wide generality) is reconciled with *particularism* (special exceptions)." (Hampden-Turner and Trompenaars, 7) Goman calls this the flexibility requirement:

> Working in a global organization requires that we all learn to live with few fixed rules, and constantly readjust to new organizational goals, objectives and strategies. Through explanation and example managers help workers understand that the most employable people in the future will be those flexible folks who can roll with changes, move easily from one function to another, and operate comfortably in a variety of environments. (Goman, 36)

Black, Gregersen, and Mendenhall argue that developing new mental road maps and behaviors is the most important process in global management assignments. They suggest that while managers are obliged to look at a matrix of international management styles in staffing, training, appraising, rewarding, and developing to discover the best internal "fit" between host and visitor, the primary concern must remain the external fit, or the balance between international assignment policies and practices with the marketplace: "The objective for a firm with a global orientation . . . is to coordinate value-chain activities on a global scale and thereby capture comparative advantages and links among countries." (Black et al, 1992, 22-23)

But these authors also admit that the way managers personally adjust to cross-cultural assignments is crucial to the success of the venture. They suggest that there is a set of dimensions beyond simple comfort and demographic factors that are controlling. And while such abstractions as adjustment to the job and the difficulty/ease of interacting with host-country nationals may well be purely personal, psychological behaviors, nevertheless, they are no less offensive if mismatched. Individual factors can neither be predicted nor prevented with any degree of certainty, hence the importance of intercultural training; but it must be recognized that there are simply some psychological circumstances of self-orientation and perceptions which just may not work and cannot be foreseen in intercultural situations. Goman speaks to this issue, advising that organizations should seek to balance intuitive individuals with analytical individuals. No one approach is sufficient in a multidimensional, intercultural enterprise; perhaps the best antidote to excesses is alternatives. (Goman, 38)

Black, et al, make an additional point for balance, warning that some managers may "go native," in the old diplomatic jargon, while

The Communitarian Paradigm

others may maintain an overarching allegiance to the parent firm. The communitarian ethic would also enforce a balance between these two extremes, or what these authors call the development of "dual allegiances" in order to secure greater role clarity and discretion, and diminish conflict. (Black, et al, 115-161)

Goman advises that the development of local and global work teams is an important management tool for global organizations. Such teams are a significant means by which to coordinate and leverage the flow of information and expertise, as well as to equip companies to respond quickly and effectively to dynamic markets. Quoting from a multinational representative's response to the Conference Board:

> We have over 75,000 employees and $8 billion in sales, 40 percent of which are from the international arena. Almost all goods sold overseas are produced overseas. We are extremely broad based in terms of products. We sell 55,000 different products. We are in niches. We have small unit sales in many areas that are related in terms of process technology. This makes global teamwork essential. (Goman, 37)

Globalization is reshaping lives and redefining political and economic thresholds. Earth-spanning technologies, immense corporate creatures, and the clash of diverse cultures, however, need not create unwholesome and destructive situations. Goman reminds us that the diversity of transnational enterprise is a valuable, not onerous, quality. A diverse work force is rich in ideas and approaches to business that can stimulate and utilize the best responses and draw the best effort from all employees. (Goman, 37) Kotkin and Kishimoto agree, taking the argument even deeper, using the "world nation" represented by American culture as a key element in preparing American society for a new era of non-Caucasian economic predominance:

> No other major nation enjoys this social flexibility. Other countries may for a time imitate or even surpass American technology. They may enjoy brief periods of economic, political and cultural hegemony. But they are confined by the limits of their own peculiar social and economic systems. (Kotkin and Kishimoto, 167-168)

Leadership and Vision

There is little doubt but that as old organizational styles have crumbled in the face of flexible specialization, networking, intercultural alliances, and diversified multinational corporations, so have old styles of leadership. Much like Fordism is passe, so is leadership based on strategy, structure, and control. What might be called the Sloan model, from Alfred Sloan, who took over General Motors in 1923, does not suit a world where, thanks to converging technologies, new markets and products often spring up between the cracks of bureaucratic divisions and subdivisions. According to Jack Welch of General Electric, "It was right for the 1970s . . . a growing handicap in the 1980s, and it would have been a ticket to the bone yard in the 1990s." ("The changing nature of leadership," 1995, 57)

The Sloan model prescribed a system that minimized the idiosyncracies of human behavior, but for today's best managers and aspiring leaders, the job is to mine idiosyncracies, rather than to discourage them. "To do this, bosses are shifting their attention from designing a single corporate strategy to shaping general organisational purposes—so that others, lower down the pecking order, can design micro-strategies for themselves." ("The changing . . . 57)

This is the interrelatedness between "the vision thing" and leadership, a relationship which comes fairly easily to corporations with strong cultures, like Procter & Gamble or 3M, and is becoming a characteristic of newer firms whose heroes are capable of inspiring great passion for enterprise. For example, Anita Roddick of the Body Shop is particularly adept at moving her company along with inspiration and passion, but she spends immense amounts of time in personal discourse with her employees, and all of her seven hundred shops are equipped with bulletin boards, fax machines, and video recorders to enable her to communicate with her employees fully and openly on both critical and mundane matters. In the post-Sloan era, leaders like Roddick are changing their organizations, not managing them. ("The changing . . . 57)

James W. Rouse, founder of the Rouse Company, says that "The surest road to success in our ventures is to discover the authentic needs and yearnings of people and to do our best to serve them." (Makower, 9, quoting Rouse) Paul Fireman, CEO of Reebok International, sees himself as a role model for how employees work; Jack Stack, president of Springfield ReManufacturing Corporation sees his role as visionary,

The Communitarian Paradigm

with the calling to his role. Many leaders have no problem discovering their image and vision; others ". . . bleed in midstream in their life; they have a crisis and grow out of it a different person. And they get it. They understand that their success and other people's success are tied together . . . ." (Makower, 50)

Hammer and Champy describe a leader as one who can turn an organization inside out and upside down, and yet persuade people to accept radical restructuring:

> The leader's primary role is to act as visionary and motivator. By fashioning and articulating a vision of the kind of organization that he or she wants to create, the leader invests everyone in the company with a purpose and a sense of mission . . . From the leader's convictions and enthusiasm, the organization derives the spiritual energy that it needs to embark on a voyage into the unknown. (Hammer and Champy, 103)

The qualities of leadership defy objective reason, being buried in charisma, magnetism, and presence. A leader does not make people do what she wants; she makes people want to do what she wants, and makes them willing to accept any attendant distress and anguish. But there are commonalities in the leadership models discovered in the literature: They are visionaries; they set personal examples; they are inspirational; they are strong, aggressive, committed, and knowledgeable. (Hammer and Champy, 105-108)

Corporate leaders are the source of corporate philosophy. And a stated philosophy is a consistent pattern in the most successful companies discovered in our research. Although, and in spite of, the profit motive in business enterprise, a company philosophy is a theme, a connecting thread between the hassles and fragmentation of day-to-day activities and the larger purpose. Most socially responsible exemplars have an equally socially-responsible corporate philosophy which is usually included in corporate value or mission statements; most strong corporate cultures have strong philosophies.

Makower provides these examples:

> The Timberland Mission Statement includes the statement that "Human history is the experience of individuals confronting the world around them. Timberland participates in this process not just through our products or through our brand, but through our beliefs

that each individual can, and must, make a difference in the way we experience life on the planet."

Tom's of Maine's Statement of Beliefs concludes with the statement that "We believe our company can be financially successful while behaving in a socially responsible and environmentally sensitive manner."

Whole Foods Market calls its Mission Statement a Declaration of Independence. In part, it states that "We recognize that our success reaches far beyond the company by contributing to the quality of life renaissance occurring here on earth. We are willing to share our successes and failures, our hopes and fears, and our joys and sorrows with others in the quality food business . . . The success of our business is measured by customer satisfaction, Team Member happiness, return on capital investment, improvement in the quality of the environment, and local and larger community support."

The Calvert Group's Statement of Shared Values concludes: "Our experience has proven that freedom to be oneself actually promotes higher levels of personal commitment and responsibility than does the more conventional, highly structured organization.

The Herman Miller Company Mandate acknowledges a belief that "all career employees should be able to own stock in the corporation. We believe that participative ownership, practiced with fidelity, can make this an exceptional company . . . we are more than participating owners in our company: We are also members of families and communities. We are committed to the nurture, support, and security of the family.

The White Dog Cafe, a 164-seat Philadelphia restaurant named by *Conde Nast Traveler* as one of the fifty American restaurants worth a journey and by *Inc* magazine as one of "the best small companies to work for in America" publishes a set of goals dealing with product excellence and workplace satisfaction, committing the company to "Making a difference" by using the business "as a vehicle for social change, promoting a more just society and world community, incorporating our values into every aspect of our work; profitability; [and] never neglecting [the] goals to achieve higher profits, nor jeopardizing the financial health of the business to maximize other goals." (Makower, 76-86)

A corporate philosophy is profoundly important as a means of uniting disparate operations, scattered about the globe, or of simply explaining to the larger society what a corporation stands for. Everyone recognizes the theme that "Quality is Job One" of Ford Motor Company; it is a corporate philosophy that energizes its behavior as an enterprise; most of its projects and goals are clearly associated with the idea of quality, right down to the Q1 flags flown by its certified suppliers.

Rubbermaid's philosophy is to create competitive advantage through quality and the innovation of the mundane. It is totally focused on purpose, recognizing its niche and the responsibility for its tradition of plain, quality products that make life easier. (Waterman, 169-191) There is no question but that it is AES leadership that has stoked its corporate flames, and sustained its values. Its founders have maintained their commitment to their values, even as a public corporation. According to Dennis Bakke: "The truth is, I feel strongly about principles and I'm not going to compromise them just to satisfy AES's stakeholders." (Markels, 1995)

Merck's commitment is to great science; P&G is committed to technology. According to P&G Chairman and Chief Executive Ed Artzt: "Technology is really what drives our business. For our company the main challenge is to maintain an edge in technology." (Waterman, 193) Motorola's vision is to make a difference, not just in a product, and not just to the company, but to the country itself. With a credo of "total customer satisfaction," Motorola endorses the notion that its customers are buying a reputation, not a product; this assumption of responsibility indicates the strength and durability of its culture, as well as its sense of a corporate self. (Waterman, 228-229)

INTERNAL AND EXTERNAL ENVIRONMENTS FOR THE COMMUNITARIAN ENTERPRISE

The communitarian enterprise arises out of a web of relationships; it is dependent on advantageous political environments and visionary company leadership. Political bodies are parameters within which corporations exist, and most states of the world are anxious to participate in the transnational economy. But the power and wealth of corporations make it imperative that the ethical strength which compels it as a body to make decisions that are right, not merely legal, is more than transitory.

Charles Handy quotes the late David Packard of Hewlett Packard:

> Why are we here? I think many people assume, wrongly, that a company exists solely to make money. Money is an important part of a company's existence, if the company is any good. But a result is not a cause. We have to go deeper and find the real reason for our being. As we investigate this, we inevitably come to the conclusion that a group of people get together and exist as an institution that we call a company, so that they are able to accomplish something collectively that they could not accomplish separately—they make a contribution to society, a phrase which sounds trite but is fundamental. (Quoted in Handy, 1998, 70-71)

The Political Environment.

Recognizing the affiliation between democracy and capitalism, the institutions of democratic, republican governments are major participants in establishing and maintaining a communitarian environment for business. From the perspective of government policy, this implies that government recognize that a healthy society cannot be sustained unless its people are able to control their own destiny through worthwhile employment, and unless business is freed from problematic and political restraints which despoil the institutional and personal work ethic.

Voters are vested with the responsibility to elect representatives and political leaders who understand that work is preferable to welfare, and that the real strength and security of a society are in the vigor and energy of its civil institutions. These presumptions would lead government to free businesses to compete by relieving them of onerous restrictions whose consequence is to reward mediocrity, restrain investment, and protect one group at the expense of another. Clark reminds us that the United States can no longer afford the existing adversarial relations among government, business, and labor that mark regulatory policy, labor relations, and many areas of social policy, arguing that cooperation among these sectors is a central factor in competitiveness. He suggests that government needs to redefine itself, exercising innovative schemes to privatize most government functions

The Communitarian Paradigm

as much as possible and creating desirable alternatives to the costly and time-consuming regulatory process. He believes that the government can ensure the provision of a service, while not engaging in its direct production by such activities as privatizing and contracting out much clerical and blue collar work and divesting itself of much of its administrative and bureaucratic functions that are bogged down in deadening rules and procedures and reasons for doing nothing. He describes the concept of catalytic government (after Osborne and Gaebler, 1992):

> Catalytic government at whatever level, then, would be fairly small and composed primarily of professionals ("symbolic analysts" to use Reich's (1991) term). It would act in partnership with business, local communities, and social groups to respond to problems creatively and to anticipate future events. It would act to spread information about successful organizations, programs, and technologies, coordinate efforts, mobilize resources, and perhaps act as what Piore and Sabel (1984) have called a guarantor of community flexible specialization and innovation—that is preventing the market dynamics of "cut-throat competition" leading to the full mass production ethic of low cost, low wage, and medium quality—a neoclassical prescription that might turn America into a Brazil or Thailand. (Clark, 57)

Clark also suggests such innovations as the easing of limitations on establishing subsidiaries; encouraging American corporate focus on sunrise, rather than sunset industries; and general government downsizing, shedding responsibilities for costly pension and health care plans. This perspective implies that the national government follow the lead of states to encourage economic growth and development, recognizing that the responsibilities of the national government are best limited to establishing standards which guard the values and common good of a society, with the devolution of responsibility to states and localities where accountability is greater and responsibility is more direct. Of course, there are needs for national standards to protect the natural resources of the commons; but the national government should remove itself as the provider of any service that can be privatized. The claim that government can do a better job than the private sector cannot be sustained. In locating responsibilities in communities, rather than in a large, bureaucratic state, the national government is freed to do its work for the greater common good, and communities are freed to pursue the kind of community they want and can control. Charles Handy suggests that citizens generally take a more restricted view of the role of government than the politicians they elect:

> Voters can understand that the prime responsibilities of government are to defend the nation against its enemies, and to provide a sound and stable economic infrastructure along with the necessary rules and regulations for an orderly market. after that it's up to us and our local communities . . . . A sound and stable economic infrastructure typically means low inflation, a stable currency with moderate government expenditure and borrowing, resulting in moderate taxes and low interest rates. That is what voters want governments to provide and they will vote for those who they think can deliver it. (Handy, 49)

Handy contends that as societies become more affluent, their citizens seek less government control and more personal control of the wealth. He proposes that the search for a balance between government intervention and personal responsibility "is likely to be the most important social change in the West in the early years of the next century and will be one change where government has to lead rather than follow." (Handy, 223)

The Enterprise.

The arrangement of the attributes of the communitarian enterprise has been revealed to be eclectic. Nevertheless, research suggests several sets of common features of the communitarian enterprise. At the network level, the communitarian perspective would direct cooperation, rather than manipulation, to include sharing of information, open communications, and decisionmaking responsibilities. There must be a presumption of trust and mutuality of common purpose; smaller firms should be considered as partners in the larger enterprise, rather than as minor children of a benevolent parent whose decisions are arbitrary, inconsistent, and secretive. There should be a sense of freedom in the network, which encourages movement of representatives of members of firms who have a shared purpose or lineage to understand their commonalities. This is a critical element in global alliances, which unites native and alien and builds a team of firms beyond the notion of the core/ring and facilitates informed decisions, rather than assumptions and conjecture. It also serves as a means of discovering the strengths and weaknesses of the system, and would expedite quick responses to crises. Smaller firms in these networks or alliances need to know that they are not "hung out to dry" by their larger partners. The need for enterprise mentoring is as critical as personal mentoring, which suggests that affiliations and buyouts should be made not on the basis of "milking" whatever is left out of a struggling sunset firm, but rather creating strong networks of sunrise and cutting-edge technologies to ensure long-term growth.

The political environment is also important in the matter of networking, in that laws should encourage excellence in performance of firms with a united purpose; anti-trust laws and regulations often have a debilitating effect on the development of these sorts of consortia. It appears that the market can be trusted with much more fidelity than government. The Japanese policies of mutual investment have provided strong evidence that success in common is a strong impulse for cooperation rather than exploitation.

The internal nature and culture of the organization is based on the same equality of purpose as we have suggested at the inter-firm level. But the market teaches us that unless a business is commercially and financially viable, unless it is profitable, unless there is return for investment made, it can do little for any of the members of its community, a community which includes its owners and investors as rightful members. The firms cited within have provided numbers of strong options to build the communitarian enterprise, among them empowered teams, shared decisionmaking, self- and peer-evaluation procedures, information sharing, profit-sharing and employee ownership, training and re-training programs, and inspirational and visionary leadership. These programs cannot be implemented, however, absent an atmosphere of trust, caring, and conviction of moral responsibility on the part of owners, managers, and workers. There are powerful forces for both autonomy and collectivity, natural and learned, discovered and contrived in drawing conclusions about corporate behavior. The communitarian enterprise is obligated, duty-bound, to reward and preserve both compulsions as a part of the human experience. But organizations, no matter the nobility of internal purpose, are also duty-bound to the larger society; clearly, unless the organizations of civil society assume their moral obligations, government becomes the Tocquevillian tutelary and remote colossus.

And it is apparent that organizations are taking up the sword where government has failed in its battle with the dragons of social despair. The communitarian enterprise is educating and re-educating its employees; it may also find it necessary to provide language study and classes in history and culture for its employees and their families who will reside and work outside their native countries. It cannot guarantee a lifetime of employment, but it should be able to insure employability. The communitarian enterprise may also find itself setting up counseling sessions for both native and visitor representatives, to ensure that grievances and unintended cultural slights do not become major problems. The communitarian enterprise will probably want to include incentives, bonus plans, and stock options for its employees. It will create and maintain a close, collaborative relationship with community political and civic leaders, inviting locals to tour facilities and make suggestions, making sure the dialogue remains open, especially when complaints and criticisms are waged. It may not have created slums or urban poverty, but it can join in community efforts to attend to immediate needs and prepare for a better future. It may not have degraded the environment, but it can clean it up, and make sure that it stays clean for future generations. The communitarian enterprise is actively involved in all its situated communities, realizing the virtues of charity and service. If successful, the communitarian enterprise provides a return to all its investors: owners are rewarded for their venture, leaders are rewarded for their vision, workers are rewarded for their toil, with society the biggest winner of all.

Organizations are, after all, just groups of people joined together with a common purpose. They are severally and jointly responsible and privileged; but they are also subject to the same pettiness and paucity of spirit that devalues the human conscience. As a democratic system cannot guarantee equality, neither can a communitarian enterprise promise that it can make everyone wealthy. At its best, it is a venue in which one discovers one's capabilities and one's responsibilities; at its worst, it can crumble into ignoble wrangling. But even out of chaos, some management experts would advise, comes a better order. The tolerance, collaboration, and cooperation manifest in a communitarian enterprise are a fine fit with the array of mankind's wants and wishes.

THE COMMUNITARIAN ETHIC AND CAPITALISM

The communitarian ethic has the capacity to reduce the institutional coercion which persists in possessive individualism and, by extension, in capitalism at a foundational level, but it does not assume an egalitarian perspective in the sense of a theory which supports an equal distribution of income. Perhaps the more basic question in this respect would be to attempt to define complete economic justice, and to address the question of whether or not it is ever attainable in any economic system. But that is beyond the scope of this study, limited as it is to seeking to discover if the application of the communitarian ethic to existing reality is a means of dealing with the complexities of the economic interactions of diverse cultures.

There is an egalitarian perspective to the communitarian ethic, but it is best perceived as the acceptance of the idea that "the interests of each member of the community matter, and matter equally . . . entitled to equal concern and respect." (Kymlicka, 4) A communitarian organization has a vision of a common good and pursuit of shared ends which enhances individual pursuit; it is perfectionist, in that it is value-laden, but it is not a tool to bring down the capitalist system; in this study, it is best revealed as a means by which to recognize and explicate the moral content of economic enterprise. It has been revealed as a theoretical companion of the capitalist economic enterprise, not an epistemological enemy. The communitarian enterprise closely resembles what has become known as the "stakeholder theory of the firm," as explained by Igor Ansoff in 1965:

> This theory maintains that the objectives of the firm should be derived from balancing the conflicting claims of the various "stakeholders" in the firm: managers, workers, stockholders, suppliers, vendors. The firm has a responsibility to all of these and must configure its objectives so as to give each a measure of satisfaction. Profit which is a return on investment to the stockholder is one of such satisfactions, but does not receive special predominance in the objective structure. (Ackoff, 1994, 37 citing Ansoff, 1965, 34)

Ackoff points out that while in the past the "failure of private enterprises to provide enough employment to distribute wealth equitably has been the principal producer of communism and socialism," (Ackoff, 42) the converse is now the case, in that communism's failure to produce enough wealth to be distributed has been the prime mover to capitalism. He concludes that from the social-system point of view, the principal functions of an enterprise are to produce and distribute wealth simultaneously, and the compensation provided by an enterprise to those whose work adds value to what they work on, is the only known way to accomplish both purposes. According to Ackoff, other schemes of equitable distribution of wealth are specious "... [S]uch employment as nationalization usually provides is usually unproductive. Therefore it does not create enough wealth to meet minimal requirements even when equitably distributed." (Ackoff, 65) The communitarian ethic is a social system ethic with clear implications for corporate behavior in this regard, because it provides a theoretical framework within which all those who have a stake in corporate decisions have an opportunity to participate directly or indirectly in their making. (Ackoff, 65)

Corporations are entities which Americans have chosen to sanction by law, tradition, and culture as discrete, legal members of the larger society for specific purposes in a capitalist economic system. Corporate responsibility to its stakeholders, including its employees, its suppliers, customers, investors and creditors, debtors, government and the public (Ackoff, 39) is basically an expression of the obligations arising out of a new body of particulars, an aggregation, a unified body of individuals. It therefore seems that such corporate responsibility, which we have examined as an expression of the communitarian ethic, is inseparable from the capitalist system, a natural extension of the created body's need to preserve and secure its place and purpose. In fact, the examination of the record of many firms who are choosing to exercise what we describe as the communitarian ethic reveals greater profit, not less, accompanied by greater worker satisfaction and increased assumptions of responsibility for one's own welfare.

Milton Friedman argues that the only responsibility of business is to make profits, and that to add anything else to that responsibility is "pure and adulterated socialism." He claims that a corporation cannot have responsibilities, only individuals can have responsibilities:

> [T]here is one and only one social responsibility of business—to use its resources and engage in activities designed to increase its profits so long as it stays within the rules of the game, which is to say,

engages in open and free competition without deception or fraud. (Friedman, 1990, 9)

But this is as thin a view of the corporate body as individualism is of human beings. Thomas Mulligan argues that Friedman's argument is based on an inaccurate paradigm:

> Friedman is right in pointing out that exercising social responsibility costs money. If nothing else, a company incurs expense when it invests the manhours needed to contemplate the possible social consequences of alternative actions and to consider the merit or demerit of each set of consequences.
>
> But Friedman is wrong in holding that such costs must be imposed by one business stakeholder on the others, outside the whole collaborative process of strategic and operational business management. He presumes too much in intimating . . . that the business person who pursues a socially responsible course inevitably acts without due attention to return on investment, budgetary limitations, reasonable employee remuneration, or competitive pricing. (Mulligan, 1990, 15)

In Mulligan's opinion, Friedman even undermines his own argument by exhorting business to refrain from deception or fraud, words which Mulligan construes as opening up a broad range of moral obligations and social responsibilities. (Mulligan, 15)

While there is no presumption of the equal distribution of wealth among all the parts of the corporate body or in the larger society in a capitalist economic system, the communitarian ethic addresses the larger question of human development in that system. We have already discovered that wealth is not the sole measure of human development in all cultures. At the core of the communitarian ethic are the developmental expectations of personal responsibility and mutual trust; it is not an economic theory by which to reduce income inequality. Rather, it is a moral voice in between the classical liberal norms of libertarian and egalitarian encampments, neither of which pay much attention to either the problem of human virtue or the goal of community, according to Spragens. (Spragens, 44)

> [N]either wing of contemporary liberalism provides a complete or compelling account of the good society. Each is committed to an

important value, and each possesses important insights. But both have only a part of the truth, and when they offer this part as a sufficient and comprehensive blueprint for social policy, their blind spots lead us astray . . . . For the purely market-driven society of the libertarians' dreams would produce a society rife with profound inequalities, deep divisions, social tensions, and selfish preoccupations, whereas the inevitably statist regime required to achieve the full goals of egalitarianism would be profoundly coercive, deleterious to excellence and efficiency, and productive of other forms of group hostility. (Spragens, 45)

Indeed, Robert Nisbet argues that the capitalist system itself rests not on nineteenth century claims of masses of autonomous, separated individuals responding to their deepest drives, but "lay in groups and associations that were not essentially economic at all." (Nisbet, 1962, 237) He claims that "Freedom of contract, the fluidity of capital, the mobility of labor, and the whole factory system were able to thrive . . . only because of the continued existence of institutional and cultural allegiances which were, in every sense, precapitalist." (Nisbet, 237) And Nisbet warns that the incentives to economic freedom and economic production are so instinctively social, so heavily dependent on social allegiance, that to separate them would be fatal. While in the past labor unions and cooperatives were the associational reinforcers of capitalism, the reality of twentieth century corporate enterprise, if Nisbet's argument may be so extended, is dependent for its survival on the creation of a personal sense of belonging to a social order:

Capitalism is either a system of social and moral allegiances, resting securely in institutions and voluntary associations, or it is a sand heap of disconnected particles of humanity. If it is, or is allowed to become, the latter, there is nothing that can prevent the rise of centralized, omnicompetent political power. Lacking a sense of participation in economic society, men will seek it, as Hilaire Belloc told us, in the Servile State. (Nisbet, 241)

REPRISE: THE COMMUNITARIAN ETHIC.

Michael Novak's notion that business is a calling, and that the business enterprise is in essence a moral institution is a succinct recapitulation of a communitarian ethic for American organizations.

Organizations do not need either-or's, but they may find new directions for establishing theories of management appropriate to intercultural interactions in the communitarian ethic as a flexible theoretical medium between the individualist perception of an atomist society and the collectivist belief in society's organic nature.

Lawrence Harrison warns that there are fundamental problems in American society with respect to trust, national unity and purpose, ethics and authority, and attitudes about work. He is not alone in his commentary; he is joined in the litany of melancholy by Drucker (1989), Brzezinski (1993), and Kennedy (1993). Others claim that it is the derogation of a sense of duty that enervates American society (Lodge, 117), or personal lack of initiative (Thurow, 1993), or social stratification and inequality. (Luttwak, 1993)

> In stark contrast with the late 1940s, the United States today is a nation uncertain, even anxious, about itself. Many of us believe that a serious erosion of our national confidence, unity, and purpose has occurred during the past few decades. The drug and crime epidemics, the street people, the budget deficit, the penury of state and local government, the trade deficit, the decline in the quality of some American products, the savings and loan disaster, Japan's phenomenal success, our plummet from the world's largest creditor to the world's largest debtor, the sleaze on Wall Street and in Washington—these are just some of the indicators of and contributors to the national malaise. (L. Harrison, 227)

There is also anxiety and uneasiness with the magnitude of global economic and political changes, an apprehension stirred by the spectre of inequality, insecurity, unemployment, disaffection, and poverty. But the moral purpose of business enterprise is inseparable from the common good of society. It is this social bond that offers the best hope for an interdependent world. Handy counsels that as mankind becomes more interconnected, understanding the social bond becomes more critical:

Almost everything we do affects other people, whether it is the pollution from our car or our decision to buy one computer rather than another. National boundaries can't control the winds that carry acid rain, the flows of money, or the messages on the Internet. In no way can we stand alone and pretend that what we do affects no one else and that no one else affects us. (Handy, 125)

According to Etzioni, the communitarian ethic affords philosophical relief of the polarized tensions between authoritarianism and the radical individualism of intellectual libertarians, civil libertarians, and laissez faire conservatives. (Etzioni, 1993, 15) Elshtain collects the latter groups within the category of "possessive individualism," a concept which directs individuals to see themselves as "... `owners' of their own person [F]used with market images ... wholly instrumental ... getting what one wants and translating that `want' into a `right.'" (Elshtain, 1995, 104) She muses that such an assumption arises out of social contract theory which "... exudes a politics of self-interest undertaken by a freely choosing, rational agent," (Elshtain, 104) a theory which reduces what is good to functionalist or instrumental criteria. But like Etzioni, who claims that "free individuals require a community," (Etzioni, 15) Elshtain reiterates that the "communitarian individual is very much an individual," (Elshtain, 108) albeit one who emerges out of a dense social ground whose "ill-defined boundaries . . . [and] ties that bind . . . paradoxically releases us into a wider world." (Elshtain, 108)

Individualism and classical liberalism were animated as a defense against the authoritarianism of popes and kings, but the popular perception of the impersonal force of classical economics which followed so closely on the heels of liberalism in the guise of narrow self-interest, has failed to provide the conditions necessary for meaningful existence. Still, the benefits of liberalism—individual rights and liberties—has a greater moral vocabulary than the aggregation of private goods. That greater moral vocabulary reprises Rousseau's vision of a harmonious pluralistic society composed of free-spirited and civic-minded individuals. According to Durkheim, "moral individualism" and the communitarian ethic are synonymous, suggestive of a middle ground between extreme libertarians and authoritarians. (Cladis, 6-9)

It is the mitigating property of the communitarian ethic which makes it appropriate in application to contemporary economic enterprise. The communitarian ethic is not merely a critique of liberalism, nor is it inherently contradictory to laissez faire economics; rather, it is the moral component of both concepts. Etzioni recalls the comments of John Leo in *U.S. News & World Report* in 1991 on the communitarian theme of rights and responsibilities. His observations assess directly the appropriateness of the communitarian ethic as an expression of moral economic purpose:

> Here, for instance, is a communitarian perspective on plant closings: If a steel plant shuts down in Youngstown, why should the suddenly unemployed workers be left alone to pay the price for what is, predictably, the occasional result of our economic system? (Etzioni, 17, citing Leo, 1991)

In this case, Leo goes on to explain, the communitarian perspective would prescribe ways in which to retrain or relocate workers, ". . . partly out of a sense of justice, partly to avoid the negative social effects of plant closings . . . ." (Etzioni, 17, citing Leo, 1991) This is not to say that the communitarian perspective would require that the owners or stockholders of the plant do not have the right (or responsibility) to seek the best course for the company under capitalism, only to provide moral direction in that course, or in his words, "social responsibility and laws based on connectedness." (Etzioni, 17, citing Leo, 1991)

Work is indispensable to the building of self-respect; it is the structure of most of our lives; it gives us self-discipline; and the job well-done is one of the most abiding sources of human satisfaction. (L. Harrison, 229) When the arrangements of our work are sufficient to our human needs, we are freed from the frustrations of self-doubt and apprehension to focus on the good of the common and the community of souls which ultimately defines human progress.

CHAPTER VI
Global Change, Cultural Challenge, and the Communitarian Response

Although united by democratization and the economic energy of capitalism, the world remains a crazy quilt of diverse societies whose ancient customs, values and social arrangements endure. The wisdom, as well as the foolishness, of the species is buried in its customs and traditions; the ways people actually and habitually live will profoundly influence how societies adapt to the momentous political and economic changes of the last decade of the twentieth century. What is customary and traditional in one society is not transferable in precisely the same form to another. (Brenkert, 39-40) Not unlike Tocqueville's vision of America, the international order lacks an institutional order, patterns of "normative, sanctioned interactions" among market, states, and civil societies which structure patterns of behavior in pursuit of common causes and generalized reciprocity, in relationships of mutual trust and tolerance. (Sullivan, 1995, 173-174)

Interdependence of diverse and dissimilar cultures is the fruit of the global community phenomenon of the 1990s. Interdependency implies relationships, and the pursuit of entwined cross-cultural economic and political relationships carries the social baggage and community traditions of both the user and the used, the buyer and the seller, the source and the producer, the native and the alien, those accustomed to freedom and the newly free.

The merits of democracy and capitalism, and their heady promise of power, leisure, and security, are only realizable within the cultural constraints of the larger society. The diverse cultural expectations of the nations of the world are likely to find themselves in tension with the institutional arrangements designed to manage surging, worldwide economic growth and development. But to trample the customs, values, and virtues of society in search of profit without munificence is to fail in organizational purpose. The social nature of man and his cultural environment are necessary variables in the formulation of the theories to guide economic enterprise.

> The great economic unions going forward in Europe and elsewhere put at risk the richness of the cultures that for ages have protected themselves behind castle walls and tariff barriers . . . . .The challenge is to make the world safe for and from ethnicity, safe for . . . those differences . . . . (D. Moynihan, 172-173)

The American and Japanese models illustrate polar approaches to the ways in which modern societies, and their organizations, choose to arrange themselves for work. In examining these two cases we are presented with two sets of options that in a number of important ways are contradictory and incompatible with each other. Just as surely as the individualist/collectivist dualities represent the major philosophical differences among most societies of the world, so do the American and Japanese organizational models represent the major organizational styles of modern economic enterprise.

In the American case we have discovered an organizational style which parallels the American cultural tradition of society as a free association of independent and self-reliant citizens who enjoy and exploit their liberties and rights. Unbounded by the structures of class and privilege, America perceived herself and was perceived by the rest of the world as the land of opportunity, a frontier society, a New World where one's fortune was to be had if one worked hard enough, took chances, and played the game of life with intensity and enthusiasm. Largely unfettered by government intervention until the 1930s, American economic enterprise was both affirmation and confirmation of the common man, the self-interested individual whose Puritan work ethic, competitive drive and rational nature, contempt for authority, and predisposition to run over others on his way to the top created a mass production model eminently successful in creating wealth and sets of reliable goods for a consumer-oriented society. But according to Clark, the negative spinoffs of the mass production model in the form of "increasing human physical waste of a `throw-away society,' and the gridlock of bureaucratized corporations . . . . [have] interacted much

Global Change

more perversely in late twentieth century America to "produce hyperindividualism and social breakdown...." (Clark, 58) The model which served America well under different circumstances is becoming "increasingly obsolete and dysfunctional." (Clark, 2) Clark declares, however:

> While such destruction can be devastating for its victims, it also opens the way for creative innovation in the construction of a new economy and society. For example, Mancur Olson (1982) attributes the "fall of nations" to overinstitutionalization which allows vested interests to prevent needed change and to reap "monopoly rents." From this perspective, Schumpeter's "creative destruction" starts the game over again. (Clark, 2)

Japanese organizations are equally reflective of their cultural traditions. In deference to its ancient tribal roots, and grounded in Confucian notions of interpersonal responsibilities and the social nature of man, Japanese society, and its organizations, seek harmony rather than confrontation, cooperation rather than dissension, commitment rather than freedom, and collectivity rather than individuality. Self-disciplined and orderly, with inordinate trust in each other and authority, the unity of purpose of Japanese society spills over into its economic organizations, building interlocked enterprises whose common bonds reflect the powerful unity of Japanese society. But, like the American model, Japan's "Organic" political economy, which proved extremely functional for promoting industrialization, is also trapped in organizational patterns that are dysfunctional in the face of new sets of circumstances outside the bounds of the economic framework for which it was designed and which it served well for many years.

Both models have been exceptionally successful, but we have found that they are not without serious imperfections. The American model is tremendously productive, energetic, irreverent, and entrepreneurial. Philosophically joined to classical liberalism, American capitalism represents the essence of self-interest and private enterprise. But driven by an emphasis on rationality and efficiency, and an infatuation with scientific management methodology, American organizations tend to roll roughshod over the very individualism which the American culture is designed to protect. The American capitalist model, with its mass production mentality, substitutes the mechanized life for the treasured individual freedom of artistic and intellectual creativity.

With responsibility for social welfare vested in the institutions of the state, organizations based on the American model offer little security and expect little loyalty in return. Indeed, the American model is locked in an adversarial relationship with the state, which regulates all forms of economic activity in order to reduce the inequities of the capitalist system. American model organizations are profit-oriented, short-sighted, detached associations of individuals who are come together for a common purpose, but whose interpersonal connections and mutual responsibilities are largely nonexistent, much like the society from which the model has arisen.

The American mass production organization model, in pandering to selfish interests, has sanctioned an unnatural estrangement between individuals which cancels out all sense of mutual responsibility. Therein lies the dilemma for the individualist paradigm: Exaggerated competition leads to the development of a disabling pride, diminishes performance to simply the goal of winning, creates hierarchies in societies, breeds distrust and fosters domination, glorifies rationality and reason; and diminishes the social nature of humankind.

The collectivist Japanese model, however, reverses this process, sustaining the social nature of humankind at the expense of individuality. Offering security in return for absolute loyalty and fealty, Japanese model organizations expect conformity, cooperation, harmony, and unity. The organization becomes the family; it represents the extension of Confucian relationships and tribal devotion. Personal ambition is expected to be channeled into team effort; self-interest is subsumed by self-discipline and allegiance to the warrior's moral code.

The state's role is interwoven into the fabric of the Japanese organization. Instead of adversary, the state is an economic partner, with state and organization thus becoming a whole cloth. But welfare responsibility rests with the enterprise; it is truly the worker's family, lifetime protector, and source of identity, its moral purpose greater than the realization of profit. Dedicated to achieving long-term stability and consistent, albeit slow, growth, the Japanese model is a powerful unifier, but it is also personally inhibiting and paternalistic. In an important sense, the selfishness of the organization simply replaces the selfishness of individuals. While the organic society is an affirmation of the natural social connection between human beings, the Japanese organizational model exceeds the ethic of care. The better ethic would enlarge, rather than displace individuality.

The conundrum between individualism and collectivism in organizations has yet to be institutionally resolved. Both major models suffer from their own excesses, the consequences of which spill over into the societies they serve. Elite economic institutions are powerful harbingers of social and personal well being; in an interconnected world the dualities of diversity and unity in individualistic and collective societies take on new significance.

We are coming to realize our membership in a community beyond our cultural boundaries. The either-or's of individualism and collectivism are displaced and interpenetrated. As we proceed to learn our way around this larger social and economic order in which we have discovered ourselves, the communitarian ethic allows us to look beyond reliance on the unfettered market or the bureaucratic regulatory state for steering and guidance through global change:

> [R]ecent thinkers have stressed the need to attend to the whole realm of organizations and associations that are neither simply parts of the market nor agencies of the state. This is the much-invoked idea of civil society. (Sullivan, 173)

The deficiencies of the corporate organizational styles of the American and Japanese models leave ample room for improvement. There are lessons to be learned from each; neither is sufficient unto itself to meet the demands and absorb the consequences of turbocapitalism. Both models have been exposed as contradictory in fundamental ways to their own presupposed values; both fail to comprehend fully the idea that capitalism requires a creative form of community in order to produce real wealth. (Novak, 126-127) And as systems, cultures, and peoples become more intermixed and mingled; as the Information Age consolidates; and as international competition becomes more comprehensive, the repercussions of a failure to comprehend the communitarian nature of organizations of economic enterprise will become more manifest. Each model is being propelled inexorably toward the other, but neither is substitutive; rather, they are recombinant.

The communitarian ethic is an appropriate theoretical bridge between these two models. Both philosophically sound and morally correct for the individuals, communities, and organizations who constitute the modern global society, the communitarian ethic tempers many of the personal ills and systemic ailments we have observed. For individuals, the ethic relieves the estrangement and alienation of both faceless and servile labor, leaving a whole human being who is more aware of her self-worth and more emotionally and intellectually equipped to meet her broader responsibilities to herself and to others. The ethic re-unites and uplifts work and civil communities of all cultural preferences, strengthening the democratic process and the intermediate civil institutions of normal life. And the ethic enables corporate organizations to forge a full-fledged partnership with all its stakeholders—the owners, stockholders, managers, workers, and the extended communities within which it discovers itself.

Above all, the communitarian ethic does no harm; it is a positive force which has been revealed as a rightful moral posture for an international order struggling to realize its political and economic fortunes while preserving the integrity of singular and diverse cultures.

Bibliography

Ackoff, Russell L. *The Democratic Corporation*. New York: Oxford University Press, 1994.

Adams, Loyce. *Managerial Psychology*. Boston: The Christopher Publishing House, 1965.

Airaksinen, Timo. *Ethics of Coercion and Authority: A Philosophical Study of Social Life*. Pittsburgh: University of Pittsburgh Press, 1988.

Alston, Jon P. *The American Samurai*. New York: Walter de Gruyter, 1986.

Armstrong, Richard. "Rudeness pervades American society, experts say." *The Montgomery Advertiser*, June 17, 1996, B1.

Baradat, Leon P. *Political Ideologies. Their Origins and Impact*. 5th Ed. Englewood Cliffs, New Jersey: Prentice Hall, 1994.

Bartley, Robert. "The Case for Optimism." *Foreign Affairs*, Vol. 72, No. 4, 15-18, September/October 1993.

Beck, John C. and Martha N. Beck. *The Change Of A Lifetime*. Honolulu: University of Hawaii Press, 1994.

Benn, S. I. "Individuality, autonomy and community." In *Community as a Social Ideal*. Eugene Kamenka, Ed. New York: St. Martin's Press, 1982.

Bennett, W. Lance. *Inside the System. Culture, Institutions, and Power in American Politics*. Fort Worth, Texas: Harcourt Brace College Publishers, 1994.

Black, J. Stewart, Hal B. Gregersen, and Mark E. Mendenhall. *Global Assignments*. San Francisco: Jossey-Bass Publishers, 1992.

Blasi, Joseph Raphael and Douglas Lynn Kruse. *The New Owners: The Mass Emergence of Employee Ownership in Public Companies and What It Means to American Business*. New York: HarperBusiness, 1991.

Blinder, Alan S., Ed. *Paying for Productivity: Look at the Evidence*. Washington, D.C.: The Brookings Institution, 1990.

Bowker, Mike. "Explaining Soviet Foreign Policy Behavior in the 1980s. In *From Cold War to collapse: theory and world politics in the 1980s*. Mike Bowker and Robin Brown, Eds. Great Britain: Cambridge University Press, 1993.

Bowker, Mike and Robin Brown, Eds. *From Cold War to Collapse: theory and world politics in the 1980s*. Great Britain: Cambridge University Press, 1993.

Brenkert, George G. *Political Feeedom*. New York: Routledge, 1991.

Brislin, Richard W. "Individualism and Collectivism as the Source of Many Specific Cultural Differences." In *Improving Intercultural Interactions*, Richard W. Brislin and Tomoko Yoshida, Eds. Thousand Oaks, CA: Sage Publications, 1994.

Bronfenbrenner, Martin, Werner Sichel and Wayland Gardner. *Economics*. 3d Ed. Boston: Houghton Mifflin Company, 1990.

Brzezinski, Zbigniew. *Out of Control*. New York: Collier Books. 1993.

Buscher, Martin. "Economic Systems and Normative Fundaments: A Social Market Economy in the Light of Economic Ethics." *The Journal of Socio-Economics*, Vol. 22, No. 4, 311-322, 1993.

Butler, David. "Eclipse in the land of the rising sun." *U.S. News & World Report*, December 11, 1995, 62-68)

Chandler, Clay. "A Market Tide That Isn't Lifting Everybody." *The Washington Post National Weekly Edition*, April 13, 1998.

Chandler, Clay. "Job Growth to Brag About." *The Washington Post National Weekly Edition*, April 8-14, 1996.

Cladis, Mark S. *A Communitarian Defense of Liberalism. Emile Durkheim and Contemporary Social Theory*. Stanford, California: Stanford University Press, 1992.

Clark, Cal. "The Role of the State in U.S. Competitiveness: Lessons from East Asia." Paper presented at the 1993 Conference on U.S. Competitiveness, Washington, D.C., October 6-10, 1993.

. . . Companies find social concern is good business." *Montgomery Advertiser*. April 15, 1996, 4D.

Corlett, William. *Community Without Unity*. Durham: Duke University Press, 1989.

Crockatt, Richard. "Theories of Stability and the End of the Cold War." In *From Cold War to collapse: theory and world politics in the 1980s*. Mike Bowker and Robin Brown, Eds. Great Britain: Cambridge University Press, 1993.

Dahl, Robert A. "A Democratic Dilemma: System Effectiveness versus Citizen

Participation." *Political Science Quarterly*, Vol. 109, No. 1, Spring 1994, 23-34.

Deal, Terrence E. and Allan A. Kennedy. *Corporate Cultures*. Reading, Mass: Addison-Wesley Publishing Company, 1982.

Denhardt, Robert B. *In the Shadow of Organization*. Lawrence: University Press of Kansas, 1981.

Dentzer, Susan. "Downsizing: Will East meet West?" *U.S. News & World Report*, December 11, 1995, 72.

DeTocqueville, Alexis. *Democracy In America*, Vol. 2. New York: Vintage Books, 1990.

Dewey, John. *The Public and Its Problem*. Athens, Ohio: Swallo Press, 1927; 1954.

Diamond, Michael A. *The Unconscious Life of Organizations*. Westport, Connecticut: Quorum Books, 1993.

Dillenberger, John, Ed. *Martin Luther Selections From His Writings*. New York: Anchor Books Doubleday, 1961.

DiMaggio, Paul. "Culture and Economy" In *The Handbook of Economic Sociology*, Neil J. Smelser and Richard Swedberg, Eds. New Jersey: Princeton University Press, 1994.

Doz, Yves and C. K. Prahalad. "Managing DMNCs: A Search for a New Paradigm." *Organization Theory and the Multinational Corporation*. New York: St. Martin's Press, 1993.

Drucker, Peter F. *The New Realities*. New York: HarperBusiness, 1989.

Ebenstein, Alan O., William Ebenstein and Edwin Fogelman. *Today's ISMS*. 10th Ed. Englewood Cliffs, New Jersey: Prentice-Hall, 1994.

Eberts, Ray and Cindelyn. *The Myths of Japanese Quality*. Upper Saddle River, New Jersey: Prentice Hall P T R, 1995.

Elshtain, Jean Bethke. "The Communitarian Individual." In *New Communitarian*

Thinking. Persons, Virtues, Institutions, and Communities. Amitai Etzioni, Ed. Charlottesville: The University of Virginia Press, 1995.

Elshtain, Jean Bethke. "The politics of resentment is killing democracy." *The Atlanta Journal and Constitution*. May 5, 1996, C4.

... *Employee Ownership Plans: How 8,000 Companies and 8,000,000 Employees Invest In Their Futures*. Bureau of National Affairs, Inc., 1987.

Enloe, Cynthia. *Bananas, Beaches & Bases*. Berkeley: University of California Press, 1990.

Etzioni, Amitai. "Old Chestnuts and New Spurs." *New Communitarian Thinking.*

Persons, Virtues, Institutions, and Communities. Charlottesville: University Press of Virginia, 1995.

Etzioni, Amitai, *Public Policy In A New Key.* New Brunswick: Transaction Publishers, 1993.

Etzioni, Amitai. "Socio-Economics A Budding Challenge." In *Socio-Economics Toward a New Synthesis*, Etzioni, Amitai and Paul R. Lawrence, Eds. Armonk, NY: M. E. Sharpe, Inc., 1991, 3-7.

Etzioni, Amitai. *The Spirit of Community.* New York: Crown Publishers, Inc., 1993.

Etzioni, Amitai and Paul R. Lawrence, Eds. *Socio-Economics Toward a New Synthesis.* Armonk, NY: M.E. Sharpe, Inc., 1991.

Fallows, James. *More Like Us.* Boston: Houghton Mifflin Company, 1989.

Fingleton, Eamonn. "Japan's Invisible Leviathan." *Foreign Affairs*, Vol. 74, No. 2, March/April 1995, 69-85.

Foster, Jack L. Conversation with Bulgarian representatives, June, 1998

Fowler, Robert Booth and Jeffrey R. Orenstein. *An Introduction to Pollitical Theory: Toward the Next Century.* New York: HarperCollins College Publishers, 1993.

Frandsen, Jon. "Companies reap benefit from ethics." *Montgomery Advertiser.* May 28, 1996, 5B.

Friedman, Milton. "The Social Responsibility of Business Is To Increase Its Profits." In *Taking Sides: Clashing View on Controversial Economic Issues*, 5th Ed., Thomas Swartz and Frank Bonello, Eds. Guilford, Connecticut: The Dushkin Publishing Group, Inc., 1990.

Fukuyama, Francis. "The End of History?" *The National Interest* 16, Summer 1989, 3-18.

Fukuyama, Francis. *The End of History and the Last Man.* New York: Avon Books, 1992.

Fuller, Graham E. "The Breaking of Nations—and the Threat to Ours." *The National Interest*, No. 26, Winter 1991/92.

Ghoshal, Sumantra and Christopher Bartlett. "The Multinational Corporation as an Interorganizational Network." In *Organization Theory and the Multinational Corporation.* New York: St. Martin's Press, 1993.

Glassman, James K. "Bad Publicity for the Way Japan Runs Its Economy." *International Herald Tribune*, 13 September 1995.

Goman, Carol Kinsey. *Managing In A Global Organization.* Menlo Park, CA: Crisp Publications, Inc., 1994.

Goodman, Neal R. "Cross Cultural Training for the Global Executive." In *Improving Intercultural Interactions.* Richard W. Brislin and Tomoko Yoshida, Eds. Thousand Oaks, CA: Sage Publications, 1994.

Bibliography

... "Half time." *The Economist*. March 2, 1996, 38.
Hamilton, Alexander. *Federalist 79*. In *Great Books of the Western World*, Vol. 43. Chicago: William Benton, Publisher, 1952.
Hammer, Michael and James Champy. *Reengineering The Corporation*. New York: HarperBusiness, 1993.
Hampden-Turner, Charles and Alfons Trompenaars. *The Seven Cultures of Capitalism*. New York: Currency Doubleday, 1993.
Handy, Charles. *The Hungry Spirit*. New York: Broadway Books, 1998.
Handy, Charles B. *Understanding Organizations*. New York: Oxford University Press, 1993.
Harrison, Bennett. *Lean and Mean. The Changing Landscape of Corporate Power in the Age of Flexibility*. New York: Basic Books, 1994.
Harrison, Lawrence E. *Who Prospers? How Cultural Values Shape Economic and Political Success*. New York: BasicBooks, 1992.
Hausman, Daniel M. and Michael S. McPherson. "Economics, rationality, and ethics." In *The Philosophy of Economics: An Anthology*, 2d Ed., Daniel M. Hausman, Ed. New York: Cambridge University Press, 1994.
Heilbroner, Robert L. "The View from the Top." In *The Business Establishment*, Cheit, Earl F., Ed. New York: John Wiley & Sons, Inc., 1964.
Herbert, Wray. "Morality's bottom line." *U.S. News & World Report*, August 21, 1995, 51-53.
Heywood, Andrew. *Political ideas and Concepts*. New York: St. Martin's Press, 1994.
Hoagland, Jim. "Japan: On Another Planet." *The Washington Post Weekly Edition*, 27 April 1998, 5.
Hoagland, Jim. "The Currents Run Deep." *The Washington Post Weekly Edition*, April 29-May 5, 1996, 28.
Hoecklin, Lisa. *Managing Cultural Differences. Strategies for Competitive Advantage*. Great Britain: Addison-Wesley Publishers Ltd, Addison-Wesley Publishing Co., Inc. and the Economist Intelligence Unit, 1995.
Hofstede, Geert. *Uncommon Sense About Organizations*. Thousand Oaks, CA: Sage Publications, 1994.
Hollenbach, David. "Virtue, the Common Good, and Democracy." In *New Communitarian Thinking*. Amitai Etzioni, Ed. Charlottesville: University Press of Virginia, 1995.
Huntington, Samuel P. "The Clash of Civilizations?" *Foreign Affairs*, Vol. 72, No. 4, Summer, 1993, 22-49.
Huntington, Samuel P. *The Clash of Civilizations and the Remaking of World Order*. New York: Simon & Schuster, 1996.

Huntington, Samuel. *The Third Wave*. Norman, OK: University of Oklahoma Press, 1991.

Hyland, William G. "The Case for Pragmatism." *Foreign Affairs*, Vol. 7, No. 1, 1993.

Hymowitz, Carol and Michaele Weissman. *A History of Women in America*. New York: Bantam Books, 1978.

Jacob, Margaret C. *The Cultural Meaning of the Scientific Revolution*. New York: Alfred A. Knopf, 1988.

Jamieson, Ian. *Capitalism and Culture*. England: Gower Publishing Company Limited, 1980.

... "Japan stimulus plan not enough for critics." *The Atlanta Journal-Constitution*, 25 April 1998, 1E.

Jervis, Robert. "The Future of World Politics: Will It Resemble the Past? *America's Strategy in a Changing World*. Sean M. Lynn Jones and Steven E. Miller, eds. Massachusetts: The MIT Press, 1993.

Johnson, Stephanie Jordan. "The women of Forsyth Landing." *The Macon Telegraph*, Business Plus, June 10, 1996, 1 and 8.

Jordan, Mary. "Changing the Way People Live." *The Washington Post National Weekly Edition*, 13 April 1998, 20.

Jordan, Mary. "Crisis? What Crisis?" *The Washington Post National Weekly Edition*, 22 June 1998.

Kegley, Charles W. Jr. and Eugene R. Wittkopf. *World Politics Trend and Transformation*. 4th Ed. New York: St. Martin's Press, 1993.

Kelley, Lane and Reginald Worthley. "Japanese Management and Cultural Determinism." In Sang M. Lee and Gary Schwendiman, *Japanese Management*. New York: Praeger Publishers, 1982.

Kelso, Louis O. and Patricia Hetter Kelso. "The Outlook for Employee Ownership in the 1990s." In *Employee Ownership Plans: How 8,000 Companies and 8,000,000 Employees Invest In Their Future*. Bureau of National Affairs, Inc., 1987.

Kennedy, Paul. *Preparing for the Twenty-First Century*. New York: Vintage Books, 1993.

Korgut, Bruce. "International Business: The New Bottom Line." *Foreign Policy*, Spring 1998, 152-163.

Kotkin, Joel and Yoriko Kishimoto. *The Third Century. America's Resurgence in the Asian Era.* New York: Crown Publishers, Inc., 1988.

Krugman, Paul. "America the Boastful." *Foreign Affairs*, Vol. 77, No. 3, May/June 1998, 32-45.

Krugman, Paul R. and Maurice Obstfeld. *International Economics Theory and Policy*, 2d Ed. New York: HarperCollins Publishers, Inc., 1991.

Kuttner, Robert. "Tipping the Income Scales." *The Washington Post National Weekly Edition*, July 1-7, 1996, 5.

Kymlicka, Will. *Contemporary Political Philosophy*. New York: Oxford University Press, 1990.

Lash, William H. III. "No Threat." *The Montgomery Advertiser*. June 2, 1996, 3F.

Lealand, Geoff. "American Popular Culture and Emerging Nationalism in New Zealand." *Phi Kappa Phi Journal*, Fall, 1994, 34.

Lincoln, Edward J. "Japan's Financial Mess." *Foreign Affairs*, Vol. 77, No. 3, May/June 1998, 57-66.

Liu, Binyan. "Civilization Grafting." *Foreign Affairs*, Vol. 72, No. 4, September/October 1993, 19-21.

Lodge, George C. *Managing Globalization In The Age of Interdependence*. San Diego, CA: Pfeiffer & Company, 1995.

Lorange, Peter. "Human Resource Management in Multinational Cooperativ Ventures." In *Globalizing Management*, Vladimir Pucik, Noel M. Tichy and Carole K. Barnett, Eds. New York: John Wiley & Sons, Inc., 1993.

Lowi, Theodore J. and Benjamin Ginsberg. *American Government. Freedom and Power*. Brief 3d Ed. New York: W. W. Norton & Company, 1994.

Lundin, William and Kathleen Lundin. *The Healing Manager*. San Francisco: Berrett- Koehler Publishers, 1993.

Luttwak, Edward N. "Our Anxious Economy." *The Washington Post Weekly*, April 8- 14, 1996.

Luttwak, Edward N. *The Endangered American Dream*. New York: Simon & Schuster, 1993

Mainwaring, Scott. "Transition to Democracy and Democratic Consolidation: Theoretical and Comparative Issues." In *Issues in Democratic Consolidation. The New South American Democracies in Comparative Perspective*, Scott Mainwaring, Guillermo O'Donnell, and J. Samuel Valenzuela, Eds. Notre Dame, Indiana: University of Notre Dame Press, 1992.

Mainwaring, Scott, Guillermo O'Donnell, and J. Samuel Valenzuela, Eds. *Issues in Democratic Consolidation. The New South American Democracies in Comparative Perspective*. Notre Dame, Indiana: University of Notre Dame Press, 1992.

Makower, Joel. *Beyond the Bottom Line*. New York: Simon & Schuster, 1994.

Malone, Julia. "Clinton to challenge Americans to return to civility, responsibility." *The Atlanta Journal and Constitution.* July 6, 1995, A7.

Markels, Alex. "Team Approach." *Wall Street Journal*, July 3, 1995.

Marshall, Edward M. *Transforming The Way We Work.* New York: AMACOM, 1995.

Matsumoto, Koji. Trans. by Thomas I. Elliott. *The Rise of the Japanese Corporate System.* New York: Kegan Paul International, 1991.

McCreary, Don R. *Japanese-U.S. Business Negotiations. A Cross-Cultural Study.* New York: Praeger Publishers, 1986.

McNeill, William H. *A History of the Human Community. Prehistory To The Present*, 3d Ed. Englewood Cliffs, New Jersey: Prentice Hall, 1990.

Mitchell, Tom. "Companies bring workers into the world of business." *Montgomery Advertiser.* April 18, 1996, 6A.

Mole, John. *When In Rome . . .* New York: AMACOM, 1990.

Moran, Robert T. and Philip R. Harris. *Managing Cultural Synergy.* Houston: Gulf Publishing Company, 1982.

Moran, Robert T., Philip R. Harris and William G. Stripp. *Developing the Global Organization.* Houston: Gulf Publishing Company, 1993.

Morgan, Gareth. *Images of Organization.* Newbury Park, California: SAGE Publications, Inc., 1986.

Morin, Richard. "So Much for the `Bowling Alone' Thesis." *The Washington Post National Weekly Edition*, June 17-23, 1996, 37.

Morong, Cyril. "Mythology, Joseph Campbell, and the Socioeconomic Conflict." *The Journal of Socio-Economics*, Vol. 23, No. 4, 1994, 363-382.

Morris, Tom. *If Aristotle Ran General Motors.* New York: Henry Holt and Company, 1997.

Morton, W. Scott. *Japan Its History and Culture.* 3d Ed. New York: McGraw-Hill, Inc., 1994.

Moynihan, Daniel Patrick. *Pandaemonium.* New York: Oxford University Press, 1993.

Moynihan, Michael. *The Economist Intelligence Unit Global Manager.* New York: McGraw-Hill, Inc., 1993.

Mueller, Frank. "Societal Effect, Organizational Effect and Globalization." *Organization Studies*, Vol. 15, No. 3, 407-428, 1994.

Mulligan, Thomas. "A Critique of Milton Friedman's Essay `The Social Responsibility of Business Is To Increase Its Profits.'" In *Taking Sides: Clashing Views on Controversial Economic Issues,* 5th Ed., Thomas Swartz and Frank Bonello, Eds. Guilford, Connecticut: The Dushkin Publishng Group, Inc., 1990.

Naisbitt, John and Patricia Aburdene. *Re-inventing the Corporation.* New York: Warner Books, 1985.

Bibliography

Nelson, Brian R. *Western Political Thought From Socrates to the Age of Ideology*. Englewood Cliffs, New Jersey: Prentice Hall, 1996.

Nisbet, Robert A. *Community & Power* (formerly *The Quest For Community*) New York: Oxford University Press, 1962.

Novak, Michael. *Business As A Calling*. New York: The Free Press, 1996.

Novick, Sheldon. "The Individual and the Community." Address at Vermont School of Law. 29 September 1995.

Ouchi, William G. *Theory Z*. New York: Avon Books, 1981.

Ozaki, Robert. *Human Capitalism*. New York: Penguin Group, 1991.

Palvia, Shaildndra, Prashant Palvia and Ronald M. Zigli, Eds. *The Global Issues of Information Technology Management*. Harrisburg, Pennsylvania: Idea Group Publishing, 1992

Parenti, Michael. *Land of Idols: political mythology in America*. New York: St. Martin's Press, 1994.

Pegels, Carl. *Japan vs. the West*. Hingham, MA: Kluwer Boston, Inc., 1984.

Pempel, T. J. *Policy and Politics in Japan*. Philadelphia: Temple University Press, 1982.

Pfaff, William. *The Wrath of Nations*. New York: Simon & Schuster, 1993.

Piore, Michael J. and Charles F. Sabel. *The Second Industrial Divide*. USA: Basic Books, Inc., 1984.

Plato. *The Republic*, Book IX. *Great Books of the Western World*, Vol. 7. Chicago: William Benton, Publisher, 1952.

Prestowitz, Clyde V. Jr. "The Time Has Come For a Frank Talk With Japan." *The Washington Post Weekly Edition*, April 22-28, 1996, 20.

Przeworski, Adam. "The Games of Transition." In *Issues in Democratic Consolidation. The New South American Democracies in Comparative Perspective*. Scott Mainwaring, Guillermo O'Donnell, and J. Samuel Valenzuela, Eds. Notre Dame, Indiana: University of Notre Dame Press, 1992.

Rawls, John. *A Theory of Justice*. Cambridge: The Belknap Press, 1971.

Ray, James Lee. *Global Politics*. Boston: Houghton Mifflin Company, 1979.

Redding, S. Gordon. "Comparative Management Theory: Jungle, Zoo or Fossil Bed?" *Organization Studies*, Vol. 15, No. 3, 323-359, 1994.

Reischauer, Edwin O. *The Japanese*. Cambridge, Massachusetts: The Belknap Press, 1981.

Reischauer, Edwin O. *The United States and Japan*. 3d Ed. New York: The Viking Press, 1965.

Robertson, Ian. *Society: A Brief Introduction*. New York: Worth Publishers, Inc., 1989.

Rueschemeyer, Dietrich, Evelyne Huber Stephens, and John D. Stephens. *Capitalist Development and Democracy*. Chicago: University of Chicago Press, 1992.

Russell, Bertrand. *A History of Western Philosophy*. New York: Simon & Schuster, 1945; 1972.

Russett, Bruce. *Grasping the Democratic Peace*. Princeton: Princeton University Press, 1993.

Samuelson, Robert J. "Why America Creates Jobs." *Newsweek*, July 29, 1996, 49.

Sargent, Lyman Tower. *Contemporary Political Ideologies*, 10th Ed. Belmont, California: Wadsworth Publishing Company, 1996.

Sartori, Giovanni. *The Theory of Democracy Revisited*. Chatham, New Jersey: Chatham House Publishers, Inc., 1987.

Schell, Erwin H. "Challenge of Viewpoint," In *The Amazing Oversight*, Graham, Ben S., Jr. and Parvin S. Titus, Eds. New York: AMACOM, 1979.

Selznick, Philip. "Personhood and Moral Obligation." In *New Communitarian Thinking*, Amitai Etzioni, Ed. Charlottesville and London: University Press of Virginia, 1995.

Sen, Amartya. Chapter in *Economics and Sociology*, Richard Swedberg, Ed. New Jersey: Princeton University Press, 1990.

Simmons, Robert H. and Eugene P. Dvorin. *Public Administration: Values, Policy, and Change*. Port Washington, N.Y.: Alfred Publishing Co., Inc., 1977.

Simon, Herbert A. *Administrative Behavior*, 3d Ed. New York: The Free Press, 1976.

Singer, Max and Aaron Wildavsky. *The Real World Order*. Chatham, New Jersey: Chatham House Publishers, Inc., 1993.

Smart, Tim. "Help Wanted: Managers (Again)." *The Washington Post National Weekly Edition*, 20 April 1998, 19-20.

Smith, Hedrick. *Rethinking America*. New York: Random House, 1995.

Smith, Rogers M. "American Conceptions of Citizenship and National Service." *New Communitarian Thinking*. Charlottesville: University of Virginia Press, 1995.

Spragens, Thomas A. Jr. "Communitarian Liberalism." In *New Communitarian Thinking. Persons, Virtues, Institutions, and Communities*. Charlottesville: University Press of Virginia. 1995.

Sugawara, Sandra. "In Japan, Survival Via a Shell Game." *The Washington Post National Weekly Edition*, 11 May 1998, 19.

Sullivan, William M. "Institutions as the Infrastructure of Democracy." In *New Communitarian Thinking*. Amitai Etzioni, Ed. Charlottesville: University Press of Virginia, 1995.

Susser, Bernard. *Political Ideology in the Modern World*. Boston: Allyn and Bacon, 1995.

Swedberg, Richard M. "The Battle of the Methods Toward a Paradigm Shift?" In *Socio-Economics Toward a New Synthesis*, Amitai Etzioni and Paul R. Lawrence, Eds. Armonk, NY: M. E. Sharpe, Inc., 1991, 13-33.

Taylor, Charles. "Liberal Politics and the Public Sphere." *New Communitarian Thinking*. Amitai Etzioni. Ed. Charlottesville: Univresity Press of Virginia, 1995.

Terry, Edith. "Asians Balk at Japanese Corporate Culture." *The Christian Science Monitor*, 26 January 1995, 9.

. . . "The changing nature of leadership." *The Economist*. June 10, 1995, 57.

. . . "The Japanese numbers game." *The Economist*. March 2, 1996, 71.

. . . "The uncommon good." *The Economist*. August 19, 1995, 55-56.

Thurow, Lester. *Head To Head*. New York: Warner Books, 1993.

Thurow, Lester. *The Future of Capitalism*. New York: William Morrow and Company, Inc., 1996.

Toffler, Alvin and Heidi Toffler. *Creating a New Civilization. The Politics of the Third Wave*. Atlanta: Turner Publishing Inc., 1995.

Tonelson, Alan. "America, Germany, and Japan: The Tenacious Trio?" *Current History*, Vol. 94, No. 595, November 1995, 353-358.

. . . "True profits." *The Economist*. June 24, 1995, 68.

. . . "Up, down and standing still." *The Economist*. February 24, 1996.

VanMaanen, John and Andre Laurent. "The Flow of Culture: Some Notes on Globalization and the Multinational Corporation." In *Organization Theory and the Multinational Corporation*, Sumantra Ghoshal and D. Eleanor Westney, Eds. New York: St. Martin's Press, 1993.

VanWolferen, Karel. "Japan's Non-Revolution." *Foreign Affairs*, Vol. 72, No. 4, September/October 1993, 54-65.

Walzer, Michael. "The Communitarian Critique of Liberalism." In *New Communitarian Thinking. Persons, Virtues, Institutions, and Communities*. Charlottesville: University Press of Virginia. 1995.

Ward, John William. "The Ideal of Individualism and the Reality of Organization." In *The Business Establishment*. Earl F. Cheit, Ed. New York: John Wiley & Sons, Inc., 1964.

Waterman, Robert H., Jr. *What America Does Right*. New York: Plume, 1994.

Weick, Karl E. *The Social Psychology of Organizing*, 2d Ed. New York: McGraw- Hill, Inc., 1979.

Weisbord, Marvin R. and Sandra Janoff. *Future Search*. San Francisco: Berrett-Koehler Publishers, 1995.

... "Why more looks like less." *The Economist*, April 27, 1996, 26.

Wilson, John Oliver. "Human Values and Economic Behavior." In *Socio-Economics Toward a New Synthesis*, Etzioni, Amitai and Paul R. Lawrence, Eds. Armonk, NY: M. E. Sharpe, Inc., 1991, 233-259.

Wolfe, Alan. "Human Nature and the Quest for Community." In *New Communitarian Thinking. Persons, Virtues, Institutions, and Communities.* Amitai Etzioni, Ed. Charlottesville: The University of Virginia Press, 1995.

Wooldridge, Adrian. "Who wants to be a giant?" *The Economist*, June 24, 1995.

Wright, Robert. "The Evolution of Despair." *Time*, August 28, 1995, 50-57.

Yoder, Edwin. "Responsible Corporation Issue Absurd." *Montgomery Advertiser*. March 27, 1996, 18A.

Zakaria, Fareed. "Bigger Than the Family, Smaller Than the State." *The New York Times Book Review*, August 13, 1995.

Zemke, Ron. "The Call of Community." *Training*. March 1996.

Zuckerman, Mortimer B. "A Second American Century." *Foreign Affairs*, Vol. 77, No. 3, May/June 1998, 18-31.

Index

AES, 163-164, 195
AT&T, 25, 87
acculturation, 99
acquisitions, 52
administrative guidance, 106
affiliation, 175, 176
affirmative action, 123
Age of knowledge, 22
alliances, 52, 72, 174, 177, 189, 192, 198199
American businesses, 86
American citizenship, 154
(The) American Creed, 155
American competitive spirit, 74
American Constitution, 66
American corporate model, 71-93, 114, 175, 177, 211-212
American corporate style, 79
American corporations, 130, 185
American culture, xix, 62, 71, 78
American economic system, 62, 91, 211
American economy, 85-93
American individualism, 63-69
American industry, 23
American managers, 83

American model, xxiv, 79, 84, 105, 116, 120, 158, 184, 210
American organization style, 73
American organization theory, xxii, 61-84, 156
American organizations, xx, 71, 74, 80, 117, 156, 157
American Revolution, 65
American society, 61, 62, 81, 205, 210
American stock market, 85-86
American worker, 58, 87-88, 91
Americans, 72
Anglo-Saxon, 40, 105
Aristotelian logic, 116
Aristotelian thought, 134
Aristotle, 63-64
Asian model, 130
"asocial society", 135
assembly line, 53, 79-80
associational crisis, 146
atomism, xix, 67
atomist/individualist, 93
atomist/organic, 107
atomized society, 61-63, 71
Australia, 62
authoritarian management, 81

authoritarianism, 110, 120, 206
authority, 62
autonomy, 163

benevolence, 69
Ben and Jerry's Ice Cream, 165-166
"Bet-Your-Company Culture", 49
Blasi, J. R. and D. Kruse, 182-183
(The) Body Shop, 168, 192
Boff, Leonardo, 7
"boundaryless organization", 189
Bowker, M., 11-12
Britain, 40
Brown, Robin, 18
"bubble economy", xxi, 125
Buddhism, 98-99, 101, 111, 113
bureaucracy, 53, 103, 120
bureaucratic organizations, 82, 129
bureaucratization, 55, 82, 210
Burke, Edmund, xv, 16
Buscher, M., 33, 36
bushido, 111
business ethics, 166-167, 169, 172-173
Businesses for Social Responsibility, 169

Calvert Group's Statement of Shared Values, 194
Calvin, John, 65
Canada, 62
capital ownership, 181
capitalism, 11, 17, 26, 67-68, 70, 74-78, 82, 84, 104, 201-204, 209
capitalist, xxiv
capitalist democracy, xv, 17-18
capitalist economy, 89, 202-204

career path, 118
catalytic government, 197
Catholic Church, 64
Catholicism, 6-7
children, 151-152
Chinese, 96-97, 189
Christianity, 141
Christians, 64, 98
citizenship, 159
civic duty, 155, 185
civic sacrament, 154
civic trust, 146, 147-150
civics, 146
civil libertarian, 143
civil purpose, 156
civil society, xxiii, 5, 16, 44, 147-150, 156, 199
civility, 145, 146
civilizations, 19, 31, 133
civitas, 146
Clark, C., 196-198, 210
"clash of civilizations", 9, 18
classical liberalism, 63, 69, 72, 135, 147, 206-207
Cold War, 9-12, 14, 18
collaborative strategies, 173-177
collective conscience, 161
collective consciousness theory
collective good, 107
collective society, 100
collective unity, 134
collective values, 104
collectivism, 95-99, 213
collectivist, xxi, 140
collectivities, 159
common good, 71, 139, 140, 141, 155, 156, 201, 205
communal values
communalist ideal, 144
communism, 11, 14, 17, 201-202

Index

Communitarian, 142
communitarian enterprise, 195-200
communitarian ethic, ix-x, xxii-xxv, 104, 133-161, 201-207, 213-214
communitarian ideal, 146
communitarian individual, 138, 151
"communitarian liberalism", 135
communitarian paradigm, xxii, 164
communitarian perspective, xiv, 207
communitarian self, x
communitarian social thesis, 137
communitarian spirit, 176
communitarianism, xxii, 134, 135, 140, 159
communitarianist theory, 134
communities of mankind, 153
community, xxiii, 33, 108, 109, 120, 133, 135-136, 139-145, 148, 150, 156, 157, 161, 165, 197
comparative advantage, 190
competition, 18, 24, 62, 74-78, 111, 128
"competitive subnational governments", 22
competitive advantage, 77
Confucian Dynamism, 40
Confucian society, 103, 113
Confucian values, 40, 96-99, 114, 211, 212
Confucianism, 111
Confucius, 95-97
consensus, 110
contracting out, 76, 130, 197
cooperation, 106, 111

cooperative ventures, 174
core firms, 24-25, 177, 199
Corning, Inc., 189
corporate citizenship, 167, 168-169, 171-172
corporate culture, 37-60, 117, 122, 161, 163, 168
corporate earnings, 91
corporate organizations, 156-161
corporate philosophy, 193-194
corporate profits, 86
corporate reputation, 172
corporate responsibility, xxiv, 167-169, 187, 202
corporate tribes, 52
corporate values, 45, 47, 119, 165
corporation(s), xvii, 26, 186, 188, 202
Council on Economic Priorities
craft economies, 175
creative destruction, 78
Crockatt, Richard, 9-11
cross-cultural, 32, 42, 43, 157, 187, 188, 209
cross-national, 40, 42, 52
cultural constraints, 209
cultural determinism theory, 110
cultural diversity, 165
"cultural hybrid", 43
cultural imperialism, 32
cultural interaction, 188
cultural nature, 157
cultural norms, 43, 116
"cultural synergy", 42
culture(s), xiv, xvi, xvii, xviii, 17, 26, 29-32, 133, 199
Cynics, 64

Deal, T. and A. Kennedy, 46-50, 59, 166-167

decisionmaking, 72, 119, 199
deTocqueville, A., 143, 147, 149, 199, 209
deficits, 85
democracy, xiii, 5, ,9, 15, 17, 18, 26, 68, 142, 147, 151, 185, 209
democratic norms, 9, 13
democratic regimes, 13
democratic society, 63, 147
democratization, xv, 4, 13, 14, 15, 17, 19, 20, 26, 32, 134, 209
dependencia, 21
depression, 59
deregulation, 86, 126, 128
desencanto, 15
developing nations, 25;
Diamond, M. and S. Allcorn, 50-51
"digital age", 23
diverse societies, 160
domination, 81-84
downsizing, 24, 76, 83, 87-88, 89, 91, 128, 130
Drucker, P., 22, 84, 108
"dual allegiances", 191
Durkheim, E., 35, 139, 144, 155, 206

East Asia, 8, 109
Eastern ethics, 98
Eastern European, 8, 9, 11, 12, 15
economic behavior, 30, 33, 34, 35
economic community, 156
economic development, 20, 104
economic ethics, 32-36
economic growth, 6, 20
economic man, 33
economic opportunity, 123
economic organizations, 157, 162

economic power, 26
economic role, 161
economics, xv-xvi, 19, 20, 29-37
economists, 30, 34, 35
education, 90, 184-186, 200
egotists, 61
"Eleven-C Circular Model", 112
Elshtain, J., 138, 147, 206
embedded self, 137-141, 154, 156
"embourgeoisement", 90
emerging democracies, 3
emerging nations, 158
employability, 58, 200
employee ownership, 180-183, 199
employee participation, 179
employee stock ownership plans, 181-183
empowerment, 163, 199
England, 87
entrepreneur, 71, 78-79, 157
entrepreneurial spirit, 72
entrepreneurship, 67, 176
ethic of care, 159, 213
ethics, 35-36, 159, 178
Etzioni, A., 33, 133, 134; 140, 142, 144, 155, 156, 158, 206
European Union, 177
existential phenomenology, 56-57
exploitation, 81-82

FDIs, 157
face, 96
Fallows, J., 107
family, 151-152
Federal Express, 163, 179
federalisms, 22
financial impact, 170
First World, 21
fiscal policy, 86

Index

Five Classics, 96
Five Dragons, 40
flexible specialization, 174, 175, 192
Florida International University, 171
Foldcraft Company, 179
Fordism, xviii, 53, 79, 81
Forsyth Landing, 176
(The) Four Mobilities, 152-153
Foxboro Corporation, 77
France, 40, 66, 87, 99
"fraternity", 135
Fred Schmid Appliance & TV Company
free agency, 134
free association, 159
free enterprise, 66
free market, 67-68, 70
freedom, 67-68, 137, 139, 198
Friedman, M., 202
Fukuyama, Frances, 10-11, 14, 18

Gardeners' Supply
gender, 39, 83
General Electric, 167
"geo-economics", 20
Germans, 72
Germany, 25, 29, 40, 66, 87, 99
gimu, 101
global community, 134, 209, 214
global competition, 93, 178
global corporations, 25
global economic enterprise, 160
global economy, 24, 84
global marketplace, 161, 174, 187
global network, xiv, 133
global organizations, 24, 190
global orientation, 190
global village, xiii, xiv, 14

global work teams, 191
globalization, xiii, xv, 24, 27, 29, 31, 43, 57, 86, 191
globalism, xxii, 32, 134
Gorbachev, 11-12
Gordon Group, 171
government, 65-67, 69-70, 91, 104, 106, 109, 124, 155, 196-200, 210
Great Britain, 62, 106
Great Depression, 70
Group of Seven, 85

Hampden-Turner, C. and A. Trompenaars, 40-41, 51, 100, 104, 107, 112-113, 189-190
han, 108
Hanna Andersson, 168
harmony, 112
Harrison, B., 24, 83, 91, 108, 174, 177-179, 189
Hawthorne studies, 55
Herman Miller Company Mandate, 194
heroes, 45, 63, 166
Hewlett-Packard, 25, 46, 48, 118, 166, 196
hierarchy, 83-84, 95, 101, 162
"high road to profitability", 178-179
Hoecklin, L., 61, 72, 107, 187-188
Hofstede, G., 37-40, 61, 62, 104
Honeywell, 168, 186
honne, 107
host culture, 133, 187, 190
Human Capitalism, 114-116, 129, 177-186
human rights, 7
humanitarian values, 121

Huntington, Samuel, xv, 3-9, 14-15, 18-19, 31

"I and We", 138, 140, 158-159
IBM, 25, 48, 118, 166
ideology, 6
independence, 65
idion, 64
idiotes, 64
income, 89, 127
individual, 30, 33, 61, 65, 68, 135, 139-140
individual creativity, 72
individual liberty, 135
individual responsibility, 146
individualism, xix, xx, 15, 62, 65, 67, 71, 73-74, 82, 92, 95, 135, 147, 206, 213
individualism-collectivism, 39, 95, 139, 165, 210
individualist ethic, 68
individualist model, 74
individualist societies, 105
individualist organization, 74
individualist/collectivist
individualistic, xix, xxiii, 61, 71, 100, 160
individualistic capitalism, 84, 91
industrialization, 104
Industrial Age, xviii, 3, 23, 24, 31, 53, 57, 80, 86
industrial society, 137
inequality, 88-89, 91
inflation, 85
Information Age, xviii, 3, 22, 24, 31, 53, 57, 86, 90, 184, 213
information technology, xvii, 23, 26, 52
"institutional specificity of culture", 31

intercultural, 43, 187, 188, 189
intercultural model, 158
interdependence, xiii, xvii, 10, 22, 52, 92, 145, 159, 209
Interdependencies, ix, xviii, 31, 33, 109, 209
Interdependent, ix, xvi, xxiii,23, 27, 29, 32, 133, 142, 205
international competitiveness, 36, 43, 130, 213
international economy, 26, 84-85
international management, 190
international organizations, 133
internationalism, 134
interrelationships, 99
investment, 20, 29, 86, 157, 199
isolation, 136

Japan, xxi, 25, 29, 40, 72, 98
Japanese, 72
Japanese business enterprise, 108
Japanese capitalism, 104-106
Japanese collective society, 105
Japanese collectivism, 104
Japanese corporations, 130
Japanese culture, 98, 107
Japanese democratic model, 102
Japanese economic growth, 109
Japanese economy, xxi, 105, 123-131
Japanese ethical system, 113
"Japan, Inc.", 109, 128, 189
Japanese individuality, 100
Japanese management style, 117, 119, 156, 189
Japanese model, xxi, xxii, xxiv, 107-131, 158, 189, 210, 212
Japanese moral thought, 112-113
Japanese organization theory, xxi, 110-111, 114, 120

Index

Japanese Organizational Paradigm, 107-116, 211
Japanese organizational style, 107, 212
Japanese society, 99-101, 111, 211
Japanese state, 101, 103
Japanese workers, 107
Jervis, R., 9
Johnson & Johnson, 25, 46
joint ventures, 52
Judaism, 141
Just Desserts, 168
justice, 70

Kantian self, 138, 139
keiretsu, 108-109, 189
Keynesian economics, 70
kigyoism, 113-114
knowledge-based economy, 92
Knowledge Society, 173
koinon, 64
kokka, 111
kone, 99
kyakkanteki, 113

labor, 106
laissez faire, 67, 68, 206-207
land values, 125
Latin America, 5, 7, 14
leadership, 50-51, 162, 163, 173, 187, 192-195, 199
lean organization, 87
lean production,
Levi Strauss, 76, 164, 170-171, 179, 185
Liberal Democratic Party (LDP), 103, 124, 129
liberalism, xix, 15, 17, 65, 67, 70, 116, 203-204
Liberation theology, 7

"liberism", 70-71
liberty, 66, 68
lifetime employment, 117-118, 128, 158, 189, 200
Linnton Plywood Association, 180
Locke, John, 67
Lodge, G., 31
lone individual, 63
(The) Longfellow Clubs, 168
long-term employment, 110, 158
"low level equilibrium trap", 178
"low road to profitability", 83, 178
Lowes Hotels
Luther, Martin, 64-65
Luttwak, E., 20, 86

Madisonian democracy, xix, 67
madogiwazoku, 128
Mainwairing, Scott, xv, 4, 5, 15
Makower, J., 170-172, 193-195
management, 51-52, 73, 79-80, 106-107, 110, 112, 116, 120, 122, 161-162, 174, 186
managers, 87-88
market culture, 91
market economies, 32, 36
market economy, 69
market-share maximization, 105
market society, 67
Marx, K., 35
mass production model, xviii, xx, 53, 79-80, 84, 92, 116, 130, 161, 164, 175, 210, 211-212
McDonald's, 48
Meiji Restoration, 98-99, 101, 104
mergers, 52
merit, 62
microcultures, 51
Ministry of Finance, 103

Ministry of International Trade and Industry (MITI), 106, 110, 126
"mismatch theory", 59
modernization, 16, 134
monetary policy, 86, 125
moral compass, 141, 144
moral convictions, 145
moral voice, 144
Moral Conduct and Social Values, 144-147
moral individualism, 139-140, 206
moral obligation, 148
morality, 143
moral pluralism, 141
moral responsibility, 44, 159
moral voice, 145
Morgan, G, 75-77, 80, 83
Moran, R., and P. Harris: 42-43
Mueller, Frank: 31; 43-44
multinational, 24-25, 189, 192
multinational corporation, xvi, 81, 157
multiple affiliations, 152
multipolarity: 10;
myth, 45, 62, 63, 92

nation-state, 26, 133, 134, 159
National Center for Employee Ownership, 179, 182
national culture, 37-44
national societies, 157
nationalism, xiii, xvi, 14, 17, 22, 26, 27, 134
nationalist, xv, 3, 12, 15, 16,
natural law, 64
natural theory, 136
"nature", 136
neonationalism, xv, xxiii, 16, 160-161

neonationalist/individualist ethic, 161
"nested" communities, 133, 156, 175
Netherlands, 40, 62
networked alliances, 174, 177, 189
networking, 24, 52, 162, 192, 198, 199
New Economic Order, 84-93
"New Enterprise Economics", 177
new world order, xiii
New Zealand, 62
Nineteenth century liberalism, 69
non-state actors, 149
"nurture", 136

Occupation, 105
organic model, xxi, 95-131
organic society, 95-97, 211, 212
organicism, 64
organization(s), x, xvi, xvii, xx, xxiii, 75, 82-83, 88, 92, 158, 159, 161, 186, 190, 199-200, 213
organization theory, x, xiv, 107, 112, 116, 159
organizational arrangements, 162, 163
organizational behavior, 107
organizational styles, 161
Ouchi, W., 116-123, 128
outsourcing, 24, 76, 83, 130
ownership plans, 179
Ozaki, R, 114-116, 177, 184

participatory communities, 154
participatory management, 57
particularism, 190
partnering, 25, 174, 178, 198
partnerships, 52

paternalistic, 103, 158, 167, 183
patriarchy, 83-84
peace, 9, 16
perestroika, 11
personal responsibility, 151
phenomenological, xxii
Piore, M. and C. Sabel, 80, 175
Plato, xxiii, 63-64, 160
Platonic thought, 134
polis, xxiii, 160
political environments, 157
political freedoms, 147
"polyocular" culture, 113
possessive individualism, 68, 105, 138. 206
Post-New Deal liberalism, 69-71
post-World War II, 123-124
postwar Japan, 104-105
power distance, 38
private enterprise, 104, 211
private sector, 105, 197
privatization, 197
"Process Culture", 49-50
Proctor & Gamble, 46, 118, 162-163, 179, 192, 195
producer economics, 106
productivity, 53, 130, 161, 163, 183-184
profit maximization, 105, 166
profit sharing, 179-183, 199
profits, 163, 202
property, 67-68, 70
protectionist, 124
Protestant ethic, 65
Protestantism, 64
Przeworski, Adam, xv, 5
psycholinguistics, 96
public service, 154
Publix Super Markets, 180
Puritan work ethic, 63, 210

Quality Control Circle, 121

R. H. Bruskin Associates, 181
"rabble" hypothesis, 136
racial discrimination, 83, 122
radical individualism, 61
radius of trust, 107
rationality, 35, 54, 63, 78, 82, 119, 154, 211
Rawls, J., 70, 138
Reagan, R., 12
"reciprocal altruism", 145
reciprocity, 109
Reebok, 168, 192
Reischauer, E., 99, 104
regime, 17
Renaissance, 64
(The) Republic, xxiii, 64, 160
Responsibilities vs. Rights, 141-143
"(The) Responsive Communitarian Platform", 145
restructuring, 87, 175
return on investment, 178
Rhino Records, 167-168
rituals, 45, 47, 76
Rouse Company, 192
Rostow, Walt W., 21
Rubbermaid, 75-76, 195
Russert, B., 9
Rutgers University, 171

samurai, 98
Sartori, Giovanni, 5, 12, 15, 64, 70
Scandinavian, 40
scientific management, 54-55, 78-81, 211
Scylla and Charybdis, xxv
self-direction, 162

self-government, 154, 169
self-interest, 61, 67-69, 71, 105, 107, 136, 206, 211
self-made man, 62
self-management, 163
self-worth, 162
sempai-kohai, 114
Sen, Amartya, 35
"seven cultures of capitalism", 40-41
sexism, 122
sexual harassment, 83
Shinto, 99
Shintoism, 113
shukanteki, xxii, 113, 131
shumi, 101
Singer, M. and A. Wildavsky, 13-14, 21-22
Sloan model, 192
small-firm-led economic growth, 175-176
Smith, A., 35, 67, 79, 105
"snowballing", 8
sociability, 137
social capital, 150
social concerns, 165
social contract theory, 67, 138
social compact, 138
social conscience, 169, 186-187
social context, 137
social good, 61
social man, 33, 210
social change, 127
social harmony, 173
social order, 95, 107, 204
social responsibility, 143, 164, 169, 170-172, 193, 202
social role, 161
social theory, 136, 159
social values, 33

sociality, 158
socialization, 136
society, 15, 30, 31-32, 36, 38, 52-53, 56, 61, 62, 70-71, 83, 92, 134, 136, 137, 140, 145, 154, 155, 210
solidarity, 106
socioeconomics, 32-36
sociological, 35
sociology, 29
solar firms, 189
solidarity, 107
Sophist, xix, 61, 63
sovereign states, 18, 159
sovereignty, 159
Soviet Union, 8, 10, 11, 12, 14, 15, 80
Soziale Marktwirtschaft, 36
Springfield ReManufacturing Corporation, 192
stagflation, 84
stakeholder theory, 201, 202
state, 62, 154, 155, 212
"state-led capitalism", 106
state sovereignty, 134
stereotyes, 188
stewardship, 158
stock ownership, 89
Stoics, 64
strategic allies, 24
"strong culture companies", 46
subcontracting, 83
subgroups, 47
subordination, 82
subsidiaries, 52
Susser, Bernard, xv, 5
Sweden, 40
Switzerland, 29
symbols, 45-46

Index

Taylor, F., 79
Taylorism, 24, 79-81
teams, 122, 161, 163
teamwork, 92, 174
technology, 52, 130, 178
Theory of the Cooperative
  Japanese, 111-114
Theory Y, 162-163
Theory Z, 116-123, 158
"Third Wave of Civilization", 22-23, 31
third wave of democratization, xiii, 3, 7, 8
Third World, 14, 21
"throw-away society", 210
Thurow, L., 77, 92, 105, 108
Timberland Mission Statement, 193
Toffler, A. and H., 22, 30-31
Tom's of Maine's Statement of Beliefs, 194
Toshiba, 187-188
totalitarian, 140
"Tough-Guy, Macho Culture", 47-48
trade, 20, 23-24, 29, 43
trade surplus, 124
training, 184-185
"transcendent collective enterprise", 144
transnational economic organizations, 133, 161, 191
transnational world economy, 133
transnationalism, 9, 18-20, 22, 31
"Triumphant Individual", 78
"Turbocapitalism", 84-90

uchi, 129
uchiwa, 111
uncertainty avoidance

unemployment, 85, 127, 129
unencumbered self, 138
United Kingdom, 66
United States, 10, 25, 29, 40, 106, 124, 177, 205
unity, 109
universalism, 189
University of Massachusetts, 171

value-added maximization, 105
value systems, 133
values, 34, 46, 57, 138, 159, 163, 164
"Velvet curtain of culture", 18
virtual corporations, 189
vision, 192, 193-195
visitor culture, 133, 187, 190

Wa, 111-112
wage labor, 88
Walker Research
Walzer, M, 135, 152
"weak corporate cultures", 47
wealth, 6, 92, 198, 202, 203
Weirton Steel, 180
welfare, 106
welfare state, xix, 70
Western capitalism, 116
Western Christianity, 6
Western Culture Thesis, 18
Western management style, 119
Western organization thought, 112
White Dog Cafe, 194-195
Whole Foods Market Declaration of Independence, 194
Wildavsky, A., 13
"windowside employees", 128
Wooldridge, A., 24
work ethic, 92
work groups, 164

"Work Hard/Play Hard Culture", 48-49
workers, 90, 174, 178, 179, 184, 186
world democratic ethos, 5
"world nation", 191
World War II, 84, 105, 121
Wright State University, 171

xenophobia, 122

yen, 125-126

zaibatsu, 108